M000239250

THE
ACCIDENTAL
PHILANTHROPIST

THE ACCIDENTAL PHILANTHROPIST

From a Bronx Stickball Lot to
Manhattan Courtrooms and Steering
Leona Helmsley's Billions

SANDOR FRANKEL

Skyhorse Publishing

Copyright © 2021 by Sandor Frankel

All rights reserved. No part of this book may be reproduced in any manner without the express written consent of the publisher, except in the case of brief excerpts in critical reviews or articles. All inquiries should be addressed to Skyhorse Publishing, 307 West 36th Street, 11th Floor, New York, NY 10018.

Skyhorse Publishing books may be purchased in bulk at special discounts for sales promotion, corporate gifts, fund-raising, or educational purposes. Special editions can also be created to specifications. For details, contact the Special Sales Department, Skyhorse Publishing, 307 West 36th Street, 11th Floor, New York, NY 10018 or info@skyhorsepublishing.com.

Skyhorse® and Skyhorse Publishing® are registered trademarks of Skyhorse Publishing, Inc.®, a Delaware corporation.

Visit our website at www.skyhorsepublishing.com.

10 9 8 7 6 5 4 3 2 1

Library of Congress Cataloging-in-Publication Data is available on file.

Cover design by Kai Texel
Cover photo credit: Getty Images

Print ISBN: 978-1-5107-6285-5
Ebook ISBN: 978-1-5107-6590-0

Printed in the United States of America

To Ruthie,
still as dazzling as the day we met,
and the beautiful family we're blessed with.

Contents

Chapter 1—Here's What Happened   1

Chapter 2—The Bronx   3

Chapter 3—Two Cambridges and Washington, D.C.   11

Chapter 4—Back to New York   33

Chapter 5—Personally   49

Chapter 6—Cases   57

Chapter 7—Defending "One Tough Bitch"   83

Chapter 8—Practicing Doesn't Make Perfect   121

Chapter 9—Consigliere, Sort Of   154

Chapter 10—Gathering Billions   176

Chapter 11—Giving Billions Away   214

Chapter 12—Trying to Cure a Disease   242

Chapter 13—Israel   258

Chapter 14—Oh, the Rich Folks You Meet   313

Chapter 15—Lawyering Redux   326

Chapter 1

Here's What Happened

The first time Leona Helmsley fired me, I never dreamed she'd wind up trusting me with more than $5 billion.

I'm a lawyer. Leona Helmsley was a client of mine for the last eighteen years of her life. She appointed me one of the executors of her estate, charged with selling her multi-billion-dollar holdings, including highlights of the New York City skyline and billions of dollars in other assets. She also named me one of the trustees of her charitable trust with complete discretion to decide which charitable organizations to give her fortune to.

Imagine yourself walking down the street and being suddenly showered with wagonloads of gold labeled "Use only for the good of mankind as you see fit." That's what happened to me, and the gold has been pouring continuously for over a decade.

Today—literally, today—I signed checks for several hundred million dollars. When you control billions of dollars, you become—I assure you—very popular. My wit is now wittier, my jokes funnier, my opinions more incisive and *always* worth listening to. Friends, pseudo-friends, former friends, would-be friends, quasi-friends, friends of friends—they all come knocking.

Life has become surreal. On a trip to Israel, I was invited to join then-President Peres for lunch, beginning at 1:00. Shortly before the lunch, I was invited to attend a meeting with Prime Minister Netanyahu, beginning at 2:00 on the same day. I responded to the second invitation with: This is a sentence I never thought I'd utter, but please tell the Prime Minister I'll be late because I'm having lunch with the President.

I pinch myself to make sure this is real. I think I'm awake. Here's how it happened.

Chapter 2

The Bronx

I was born in 1943 in the Bronx, and lived at 690 Gerard Avenue, one short block from Yankee Stadium. My parents divorced shortly after I was born. I was their only child. I lived with my mother in a small one-bedroom apartment. I slept in the bedroom, my mother in the living room. She was an elementary school teacher.

We didn't have money. I was not aware of that, didn't know anyone rich, and had no concept of "rich." Next to my apartment building was a vacant lot, dirt-topped and littered with rocks and broken glass. When I wanted to play, I went downstairs to the lot; kids were always there.

Mostly we played stickball. Nobody had a bat. We'd dismantle an old discarded broom and use the handle. The ball was always a "Spaldeen"—a pink rubber ball that cost a nickel. I never bought one, but kept whatever leftover I'd find and use it until the seam split open. If nobody had a broom handle, we'd play punchball: same ball, but you'd hit it with your fist.

We also played stoop ball. One of the apartment buildings on the block had half-a-dozen steps leading up to the entrance. You'd stand on the sidewalk in front of the steps and throw a ball against them to make the ball ricochet backward toward another kid who was the fielder. If he caught it on the fly, you were out. One bounce before he caught it was a single, two bounces a double, etc. If you hit the edge of a step at a perfect angle, the ball would fly back over the fielder.

My grandparents, Enny and Poppy, who had emigrated from Russia with only the shirts on their backs, lived on the sixth floor of one of the buildings that surrounded the lot. When I'd get hungry while playing, I'd yell "Enny!" and shout for food. Shortly, she'd toss a sandwich wrapped in a brown paper bag out the window, and I'd have something squashed to eat as soon as it hit the ground.

Enny and Poppy had a little tin box—called a *pushke*—in their apartment, in which they or a visitor would drop any pennies or nickels they could spare. When filled, the box would be returned to the Jewish National Fund. Those given-out-for-free little tin boxes now retail for $117 on eBay.

I created an indoor basketball court in my bedroom. I found a discarded wire shirt-hanger and bent it into as close to a circle as I could. Then I wedged the hook of the hanger between the top of the door and the doorframe; presto, a wire basket protruded from the door. My basketball was a rolled up pair of socks. I'd be all ten players, and invariably the game would reach the final seconds before I'd score the winning basket.

I played outdoor basketball a few blocks away at McCombs Dam Park, across the street from the stadium. Teams were choose-up. Winners kept playing; losers had to wait for "next." The basketball court disappeared years ago, squashed like a bug: The new Yankee Stadium was built over it.

Although the stadium was just seconds away from my apartment building, I never had money to get in. Some kids could afford bleacher seats, and by the sixth inning, friendly ushers would let others sneak in. That seemed dishonest, even with the ushers' okay, and I didn't.

Sounds occasionally gave away the taste of what was happening on the field. You could tell a home run by the cheering. A long out would begin with the same sound, followed by a collective groan.

I didn't like the Yankees. They were one of the last all-white teams, and that seemed wrong. I rooted for the Dodgers, who had Jackie Robinson and other blacks on their roster. I memorized the Dodgers' batting averages to the fourth digit. We eventually got a small TV (black-and-white, with just a few channels), and I'd watch the games and keep a box score.

Our home had one luxury: a Steinway grand piano which took up most of the living room. My mother had been a talented pianist in her youth, winning several gold medals in concert competitions. But she became nervous in front of audiences and never reached the highest level.

I was forced to take piano lessons at an early age, and hated it. My teacher was Mrs. Grier, a tall, slim, unsmiling woman who clearly derived no satisfaction from my inability to master even the scales or my refusal to practice between weekly lessons. I'd wear my Little League baseball uniform to the lessons as a silent protest against enforced culture.

Charlie the barber, a short, fat, bald man with a pronounced limp, cut my hair every five or six weeks for fifty cents plus a ten cent tip. My next-door neighbor, Guy, went to Tony the barber two blocks uptown, for seventy-five cents and a twenty-five cent tip, and seemed rich to me. We're still close buddies after seven decades.

I'd get a special treat every month or so: a double-feature at the

Earl movie theater. A ticket cost twenty-five cents. Popcorn and candy were sold there, but buying any was out of the question.

My school was P.S. 31, a five-block walk from my apartment house. Today, it's a dangerous walk. Then, it was simply part of the day.

The school gave us autograph books at the end of each year. We would sign each other's books with a best wishes, or a poem, or joke. One of my fifth-grade classmates signed mine: "Best wishes. Remember, money talks." At that time, I had no idea what he meant. Many years later, I wondered how he got so wise so young.

A sixth-grade classmate of mine named Dennis walked nearly the same route to school as I did. But he used to cut through the park, and began to hang out with kids I didn't know. He sat next to me in class. He was the first person I knew whose name appeared in the newspaper, when he was shot to death by a zip-gun in the park. His older sister looked so sad when she came to our class to pick up his papers and assorted things from his desk.

Our desks were multi-purpose. We could write on them, and store our books on a shelf beneath the writing surface. They also had inkless inkwells in the corner for, well, ink. And there was enough empty space under each desk for us to hide, as we periodically practiced doing, in case the Russians decided to aim an atomic bomb at P.S. 31.

I'd see my father every third Sunday. He was a lawyer. "I had some ten-dollar cases and also some small ones," he'd later quip. He worked his way through night law school at St. John's in Queens. I'm told that his father, whom I never met, was a sweet man who never had much of a head for business. With his life's savings, he had bought a neighborhood movie theater, and the only due diligence he'd done was to look at what the seller said were the theater's business records and stand outside the movie house one Saturday afternoon to see kids pouring in beyond capacity. After buying the theater, he learned that the seller had handed out free tickets the previous weekend throughout the neighborhood. The theater was nearly empty, and soon went kaput.

There was a junior high school program in New York City in those years called "SP"—"Special Progress"—in which supposedly gifted students completed three years of study in two. Though I was already one of the youngest children in my class, having been born in November, it was a foregone conclusion that if I were accepted to "SP" I would go, despite my being far younger than most others for the balance of my education. I was accepted, and I accepted.

The school was a long distance from Gerard Avenue. I'd walk there and back daydreaming. I developed a talent for procrastinating about homework, and played with other kids in the lot after school or, if nobody was there, played catch with myself, throwing a ball against a wall and fielding endless bounce-back grounders, line drives, and high flies before trudging upstairs to study.

I went to Hebrew school and was bar mitzvahed in a synagogue on the Grand Concourse three blocks from the lot. The temple had two rabbis named Katz. I got the older one, who made all his students memorize Hebrew words they'd soon forget. I did very little—no, nothing—that pleased my Rabbi Katz. He was an intimidating man although, looking back, I think he was much younger than I am now.

By the time I was ready for high school, my mother found a one-bedroom garden apartment in a suburb, and I spent three years as the youngest member of a seven-hundred-plus class at White Plains High School. The boy who sat behind me in home room, Jethro Lieberman, remains a close friend to this day. I was bored by what the teachers were teaching, was placed in mediocre classes for mediocre students, and my performance was mediocre.

As a high school graduation gift, my mother promised to take me to Israel. We didn't have enough money to go that year, but went the next. We spent one day on that trip attending the trial of Adolph Eichmann. He was seated in a closed glass protective booth, with several young Israeli policemen guarding him. The civilized court proceeding was eerily quiet and antiseptic, starkly contrasting with the beyond-inhuman events being recounted. I wanted to smash Eichmann's bullet-proof glass enclosure and rip him to shreds, but simply listened to the witnesses describe horrors.

When the time came for college, I barely got into NYU, which in those days, 1960, was not the caliber school it is today. NYU had a liberal arts branch in the Bronx, which accepted me. My father paid my tuition. By then, my mother had moved back to the Bronx, with me in tow. Money was too scarce for me to live on campus. Our new apartment was three bus rides away from the school—three eternal outdoor waits in the cold of winter.

I developed an interest in writing and became editor-in-chief of the college's daily newspaper, yearbook, and handbook. The biggest challenge in publishing a daily college newspaper was finding news worthy of reporting five days a week. The trick was to magnify the inconsequential in print.

Even after looking under stones to find news to print, the physical production of the newspaper was challenging. The printing plant was in lower Manhattan. Five late afternoons a week, someone on the newspaper's staff, often me, had to trek down from the Bronx campus to lower Manhattan with typewritten stories, deliver them to the printer, and stay there until early morning, proofreading text coming off the presses—and then, without sleep, attend classes in the morning.

I managed. Reading course material on the subways, and while waiting for galleys to be printed late at night and early in the morning, became second nature.

Through hard work, luck, belatedly developing an interest in learning, and gentle grading by several professors, I did well enough to be accepted into Harvard Law School. Though Harvard accepted me, I wasn't sure I wanted to go. First, I would be twenty years old, far below the age and experience I assumed most others there would be and have. Second, I figured everyone else there was especially smart, and I certainly wasn't. And third, I hadn't had any real-world experience: I'd had summer jobs selling household goods at a department store, delivered newspapers, been a "stringer" for the *New York Times* phoning in high school football game scores, been a summer camp counselor, and worked one summer in the New York City Department of Welfare evaluating welfare recipients' needs. Additionally, I had no idea what lawyers actually do, but it seemed far less exciting than writing the great American novel, which I had several times started.

My father said he'd be happy to pay the law school tuition, but I told him that I wanted to go to graduate school in English literature instead. He was a practical man, and said that would be a big mistake. When he couldn't pierce my stubbornness, he said he wanted me to meet a man he knew named Larry Wein. Wein was an extraordinarily successful lawyer-businessman who had invented the concept of real estate syndication with some famous properties in New York City, including the Empire State Building.

I had no idea what "real estate syndication" meant, but agreed to meet Wein. My father accompanied me to Wein's 48th-floor office in the Lincoln Building in mid-Manhattan. Wein led us to plush armchairs and, doubtlessly prepared by my well-meaning father, regaled us with the glories of the practice of law and the riches it could bestow. He was a man whose time was very valuable, and as we said goodbye I thanked him for having taken the time to meet with me.

As soon as my father and I were in the elevator going down, I told him I was even more determined to do post-graduate work in English. I couldn't imagine spending my life in work as dull as Wein's seemed to be.

My father kept encouraging me to go to law school, pursuing the world's most difficult carpentry job: screwing an older head onto young shoulders. Because of his persistence, plus a combination of the prospect of being confronted with yet another series of post-graduate applications and curiosity about what Harvard Law School might be like, I decided to head up there.

Chapter 3
Two Cambridges and Washington, D.C.

My high school buddy, Jethro, had also been admitted, and we decided to share an apartment in Cambridge. The apartment was on the top floor of a run-down four-story walk-up at 901 Massachusetts Avenue with a rickety dumbwaiter for garbage removal, next door to the Daniel F. O'Brien Funeral Home and precisely a seventeen-minute walk from the law school campus. An old doctor I knew, whose office was in the middle of Harlem, offered us some dilapidated furniture he was about to throw away. Jethro and I rented a small U-Haul, and late one night packed it full of the doctor's beaten-up chairs and tables. As we were pulling away from the curb, a drug addict or drunk or lunatic grabbed onto the open passenger window of our car and tried to crawl in. We pried his hands off the door and pulled away, leaving him sprawling in the street.

In the middle of the night, we pulled into Cambridge and parked the U-Haul in front of the funeral home. There was a parking ticket on the front window the following morning, and an irate funeral director berated us for having blocked a funeral.

The law school was intimidating. Everything was imposing— the buildings, the history, the reputation. I was raw and insecure, and assumed that most of the others were more qualified than me to be there. The insecurity was only somewhat relieved by an introductory address to the 535 members of the class by Dean Erwin Griswold, a legend of the law school and lawyerdom, who introduced himself as the maître d' of this bevy of prima donnas. Years ago, Griswold told us, entering first-year students here would be told to look at the classmates to your left and to your right, because by the time you graduate one of the three of you will be gone. Those days were past, he assured us—now, the law school picks its students far too selectively for that to happen. Blessedly, I had become part of the chosen can't-miss few.

True or not, the butterflies in my stomach soon subsided. For sure, there were many accomplished, experienced, and self-assured people sitting in that auditorium, and I had no expectation of starring. I knew I wasn't going to be near the top of the class, so the tension of trying to excel didn't exist; and nestling comfortably in the middle seemed doable without too much hard work or stress. In any event, if things didn't work out, there was always the fallback of post-graduate work in English.

My half of the rent at 901 Mass. Ave. was $62.50 per month, narrowly within my budget. As a special hidden feature of the apartment, water poured through the roof and into my bedroom during the first rainstorm after we'd moved in. When I complained to the landlord, he asked what we had expected for $125 per month, but fixed the leak.

The entering law school class was divided equally into four groups. The students in each group took all courses together. None of the teachers was a woman, and only 5 percent of the students were.

Classrooms had a lectern in the front, surrounded by tiered concentric semi-circles of attached desks. The professors had seating charts, with the names and pictures of all students and their assigned seats.

Professors used the Socratic method to teach—instead of lectures, they grilled students about cases collected in casebooks, probing each student's understanding of the facts and issues, the courts' reasoning and underlying assumptions, and the value judgments and logic underlying their conclusions. Certain professors were humane, and others vicious, in their questioning.

Some professors would ask a few questions of a student picked at random, and then go on to another student similarly selected. Another professor would pick on one student for the entire fifty-minute session, working his way through the seating chart in order day by day. You couldn't escape the grilling. If it was your turn and you skipped that day's class, he'd get you the day you returned. His only sign of humanity was when the target one day turned out to be a chronic stutterer. After a few questions followed by painfully stammered answers, the professor went on to the next student, asked him a few questions, and spent the rest of the class questioning several other students seriatim.

Every professor expected full preparation every day—that is, reading and absorbing the required materials for that day's class. My contracts professor had a moderate mercy rule: If you were not prepared, simply write your name on a piece of paper and leave it on his desk before class began, and you would not be called on that day—but you'd better be prepared the day after. On most days, a handful of the timid would leave scraps of paper at his lectern, silently confessing their unpreparedness. On a day the professor was absent, he was replaced by another professor who had taught at the law school for decades and doubtless knew of this mercy rule. The substitute picked up the pieces of paper with the names of the confessed unprepareds, and said: These must be today's volunteers. For the next fifty minutes, he badgered each of them mercilessly about cases they had not read and had no idea about.

Courses ran the gamut of topics. During our first year, everyone took the same required courses: contracts, property, civil procedure, criminal law, and torts. We had some freedom of choice during the second year, and almost complete freedom of choice during the third.

Several of the professors were legendary, larger-than-life figures in the law. Some were less rough than others, intent more on exploring a principle through focused questioning than in putting someone on the hot seat.

I often wondered about the professors' lives outside the classroom. When one invited me for dinner at the faculty club, two renowned constitutional scholars, Paul Freund and Ernest Brown, sat together at a nearby table. The two, I learned, were regular dinner-mates. They barely uttered anything to each other throughout their meal, staring at their food. Another professor, years after I graduated, left his entire multi-million dollar estate to the law school; he apparently had no family.

For me, several courses were interesting, many not. Watching Professor Freund explore the scope of the Constitution's free speech clause and other constitutional safeguards held my attention far more than learning the niceties of commercial transactions or turgid rules of accounting. But disinterest could lead to humiliation. In my accounting class, I couldn't care whether an expense was reported in one year or another and so answered the professor's question by saying that in the long run it didn't matter; he skewered me with: "Yes, Mr. Frankel, but as John Maynard Keynes said, 'In the long run we're all dead,' so I suppose nothing matters."

The grading system at the law school was odd. Numerical

grades were used, and 75 was an A; 70 a B; 65 a C. I had no pretensions of excellence against the competition, many of whom studied day and night, and believed that simply graduating, undistinguished, would be sufficient. Grades were essentially based on final exams; mid-terms were rare. The week or two of finals were tension-filled—one exam after another, sometimes with no day in between, with the year's grade depending on one test result; not much time for catch-up if you hadn't followed the coursework during the term.

My grades weren't too shabby but not terrific—all in all nothing to write home about, and I didn't. By the third year, I'd become a cross between complacent and cocky. I began the year by missing the first few classes in one course, and then simply didn't bother going but read the book. Toward the end of the semester, a classmate told me that the professor, who'd known me from another course, saw my name on the seating chart and mused that he hadn't realized I was taking the class. The final exam was submitted anonymously; the professor didn't know whose paper he was grading, and it was the only A I got in three years.

Some of the courses sounded more interesting on paper than in the classroom. I signed up for an antitrust class, but neither understood nor cared much about the topic. My performance mirrored my disinterest, but I figured out a way to outsmart the professor, I thought. My handwriting has always been indecipherable. The final exam was all essays, so I hand-wrote my answers rather than typing, figuring the distinguished professor would have neither the interest nor patience to try to decipher my answers and I'd be graded somewhere in the middle of the class. But Professor Areeda's secretary called me to say he would appreciate my coming to his office and typing what I'd written, as he was having some difficulty reading it. I had no choice, and barely passed.

Professor Charles Allen Wright, a visiting Texas professor who later represented President Nixon in the Watergate scandal, had several affectations. He would never bring a book to class and would refer by memory to page numbers where cases began and quotes appeared. He would never wear an overcoat, braving the 0°F. Cambridge winter in only a suit. Nor would he call on any of the few women in the class, deliberately bypassing them as he scanned his seating chart deciding whom to question. Then one day, without warning, he had his "ladies' day," calling only on women.

Law school is designed to make you "think like a lawyer"— applying complete rationality and focused thinking to legal problems. "Justice" is done by applying the law to the facts, not by an abstract notion of what should be the right result. At a law school luncheon one day, I sat at a table with Professor Archibald Cox, who later became Watergate special prosecutor, so upright that Nixon's order that he be fired was refused in the "Saturday Night Massacre" by several layers of Justice Department officials and helped accelerate Nixon's downfall. Cox told a story illustrating the limitations of thinking like a lawyer. Early in his distinguished career, he had clerked for Learned Hand, a renowned federal judge of the U.S. Court of Appeals in Manhattan. One of the other judges on that court was Hand's cousin, Augustus Hand. Cox recounted how he had been at a meeting between the cousins. Learned Hand had analyzed the issues in a case with impeccable logic, going inexorably from A to Z to the conclusion. When he finished, said Cox, Augustus turned to Learned and asked, "But you don't really believe that, do you?"

I didn't lose my interest in writing. Jethro and I tried our hand at humor. One summer, we wrote a book-length spoof titled *A Frank Look At Emotions* under the pseudonym "Frank Look." It purported to trace the history of emotions, from their invention on April 17, 1153 by Francesco Francisi, a wine-maker and chemist who first extracted the feeling of happiness from the earth's sediments on the banks of the Euphylo River in a small town named Phleri in southern Italy and fed it to his beloved dog, Alfonso, who jumped up and down with joy and smiled rapturously.

We were at an age and stage where we thought that was witty. Neither of us had an agent or knew a publisher, and we let the finished manuscript languish in our files, where it still languishes.

During the summer following my first year at law school, I got a job in Washington as a reporter for the *Washington Daily News*, a second-rate tabloid newspaper that went out of business long ago. It was an afternoon paper, which means it went to press in the morning. While many of my classmates had opted for cushy and lucrative summer jobs at fine law firms, my days that summer began with an alarm clock ringing at 4:00 a.m. I'd get to the newspaper office by 5:00 a.m., put a quarter into a vending machine to buy a cup of yesterday's coffee, and sit down at a desk where that day's *Washington Post*, a morning newspaper, would be waiting for me. My first job each morning was to rewrite the morning *Post*'s obituary section, for publication in the afternoon's *News*.

As the summer progressed, my future as a journalist, particularly at the *News*, evaporated. Though I managed to master the art of rewriting obituaries while half asleep, my skill at the *News*'s style of journalism soon proved wanting. A heart-wrenching tragedy occurred in mid-summer when two brothers with mental disabilities drowned in a pool; one drowned trying to save the other. My editor assigned me to visit their mother, with the newspaper's photographer, to interview the mother and write a story describing her reactions to the tragedy. When we returned to the office, the photographer had photos, but I had no quotes from the mother. I explained to my editor that the tragedy was so horrible, and the woman's grief so deep, I hadn't had the heart to ask her any questions. The editor berated me for not getting quotes.

My journalism career ended a few weeks later. The same editor asked me to re-write a feature story that had appeared in the *Post*. Though the *Post* was a first-rate newspaper, that particular story—when read through the lens of someone who had finished a year of law school and had developed some ability to analyze sentence construction carefully—was nonsense: full of what someone "may have" felt, how someone "probably" reacted, and what "likely" occurred. The article was speculation masquerading as news. When I pointed that out to the editor and said that rewriting it would be foolish, he disdainfully looked away from me and said that he had told me to do something and I should do it. I obeyed, in a manner of speaking: I wrote what I thought was a clever parody of the *Post*'s article, handed it to the editor, and stood over him as he read.

He finished reading, glared at me, and demanded: "What is this?" I told him it was my resignation, walked out the door, and never returned.

The summer following my second year in law school was a noticeable improvement. I had taken several courses in criminal law, and they were the only ones that held my interest. Many second-year students at the law school traditionally apply for summer jobs at prominent law firms, where they are highly paid, treated liked potential pashas of the bar, and hope to secure offers of full-time high-paying employment after graduating. I landed a summer job as an intern at the U.S. Attorney's Office—the federal prosecutor—in Manhattan. The pay was $3 per day. (Many years later, when I met my old boss and reminded him of the salary, he told me I'd been overpaid.) I lived for the summer with my mother in her apartment in the Bronx and took a series of subways to the office in lower Manhattan. The subways and lunch cost more than my daily pay, but I would have paid for the job if I'd had money.

Each summer assistant was assigned to a prosecutor, and we did whatever was asked—legal research, attending witness interviews, arranging exhibits—anything. I was lucky: The prosecutor I worked for had two trials that summer. I sat next to him and watched him select juries, make opening statements, examine witnesses, make objections, deliver summations—the whole range of a trial. It was intoxicating, and I was hooked.

While law school helped teach about the rights of the accused, I learned from real-world exposure in a prosecutor's office that most people accused of crime are actually guilty. I learned other practicalities of the law. Arraignments of dozens of indicted defendants—the preliminary stage at which an accused is formally advised of the charges against him and pleads either guilty or not guilty—were conducted in a large courtroom. The spectator gallery would be packed with defendants and their counsel waiting for their cases to be called. One judge had an effective way of reducing the backlog by reducing the number of trials. Before calling the first case for arraignment, he'd announce to the gallery: Anyone who wants justice, sit on the left; anyone who wants mercy, sit on the right. As people moved, you could almost feel the courtroom tilt to the right.

By the time my last year of law school began, I knew I wanted to be a criminal lawyer, or certainly a trial lawyer. But by then—I graduated in June 1967—the Vietnam War was exploding, military service was compulsory, and graduates at all levels, college and post-graduate, were being drafted. Many of my classmates sought a way out, and I thought more education could be my ticket. I applied to a special post-graduate program in criminology at the University of Cambridge in England. They said yes. Now all I had to do was get my draft board to defer my call-up.

My local draft board called me for an interview to consider my deferment request shortly before I graduated. The board met in the heart of the Bronx, near where I'd grown up. When I appeared for my interview, the waiting room was filled with young men from minority groups, all apparently from low economic backgrounds. When my name was called, I walked into a small room. The chairman of the committee had my file in his hand and said: Let's see, you graduated from NYU, you're graduating from Harvard Law School, and now you want to study criminology in England while everyone else is fighting in Vietnam? He was not impressed, and my application was denied.

I graduated from the law school soon after. I probably graduated around the middle of the class, but I don't know for sure. Only the top 25 percent got ranked, and I wasn't among them. The bottom 75 percent don't know where they ranked in that large pot. My speculation is that I wasn't near the top of the unranked, and I'll settle for speculating that I wasn't at the bottom.

The graduation ceremony at Harvard is impressive. I don't recall at this point who spoke or who was honored, but the war was on most people's minds and a common theme of the speakers, partly because of the war's unpopularity but especially because of most graduates' vulnerability to the draft.

I received an LL.B. degree—Bachelor of Laws. Some law schools were by then conferring JD degrees on their graduates—"Juris Doctor," or Doctor of Laws—instead of LL.B.'s. The switch had nothing to do with the rigor of the programs, but was simply an elevated form of nomenclature—a free upgrade because federal agencies that hired lawyers paid higher salaries to those with doctorates. Harvard hadn't yet made the switch. Several years after I graduated, everyone in my class received a letter from the law school dean advising that the law school would henceforth be awarding JDs instead of LL.B.s to its graduates, and offering to replace our LL.B. diplomas with JDs if we would simply mail in a $25 check (or $35 if we wanted it in Latin). I discarded the letter and retained my LL.B. diploma, but a more ornery classmate wrote back to the dean: Thanks, but I'm content with my LL.B.; however I've always wanted a Harvard doctorate in nuclear physics, and since the university is now offering doctorates for $35, enclosed is my check for one of those instead.

Graduating from law school did not make me a lawyer; I still had to take the bar exam. I enrolled in a prep course with hundreds of other recent graduates. Rather than the abstract thinking I'd been exposed to for three years at Harvard, I had to suffer through six weeks of memorizing a compendium of useless legal rules, most of which were soon forgotten and any of which could simply be looked up when needed.

When the bar exam ordeal ended, I had to face another challenge: avoiding military service now that my University of Cambridge gambit had failed. Fear of getting killed or maimed in a pointless war overcame my sense of fairness to those who served, so I resolved to avoid the draft if possible. My only defense, and I acknowledge its meagerness, is that trying to avoid serving was commonplace at the time.

My physical examination by an Army doctor was scheduled to take place soon. After three years of legal training, I figured the Selective Service System must have rules establishing exemptions from service. I'd be my first law client. In those pre-internet days, the only way to find out the rules, and whether I could find a loophole to squeeze through, was a trip to the Library of Congress in Washington.

I took a long bus-ride to get there, spent hours poring through a mountain of regulations, and extracted two nuggets: wool allergies (because Army uniforms contain wool), and strains of hay fever with specific Latin names, were grounds for exemption. I was allergic to wool and some types of ragweed. I xeroxed the applicable pages from the manual of regulations, returned home, and through an acquaintance got the name of an allergist. I visited him, showed him the regulations, let him examine me, paid his fee, and walked out of his office holding his letter attesting to my suffering from wool allergies and the requisite Latin-named hay fever.

A few days later, I took a subway ride to Whitehall Street in lower Manhattan, where Army physicals were given. There was a long line of call-ups, and Army doctors were processing them like cattle, seconds per candidate. When I gave the doctor my allergist's letter, he cross-checked its phraseology against the language of the regulations in the book in front of him, barely looked at me, and classified me 1Y—not draftable except in an emergency. Now I could study criminology in Cambridge.

But that didn't happen. Shortly before my scheduled flight, a law school professor of mine called. In my last year at the law school, I had done legal research for a book he had been writing. Now, he was calling to say that he'd been asked whether he knew someone who might be interested in joining the staff of a newly formed White House Task Force On Crime, working out of the new Executive Office Building across the street from the White House.

It sounded interesting. I went to Washington for an interview by the executive director of the Task Force, and learned that I would not simply be joining the staff—I would *be* the staff. The Task Force itself consisted of twelve eminent personalities, including Warren Christopher, who would later become U.S. Secretary of State. They would meet in Washington every few weeks. The only full-time employees would be the executive director, who had recently finished clerking for Chief Justice Earl Warren, and his staff of—me.

Our job was to draft proposed anti-crime legislation for President Johnson to submit to Congress. The life of the Task Force would end in a few months, as the President wanted to present this signature piece of legislation soon. I was offered a salary of $151 per week and accepted immediately. I called the University of

Cambridge to say that I'd be delayed in arriving but would catch up when I got there.

At the age of twenty-three, saying that you work for the White House is intoxicating stuff. White House stationery is thick. My letterhead said simply

The White House
Washington

On my first day at work, I used it to send a handwritten note to my mother, saying only: "Hi Mom." I found the letter among her belongings when she died thirty-seven years later.

When I'd call someone and tell the secretary it's "Sandor Frankel from the White House," the call was always taken. The chairman of the Task Force told me that with all his experience, even he had learned from his exposure to this kind of power. When he was in the office of the President's chief domestic advisor, Joe Califano, and the phone rang, a slew of secretaries was available to answer; but on the several occasions when the phone button labeled "POTUS" lit, Califano himself would pick up on the first ring.

After several months, the executive director and I presented a list of recommendations for anti-crime legislation; the Task Force members convened, selected, and edited what they thought were the most worthy; and the final recommendations were submitted to Califano for submission to the President, who submitted a version to Congress. That is how the Omnibus Crime Control And Safe Streets Act Of 1968 came into existence.

During my stint with the Task Force, protests against the Vietnam War were raging across the country. Huge crowds, often unruly, gathered at the Pentagon and at powerful symbols of the government, including the White House.

I met several people who worked at the White House, discussing the potential physical dangers: What if the protestors scaled the fence surrounding the White House grounds? Should guards shoot to kill? Then I would leave my office across the street from the White House, slip off my tie, and join the mass of protestors.

Heady as my exposure to power was, the job ended in three months when the Task Force submitted its recommendations to the White House, and I had to decide what next to do. I flew to England and walked in unannounced to the office of the director of the post-graduate criminology program at the University of Cambridge. I introduced myself and apologized for being three months late. He wondered if I'd be able to catch up. I told him not to worry, and asked for the course material and required reading list. He gave the list to me, along with an armful of books, and took me to an empty dormitory room, saying he admired what he called my gumption. After wishing me good luck, he left me alone.

I sat on the bed, read the list of books, and thumbed through several of the books he had left with me. I quickly realized, having been exposed to the exhilaration of working for the White House for several months, that my days of formal education were behind me and I had no patience for further studies, and was ready for the real world. I spent the night in the Cambridge dorm, and the next morning walked into the director's office, thanked him but said no thanks, and said goodbye.

When I returned to the States, I moved into an unfurnished one-bedroom apartment across the Potomac River from Washington D.C. I had saved enough for a few months' rent and some cheap furniture, and figured I'd find a job quickly. After signing the lease, I called my father to tell him I'd found a nice unfurnished place that I'd soon be filling up. The next day, two deliverymen rang my doorbell and brought in furniture for the apartment, a present from my father.

While I was working for the White House, I had met Califano's chief assistant, Matthew Nimetz, who worked near Califano in the White House. When I returned from England, I called him and said I'd like to work for the U.S. Attorney's Office in Washington. I knew there was a requirement that candidates have at least two years of post-law school experience, but said I was confident I could do the job now, and asked if he could help.

At the time, the U.S. Attorney in Washington was David Bress. He had been a distinguished Washington attorney before being appointed U.S. Attorney, and it was known in the Washington legal community that he coveted an appointment as a federal judge. Nominations for those judgeships are made by the President.

Nimetz told me to submit an application to Bress. I did. Shortly, I received notice of an interview, and an offer. Clearance by the FBI would take about six weeks, after which I would be sworn in as a federal prosecutor.

That was my first experience with political influence. Nimetz also exposed me to a stark example of American democracy at work. After I had been in the U. S. Attorney's Office for half a year, he invited me to lunch at the White House mess—a cafeteria in the White House open to senior White House staff, cabinet members, and other high government officials and their guests. The invitation was for election day in 1968. Sitting at other tables all around Nimetz and me were front-page political figures. The talk at every table was speculation about who would win the election that day. In the highest corridors of power, among the highest levels of American government, a few steps from the oval office, nobody knew any more than me about who would be announced later that evening as the next President of the United States.

During the time it took for the FBI to do a background check and certify that nothing in my past disqualified me from being a federal prosecutor, I needed to eat and pay the rent, and in any event, I didn't want to sit around uselessly. I got a short-term position with the National Commission for Reform of Federal Criminal Laws, established by Congress to propose revisions to the United States Criminal Code. They knew my stay was short-term, and assigned me to analyze an extremely boring subsection of a very unexciting statute.

The six weeks the FBI needed to decide that I wasn't a security risk passed quickly enough, and was, in hindsight, not without interest. One of my bosses was a few years older than I. He was highly sociable and often invited me to join him for mid-afternoon coffee. He always wore a tie and suspenders decorated with configurations of elephants, and I was told he was very active in Republican Party politics. His name was John Dean. I felt sorry for him when he testified before the Senate Watergate Committee several years later about how he had helped obstruct justice as counsel to President Nixon, and when he was sentenced to prison.

After the FBI cleared me, I was sworn in as an Assistant U.S. Attorney. My starting salary was $7,850 a year. It was more than I needed, and anyway I didn't care about money. I cared about learning to try cases in a courtroom, and the U.S. Attorney's Office in Washington was a good training ground for aspiring trial lawyers. Because of the District of Columbia's unique governmental status, prosecutors have an opportunity to try crimes traditionally prosecuted by local district attorneys' offices, from petty theft to murder, as well as federal offenses. Washington was rife with crime, and prosecutors in the office were always busy.

My service in the office began two weeks before the assassination of Martin Luther King and was a baptism by fire. When Dr. King was killed, riots broke out all over Washington—fires, smashing of store windows, looting. A curfew was declared. Soldiers were stationed with machine-guns on the courthouse steps. Hundreds of rioters were arrested and processed through the local Court of General Sessions.

I was an inexperienced twenty-four-year-old, learning on the fly, making decisions about whom to prosecute and for what, handling dozens of arraignments. One morning, after I'd been a prosecutor for a few weeks, my supervisor handed me a file and told me to go to a particular courtroom and try the case. He said the judge was waiting there with the defendant and his lawyer, a jury panel was waiting, and the judge was furious that no prosecutor had yet arrived in the courtroom. I was apparently to be the designated sacrificial lamb for the judge's fury. I took the file but protested to my supervisor: I don't think you should send me—I've never tried a case or been trained to try one. He assured me: Don't worry, this is a simple case, you can do it, the most important lesson to remember is that whenever there's a recess, use the bathroom because you can't control when the next recess will be called. I went to the courtroom. The judge excoriated me for being late, and the defendant pleaded guilty.

Over the three years I spent in the office, I was given a wide variety of cases. In the beginning, I was assigned, like all newcomers, to the general intake part, deciding which among an array of crimes warranted prosecution. I also learned the ways of the Washington streets, riding in the rear of patrol cars to learn what police work is really like. The academic world of casebooks is very different from sitting in the back of a patrol car next to rifles, when the cars are racing through dangerous streets, sirens blaring, and you are wondering what awful surprise may lurk around the corner.

After learning my way around the courtroom prosecuting petty crimes, I graduated to appellate work, writing and arguing the government's opposition to appeals by convicted defendants. In

Washington, there are two court systems—local (like the state systems) and federal—and I argued appeals in both. The next step
was trying serious crimes—murders, armed robberies, frauds—the
gamut of crimes that exposed the raw underbelly of human emotions and greed.

Several of my colleagues in the office became lifelong friends.
We'd strategize about each other's cases without being competi-
tive. On weekends, we had access to a ballfield across the street
from the White House—softball in summer, football in winter, all
played with enthusiasm, laughs, and proof beyond doubt that
sports was not our calling. And we became real trial lawyers after
trying cases on a regular basis. At the end of each week we'd meet
at a local bar called The Bull, regaling each other with exaggerated
stories of our successes and others' follies, until we had to change
venue when a detective told us that the owners of The Bull were
under investigation for serious crimes.

T he criminal courtroom is a laboratory where human passion,
depravity, and greed are told in the often cold and dispassionate
words of witnesses and lawyers bound by rules of evidence and
decorum. At times, a slice of humor slides under the door:

I PROSECUTED AN ARMED ROBBERY CASE before Judge Hart, a
curmudgeonly federal judge who never cracked a smile on the
bench. The evidence of the defendant's guilt was overwhelming,
and the jury should have returned a guilty verdict in minutes.
Instead, after more time than should have been necessary, the jury
sent a note to the judge, asking: One of the jurors is hard of hearing; what should we do?

Judge Hart sent back a note: Talk louder.

The jury sent back another note: Juror #7 hasn't heard a word of the testimony.

Judge Hart summoned juror #7 back to his seat in the jury box and asked him: I understand you haven't heard a word of the testimony. Is that right?

Juror #7 looked back, cupped a hand to his ear, and asked: What did you say?

This time the Judge yelled at him: Why didn't you tell me you couldn't hear when I asked at the beginning of the case whether anyone had a reason he couldn't sit as a juror?

The juror answered: Because I didn't hear the question.

The Judge declared a mistrial. We retried the case the next day, and the jury returned a guilty verdict in minutes.

JIM SHARP WAS a down-home young lawyer from Oklahoma who claimed that he didn't know how to find the library, but who knew how to make a point with a jury. He was prosecuting a bank robbery case. His only evidence was grainy security film, and a single thumbprint matching the defendant's that had been lifted from the teller's counter where the robber had vaulted over to get the cash. The defendant claimed never to have been in the bank, and not even to have been in Washington on the day of the robbery.

Jim summed up to the jury: Folks, the defendant may be telling us the truth when he says he didn't rob the bank and has never even been there. I didn't see him there. You didn't see him. The judge didn't either. So maybe he wasn't there. But one thing we know for sure: his thumb was there.

(Jim later represented President Bush ("W") in a CIA leak investigation. They became friendly. The President called him one day while Jim was driving with someone. Their conversation began:

Jim?

Jim recognized the voice and answered: Yes, Sir.

You with someone?

Yes, Sir.

If he's a client, don't call me Sir. Call me Mr. President—you can raise your fee.)

T oward the end of my third year in the U.S. Attorney's Office, I was prosecuting a murder case in front of Judge Jones, a highly regarded United States District Judge before whom I'd tried several cases. The defendant pled guilty after I cross-examined him. Following the plea, Judge Jones asked me to come into his robing room.

I'm friendly with Colonel Spiegelberg, the judge told me. Spiegelberg was a founding partner of Strasser Spiegelberg (now known as Fried Frank), a large Wall Street law firm. He had asked Judge Jones to recommend a good young trial lawyer for the firm. Judge Jones knew I was from New York, and asked whether I was interested. I told him I was.

He said he'd give my name to Spiegelberg, and was certain I'd get a call.

M y interest in writing hadn't dried up while I was in the U.S. Attorney's Office.

President Johnson had appointed a committee to study obscenity in the United States. The committee's work continued under President Nixon, and my friend Jethro and I anticipated their publishing an absurdly puritanical tract screaming for parody. We preemptively obliged, and anonymously wrote a book titled *Report*

To the President's Commission on Obscenity and Pornography, which purported to be the government committee's report. We took it to a small publishing house whose owner thought the manuscript was clever and bought it. Our "report" hit bookstores in the United States and England soon afterwards. We were thrilled to spot it at the checkout counters at several New York City bookstores.

The major book-trade publications prominently reviewed it. *Kirkus,* one of the most important, thought it was funny, citing as an example our graph of "Percent of frequency in total verbiage of specified work in ascending order of verbal grossness." *Publishers Weekly,* alas, was humorless, mistaking the parody as being the real presidential report and criticizing the "committee of distinguished citizens" who supposedly wrote it for having produced "a 40-karat gem of unconscious parody and humor."

Several government agencies were not amused. Soon after publication, the Federal Trade Commission and the New York State Attorney General threatened us for deceiving the public into buying a parody thinking it was the real report, and the real Presidential Commission wrote to tell us they had brought the book to the attention of the U.S. Department of Justice.

Jethro and I thought government agencies trying to prevent two young amateurs from mocking a government report was free publicity from heaven, an ideal launching-pad for the book, and urged our publisher to publicize the threats. But the publisher had no stomach for litigating against Big Brother, pulled the book, and short-circuited our incipient career as parodists.

My next literary foray arose shortly before I left the U.S. Attorney's Office. Though some of the cases we prosecuted were open-and-shut, many weren't. One in particular struck me as particularly dramatic: The prosecution of two men accused of murdering three people in a carwash combined a poignant picture of

life in the ghetto with the uncertainties of proving guilt or innocence in a courtroom. I thought the case would allow a clear and
hopefully popular presentation of the criminal justice system at
work. The key to making the case bookworthy would be a man
named Robert Roscoe, who lived in a seedy section of Washington
and knew many out-of-courtroom aspects of the case and the dra-
matis personae.

I phoned Roscoe, introduced myself, and said I wanted to interview him for a book about the carwash case. He agreed to meet at
a dingy bar he selected in a dangerous section of Washington. We'd
never met but he said he'd be able to spot me as soon as I walked
in.

When I got there, he approached and led me to a corner of the
bar. The place was filled with rough-looking folks, none of whom
looked as though they had post-graduate degrees. I was the only
white person.

He asked how much I would pay for an interview. My yearly
salary had climbed to $8,000, and my bank account had little
more than next month's rent money. I asked how much he wanted.

I'll talk to you for $10,000, he said.

I said I had $50, took the bills out of my pocket, and offered
them. He accepted.

I spent hours with him at the bar that night, taking copious
notes. When we finished, I had barely enough money left to pay
the bar tab. I thanked him and walked the several miles back to
my apartment, thinking. By the time I got home, the outline for
Beyond A Reasonable Doubt was clear.

Chapter 4

Back to New York

With Judge Jones's stamp of approval, I was in Colonel Spiegelberg's spacious office in lower Manhattan being interviewed for a job. Over the years, I had heard stories of young lawyers being buried in the minutiae of never-ending cases, and wanted to be certain the same fate wouldn't befall me. Empowered by the arrogance of youth and the misimpression harbored by many ex-prosecutors that I was good enough to try skillfully any case at any time, I expressed concern to Colonel Spiegelberg about being assigned as low man on a large-case totem pole. He assured me that would not happen. I accepted a position in the firm's litigation department at $15,000 per year, the rate top firms paid lawyers in those days and almost double my government salary.

Several weeks later, I arrived at the firm ready to conquer the world of New York City trial work. The firm's reception room was large, with plush furniture and lush gold carpeting. I was given an office with a window looking across a small, dark courtyard. The office was lined with gigantic file cabinets. I was so inexperienced I hadn't known that filing cabinets that large were manufactured.

I was assigned to work for a senior partner named Larry Rosenthal. I assured him I would quickly master all the cases in the cabinets. He corrected me: The cabinets contained files of only one case, which had been pending for many years. My job was to learn the case. I was to begin reading from the upper left of the cabinets, and keep reading until I'd reached the lower right. Larry had litigated the case over several years, and now I also was to learn it, at the expense of the law firm's public company client, Linn Broadcasting, so that when I carried Larry's briefcase and sat silently by his side, I would do so knowledgeably.

The following day, I told the head of the litigation department that reviewing years-worth of Linn Broadcasting files wasn't what I had signed up for. Though the firm insisted I continue to work on—that is, uselessly read the files of—the case, when they realized the depths of my dissatisfaction they also assigned me to work on a case that had recently come into the office—a breach of contract lawsuit in which the firm represented a then-popular recording artist named Melanie. I would assist the partner in charge of that case, interacting with Melanie's outside counsel. My primary job, though, would continue to be plowing through the bottomless Linn Broadcasting files and generating time-sheets.

Though big-firm law practice made me miserable, it provided an element of financial security and stability I'd never felt. I hadn't thought about issues of money before. My financial needs at law school were small, the modest salary at the U.S. Attorney's Office had been enough for me, and my present financial needs were limited. But exposure to big money, even for a short time, had its impact. I doubted that any of the lawyers at Strasser Spiegelberg, even the older ones, had tried as many cases as I had in my three years at the U.S. Attorney's Office, and I knew if I stuck out the tedium I'd eventually become a partner and financially secure. Yet the professional lifestyle didn't seem worth bearing for the ultimate prize. I discussed with my father my disappointment at being stuffed in an office with reams of boring paper, and asked his advice.

"You've got to break an egg to make an omelet," he advised.

I resolved to leave. I needed an escape hatch, but having only recently moved back to New York City, had no connections. I called everyone I could think of, and after a few weeks finally found someone who had once been a neighbor of an attorney named Boris Kostelanetz.

I had heard the name Kostelanetz before. Andre Kostelanetz was an internationally known music conductor, and his brother Boris was one of the two preeminent New York City tax fraud lawyers at the time. The other was Lou Bender.

I dialed Kostelanetz' number, got past his secretary, introduced myself, and told him my circumstances: that I'd been trying cases for several years in the U.S. Attorney's Office, and was eager to escape a large law firm before professional rigor mortis set in. He said he had a small firm and no positions open. I asked whether he'd meet with me simply as a sounding board, and said I had no expectation of a job with him. He asked when I'd like to meet, and I said as soon as we end this conversation. We met that afternoon.

These days, many large firms have tax fraud and other white-collar criminal law departments. In 1971, Kostelanetz and Bender were the only lawyers you'd go to see if you had a tax fraud problem. They had written the book, figuratively and liter-ally (*Criminal Aspects Of Tax Fraud Cases*). As a summer intern years earlier in the U.S. Attorney's Office, I had met Kostelanetz. My boss at the time had invited me to sit in at a meeting he was going to have with him, and told me that I could learn by watching the man operate.

As I now sat in his office explaining my plight, Kostelanetz listened patiently and with apparent empathy. He repeated that he was sorry he had no position to offer and said he would ask some other lawyers he knew whether they were looking to hire someone with my background. I sized him up as being a very bright and decent man, and knew that his reputation was stellar. I decided on the spot to offer to work for him for clerical pay, just enough to pay my rent and eat, if he had space and a desk for me.

Before I could make the offer, his secretary interrupted to say that someone was calling him. I offered to step out, but he motioned for me to stay and took the call. As the call was winding down, Kostelanetz asked the caller whether he wanted to hire a lawyer. The answer was plainly yes, because Kostelanetz handed me the phone and said, "Say hello to Lou Bender."

Bender asked when I could meet him, and I was in his office within an hour. He was in his early sixties, had been a single practitioner with one associate for many years, had recently grown disappointed with the associate, and wanted to replace him. He offered me a job, and I accepted. We remained associates, and then partners, until he retired twenty years later.

The transition from the stuffiness of a big law firm to a two-man practice with Lou was refreshing. He was famous among his contemporaries. He'd been an All-American basketball player at Columbia University, and played professional basketball with the original Celtics in the days when a six-foot-two-inch athlete could play center. People would still stop him on the street, decades later, to say how much they'd enjoyed watching him play.

Like Kostelanetz, Lou was a tax fraud specialist, and I learned how to defend tax fraud cases by watching him do it, then doing it with him, and then doing it myself. Neither of us was a tax expert. If you wanted to figure out how to structure a transaction in the most tax-efficient way, or to get the answers to substantive tax questions, you wouldn't come to us. But if the IRS was investigating whether you had cheated on your taxes—deliberately underreporting your income, or taking phony deductions—or if you'd been charged for allegedly having done that, you might find yourself in our office, and we might be able to help: poking holes in the government's case, establishing defenses, occasionally establishing that you were actually innocent, or trying to convince the sentencing judge that you'd lived the life of Mother Teresa and should be forgiven the one sin.

Over the years, we represented a rogues' gallery of alleged tax fraud and other miscreants:

A LAWYER WHO DIVERTED payments from one of his firm's clients, deposited the checks into his own account, and then failed to report the money as income on his personal income tax returns.

AN ACCOUNTANT WHO BRIBED an IRS agent to get a favorable result on an audit. We had quite a few of these. The agents would invariably follow the same script: asking the accountant to count the bribe money out loud, while surreptitiously recording the counting on a concealed body recorder, and then asking the accountant what he wanted the agent to do for the money. Several accountants who had been arrested and came to us for representation were amazed that we could tell them what happened before they told us.

A TRADESMAN TRANSACTED MUCH of his business in unreported cash. He would keep the cash in a bank vault, and periodically visit the vault to count and fondle the money. He picked one wrong day to count and fondle: Robbers came into the bank, he had more cash readily available than the tellers, so the robbers took his money and left. They were captured soon after, with the cash. The F.B.I. wanted to interview him. If he acknowledged that the money was his, he risked an IRS investigation; if he didn't, he'd lose the money. He wanted our advice.

A TAXPAYER RECEIVED AN IRS request to send proof of charitable deductions reported on his tax return. He mailed in copies of receipts on the letterheads of several ostensible charitable organizations. The names, addresses, and phone numbers on the receipts were fictitious, and he had printed the receipts himself. He had received a notice to appear at an IRS audit with the originals of the receipts, and retained us to represent him.

I told the auditor that the taxpayer was withdrawing the documents previously submitted. The auditor said there was no IRS procedure for withdrawing documents. I said the taxpayer was withdrawing the documents anyway, and also was withdrawing the charitable deductions on his tax returns. The auditor said there was no IRS procedure for withdrawing the deductions. I said the taxpayer withdraws them anyway. The taxpayer got lucky: He only had to pay an additional tax plus interest and a small financial penalty, but escaped criminal charges.

THE OWNER OF A small business wanted to sell his business and retire. A prospective buyer sounded serious, and asked to see tax returns. The returns showed little revenue. The owner told the buyer that he reported whatever number struck his fancy, and the true revenue was recorded in a separate set of books, which he then showed. The "buyer" was an undercover IRS agent, and the seller was arrested.

A DOCTOR'S LONG-TIME bookkeeper would hand him patients' receipts at the end of each day, but log only a handful of them into the doctor's "official" record used for tax reporting. After many years of loyal service, the bookkeeper asked for a raise which the doctor thought was excessive, and he fired her. She visited him shortly afterwards, and showed him years of crumpled patients' receipts which she had been removing from his wastebasket and meticulously saving for years. She offered to sell them back to him.

THE CHIEF EXECUTIVE AT A successful business decided to redecorate the corporate offices. Payments to vendors were made by his assistant. When the project was nearly completed, the assistant left the company. After she left, one more bill came in, for a new lamp he had never seen. The executive soon discovered that the assistant had furnished her entire apartment at the company's expense. The assistant came to us—she hadn't reported any of the stolen property as income on her tax returns.

THE PURCHASING AGENT OF a department store chain had the job of deciding which goods the chain would carry. He struck a deal with one sales representative: That rep would be a chosen supplier, but would "kick back" a percentage of the sales to the purchasing agent in cash. After a few years of this cozy relationship, the sales rep, who had struck similar deals with other purchasing agents, was investigated for bribery, and thought his best chance of escape would be to cooperate with the investigators by naming those he'd given cash to. The purchasing agent came to see us because, of course, he hadn't reported any of the cash on his tax returns.

A HIGH-BRACKET TAXPAYER devised what he'd thought was a clever scheme. He would write out checks to charities, but after the charities had deposited the checks and they were returned with his bank statements, he would alter them with the same pen he'd used to write them—for example, changing a "1" to "4," and writing "four" in front of the word "hundred"—and deduct the altered amounts on his tax return. He hadn't realized that a computer prints the amount of each check in the lower right-hand corner as the check passes through the banking system. He came to see us after an IRS agent, during a routine audit, noticed discrepancies between the computer notations and the face amounts of the checks.

A GOVERNMENT PURCHASING AGENT in charge of extensive renovations of several government buildings conspired with a building contractor to have building materials supposedly ordered for the government project delivered instead to the purchasing agent's own home. After an auditor raised questions, inspectors showed up at the purchasing agent's home and discovered items bearing serial numbers of government-purchased goods. Not only had he stolen government property, but of course he hadn't paid taxes on it either. The prosecutor described our client as having an edifice complex.

A FAMOUS MUSIC COMPOSER tried to lower his taxes by increasing his deductions. He donated his original musical scores and arrangements to a university, and took a large charitable deduction on his income tax return based on what he claimed was the fair market value of the contribution. He supported the deduction with letters from highly reputable institutions and musicians who were household names. The signatures were forged.

A HOTEL OWNER HAD two business bank accounts. He deposited into one account the receipts he intended to report to the IRS, and deposited into the other account the receipts he intended to keep for himself. Hotel guests were unaware, since the backs of all checks indicated they had been deposited into the hotel's business account. Very simple plan, but he got caught.

A LAWYER LOVED ARTWORK. He regularly visited the Metro-politan Museum of Art in Manhattan with one of those large port-folios you've seen artists use to carry their drawings. He'd visit one of the drawings and prints rooms at the museum, and leave with choice selections stowed inside the portfolio. The museum noticed a pattern of missing artwork after his visits, and asked the police to stake out the room. The next time he came, they arrested him leaving the museum with that day's loot in tow. He is no longer practicing law. He became an art dealer.

A LAWYER CAME TO see me with a client who had a problem, and I gave some advice that worked. The lawyer called me soon after. This time, he himself had a problem. He'd "borrowed" money from his escrow account. Money in an escrow account is held in trust by the lawyer, with no right to touch it, temporarily or otherwise. The lawyer said he'd intended to replenish the account, but now his client was pressing for the money and the lawyer was a bit short of funds. He asked what I thought he should do. "Return the money immediately" took longer than it should have to sink in.

WE REPRESENTED A WEALTHY businessman indicted for tax eva-sion. I couldn't understand why someone with far more money than he'd ever need would jeopardize his life by doing what he'd done, but this man functioned in a different world. As his trial date approached, he asked, Who do I pay off, and how much? We had to explain that that's not how our legal system works.

SOMETIMES YOU CAN END up with egg on your face. Federal agents conducted an investigation into phony contributions to a major cancer charity by numerous otherwise upstanding citizens. These folks had bought poker chips at the cancer center's "casino night" by checks payable to the charity, and deducted the amounts of the checks as charitable contributions—improperly, since the payments were for gambling chits, not charity.

Because so many people had been caught in the scheme, the U.S. Attorney's Office announced that it would prosecute only those whose "contributions" exceeded a certain threshold. They offered a lenient plea agreement to anyone over that threshold, but threatened to prosecute vigorously anyone over the threshold who refused to plead guilty. My client was barely on the wrong side of that line. So was his business partner, who had attended the same event.

My client said his partner was going to tough it out and hope he'd not be charged. I told him that that office does not bluff, and he followed my advice and pleaded guilty. He received a no-jail sentence, plus a fine. His partner was never charged.

There are judges who reveal their inclinations when they question you from the bench, and those who don't. Soon after joining Lou, I argued an appeal of a client's conviction based on what we claimed was a violation of his right to a speedy trial. Judge Harold Medina, one of the oldest judges serving on the federal bench, asked me a series of softball questions during oral argument, suggesting that the violation of my client's rights was clear and egregious; he then wrote the court's decision affirming the conviction.

In federal court in New Jersey, when I stood up before Judge Frederick Lacey to begin arguing a motion (a request that a judge rule a certain way on an issue), he interrupted my first sentence to ask whether I had anything to add to what he characterized as the excellent set of papers I had submitted. Taking that as a signal that

I'd won, I said I had nothing to add and sat down. As soon as I sat, he ruled against me.

Lou and I tried some cases together, sometimes separately. I was studying under an experienced master, hoping it would rub off on me. Many of our cases required a legal oncologist. If you ever need a lawyer and find one who tells you he's never lost a case, look for someone else more experienced or more honest.

I won't regale you with tales of those we won and lament those we lost, or how (or if) we excelled. We won a fair number, but also lost some. We lived them and we cared. I kept a pad and pencil on my night table, hoping to be able to read, in the morning, thoughts in hieroglyphics I'd jot down in the middle of the night while mentally gnawing at the day's bones. I gave new meaning to the word "obsessive."

Rarely, I'd get a case that was a trial lawyer's dream. Once, I was defending a tax evasion case at trial. The government's chief witness was a crooked lawyer who had pleaded guilty and was cooperating with the prosecution in the hope of getting a reduced sentence. My cross-examination began shortly before lunch. I asked the witness, routinely, whether he'd brought his files on the case to court. He said no. The judge declared a lunch break and ordered the witness to return to court with his files.

After lunch, before the jury returned to the courtroom, the judge ordered the witness to give me his files. The witness was a crook who would have removed from the files anything potentially useful to me—if he'd had time to review them. But the lunch break had been short, he'd had to drive round-trip to get the files, and hadn't had enough time to review them.

In his files was a handwritten transcript of what appeared to be his grand jury testimony, written with the sort of shorthand abbreviations that you or I might use when hurriedly taking notes. Grand jury testimony is transcribed by a court reporter on a piece of equipment—never by hand. As required by law, the prosecutor had earlier given me a typed transcript of the witness's grand jury testimony. What was this handwritten, abbreviation-filled version of the transcript in his files? When he re-took the witness stand in front of the jury, I played a hunch.

I asked him: Did you meet with the prosecutor before testifying?

Yes.

Did he show you a transcript of your grand jury testimony?

Yes.

Did he leave you alone to read it?

Yes.

Prosecutors generally don't allow witnesses to retain copies of their grand jury testimony, to prevent a defense lawyer from suggesting that the witness is simply parroting a memorized transcript. So I asked:

Did he instruct you not to xerox the transcript?

Yes.

Did you xerox it?

No.

Then I showed him the shorthand transcription of his grand jury testimony.

Is this your handwriting?

Yes.

I had him compare, out loud and to the jury, his handwritten notes vs. the typed transcript of the grand jury testimony. They were identical.

Did you hand-copy the typed transcript when the prosecutor was out of the room?

Yes.

So you followed the prosecutor's instructions and didn't xerox it, but you fooled the prosecutor by copying it by hand instead?

Yes.

Which invited a convincing summation to the jury: he admits he fooled the prosecutor, and now he's trying to fool you.

The jury acquitted.

My lawyering developed a second track. After resigning from the Wall Street law firm, I had called up Melanie's general counsel to tell him I was leaving the firm. He said that was good news. Melanie had been sued again, for millions of dollars, by someone claiming to have been her manager and to be entitled to a percentage of her earnings. Though I had done most of the work on her first case, the law firm's partner-in-charge had made sure he had the client contact and received credit for the good result we got. But neither Melanie nor her general counsel liked him, and they intended to hire someone else for this new case.

The general counsel asked if I would take it on.

I jumped at the chance, but confessed that I didn't even have stationery yet at my new job. He said Melanie wouldn't care about stationery, and he sent the legal papers to me immediately.

And so began a second new career which developed alongside the tax fraud work. Melanie was the first client I'd ever had on my own, and I was determined to win.

The alleged manager, represented by a prominent entertainment litigation lawyer in New York City, claimed to have had an oral agreement with Melanie entitling him to 15 percent of her earnings. Many oral agreements are enforceable. But there is a "Statute Of Frauds" in New York, barring enforcement of an oral contract which by its terms cannot be completed within one year. The alleged manager seemed to be aware of that provision, and tailored his claim around it by testifying that under the oral contract he claimed to have had, Melanie could terminate his services at any time, even within a year. However, before the date when he claimed Melanie had terminated him, she had signed an enormous multi-year recording contract and he was therefore entitled, he said, to 15 percent of all money she would ever receive from the record company under that contract.

I spent hours in the library, and found an ancient but nearly identical case in which the court had decided that the Statute Of Frauds bars recovery, even if the contractual relationship could end within a year, if the obligation to pay extends beyond a year. On the strength of that precedent, the alleged manager's case was dismissed.

Winning made me a hero in Melanie's eyes and attracted a bit of attention among several New York entertainment lawyers. When you win a big case, people think you know what you're doing, and some think you're an expert. Litigation matters began coming to me, many in the entertainment area, along with some commercial non-entertainment cases.

Most of the lawyers on the other side of these civil cases didn't have the trial background I had. Ultimately, cases go to trial if they are not disposed of beforehand—by dismissal, by summary judgment, or by settlement—and a litigation lawyer who isn't ready to actually try a case in court operates at a severe disadvantage. You can't threaten someone with a shoot-out if he knows your gun is empty.

Rewind.

As I learned the profession and built a law practice, life happened.

Soon after I left Fried Frank, *Beyond A Reasonable Doubt* was published and received wide critical acclaim. The Sunday *New York Times* book section gave it a full-page review along with a new book by F. Lee Bailey, then one of the nation's most famous criminal lawyers. The review slammed Bailey's book and gave effusive praise to mine, calling it "a rare find . . . brilliantly narrated" and making me feel momentarily like a literary poobah.

Every year, the Mystery Writers Of America, an organization of mystery and crime writers, hosts a dinner with an awards ceremony—their equivalent of Hollywood's Academy Awards, without the entertainment or the stars—and gives out its version of the Oscars: Edgars, named after Edgar Allan Poe. *Beyond A Reasonable Doubt* was nominated for Best True Crime Book Of The Year. I had no expectation of winning, but the experience seemed like one I could someday tell my grandchildren about. So I went.

Following the dinner, the lights in the ballroom dimmed and a spotlight shone on the dais. As the emcee announced the nominees in each category, the spotlight jumped to each. When he finally announced the winner in each category, the spotlight stayed on the winner as he or she walked up to the stage to receive an Edgar and express thanks.

After a few preliminary awards, the best motion picture award went to *The French Connection* and its director bounded up to the dais to accept and thank those who, he said, were responsible for the movie's success. After a few more awards, the emcee announced the candidates for Best True Crime Book—one of the top awards— and I felt momentarily important when he mentioned my name and the spotlight shone on me. That would be my fifteen milliseconds of mini-fame.

The emcee then announced the winner of the award and, amazingly, it was I. I walked onto the stage to accept the Edgar without having given any thought to what I might say if I won. So I freelanced—thanked my publisher, agent, editor, and the association, and then added my deep thanks to the director of *The French*

Connection, without whose help, I said, *Beyond A Reasonable Doubt* could never have been written. Of course, I had never met him, and saw a perplexed look on his face as I thanked him from the podium. Then I stepped down, walked over to his table, introduced myself, and told him I'd like to send him a copy of the book if he would read it and consider it for a movie. He gave me his address, I sent him the book, but never heard from him.

Beyond A Reasonable Doubt made the *New York Times'* "New And Recommended" list, but I experienced the difficulties of an unknown writer attempting to crack the bestsellers' list. My publisher sent me on a week-long national tour. I went to a book-signing at Los Angeles's largest bookstore, but no copies of the book were there. I appeared before a ladies' literary convention in San Francisco along with Lawrence Welk, where everyone in the audience seemed to have blue hair and be far more interested in listening to the famous bandleader than hearing about a triple-murder at a carwash. I showed up at 4:30 a.m. to tape a television talk show in Baltimore, paired with Divine, a very large drag queen dressed in full regalia and surrounded by an unusually coifed and outrageously dressed entourage.

My father was very proud of the Edgar and, without telling me, hired a press agent for $100 a week to help generate publicity for the book. A friend sent me a gossip column in the *New York Daily News* by a syndicated columnist, featuring a picture of a stunning sexpot with plunging décolletage and a come-hither-real-quick look. Next to her picture was the caption: "Duo at Nell Gwyn's: novelist Sandor Frankel and British thrush Leonie Collins." I'd never heard of Ms. Collins, never written a novel, and never been to the restaurant. I presumed that she and the restaurant were also on the P.R. flak's roster, and he'd killed three birds with one stone by paying part of my father's, Ms. Collins', and the restaurant's fees to the gossip columnist.

Chapter 5
Personally

June 9, 1974 was a hot, sunny Sunday. I lived in an apartment on the upper east side of Manhattan, in a building that had one of New York City's rarities: a rooftop swimming pool. I was alone, and brought a book to the pool—*Alive,* the true story of the survivors of an airplane crash in the Andes mountains, stranded without supplies in sub-zero temperature and staying alive by eating their dead compatriots until being rescued weeks later. After a while, I put the book down to ponder the absurd contrast between my circumstances—relaxing pool-side on a chaise lounge in sunny mid-Manhattan—against the haunting events the book described.

As I was pondering, I noticed a girl who appeared to be a few years younger than I, several chaise lounges away. She wore a beaded bikini; her face was beautiful and exotic; she held her head high, shoulders squared, stately; her figure was magnificent. She was seated with two guys my age.

Nobody was in the pool. I put down the book and went in,

swimming laps until I was exhausted. I pulled myself out of the water in the area where the gorgeous girl was seated. The guys were no longer there.

As I stood up, the girl asked me: "How's the water?"

I answered: "Refreshing. Is that an Israeli accent?"

"Yes," she said.

And so began a love story. I sat down next to her. She was a fashion designer and model for Israeli high-end swimwear and clothing manufacturers, studying at Manhattan's Fashion Institute of Technology and scheduled to return to Israel soon. She and an Israeli girlfriend had met two brothers who lived in the same building as I, and the brothers had invited them to come over for the afternoon. Her friend had become ill, so she had come herself. They had invited her to join them for dinner they were making for their mother, and had gone down to their apartment to begin cooking.

We talked. And talked, until one of the guys returned. He told her that dinner was ready.

I didn't know the girl's name, address, or phone number. She didn't know mine.

If I may be permitted a generalization: Israelis think quickly and learn to improvise. The girl asked if I had a piece of paper, and I gave her my bookmark. She reached into her purse and took out an eyeliner pencil. The guy was standing over us.

"So I'll give you my friend's name and number," she said, and wrote down a name and number. "Don't forget to call her."

I wasn't quite as quick, but got the point. I tore off a piece of the cover page of my book, wrote my name and number, and gave it to her: "And give your friend my name and number."

Then Ruthie Motola went down for the dinner. A few hours later, she answered my phone call, and we met for a long walk and more talk.

Fast-forward: Marriage eight months later in the Ramat Aviv Hotel, on the outskirts of Tel Aviv.

Fourteen months after that: A twenty-six-hour labor, with me at her side. Ruthie refused an epidural until shortly before delivery. And then I am holding a miracle, Jennifer, swaddled in a blanket and screaming.

Ruthie: Is she all right? Does she have everything?

Yes, she has everything. She's perfect. And then both of us started crying with joy.

Twenty-two months later: a sister, equally perfect. Annette.

Then, seven years later: Ruthie's pregnant. She is now at the age where she undergoes an amniocentesis, to determine whether the baby is healthy—and, if we want, to learn the baby's sex. Ruthie is too nervous and encharges me with finding out whether the baby is okay, but she insists I not ask the doctor the baby's sex. The obstetrician is the same doctor who delivered our daughters. I am in the midst of a trial, and during a recess I call the doctor. He tells me everything is fine. Thank you so much, I answer.

The doctor: Don't you want to know the sex of the baby?

Me: Ruthie has made me promise not to ask.

Doctor: I can understand that.

A pause.

Doctor: By the way, didn't I deliver your two other children?

I'm surprised he has to ask.

Me: Of course you did.

Doctor: Yes, I thought so.

Another pause.

Doctor: They were both girls, weren't they?

Me: Yes, of course they were.

Another pause.

Doctor: Are you sure you don't want to know the sex of the baby?

That was how I learned I would have a son.

Ruthie and I took the girls out to dinner that night. As we were driving, the girls kept asking whether they'd be having a brother or another sister. I finally pulled the car over, turned around to them in the back seat, and asked if they'd promise not to tell Mom. They promised. I got out of the car, opened the rear door, and took them a few car-lengths behind our car, leaving Ruthie in the passenger seat.

Are you sure you promise? I asked.

They promised. Jennie was eight, Annette six.

I told them. They became very excited. I led them back to the car, and closed the door behind them.

"Guess what we're having," Annette immediately blurted out.

I turned around. "You promised."

Annette was unfazed. "A boygirlboygirlboygirlboygirl!"

Ruthie let us tell her over dinner.

When Ruthie was about to give birth to Michael, I drove her to the hospital, leaving Jennifer and Annette with Ruthie's mother, who had flown in from Israel for the birth. The birth took place around midnight. I stayed at the hospital until close to 4 a.m., and then drove back to our house. I pulled up to the curb, quietly. I didn't want to wake the girls. I eased the car door shut silently, and began walking to the front door. Standing there, in the door-frame, exhausted but with big smiles on their faces, were Jennie and Annette, Michael's big sisters, waiting. We had a three-way hug I will never forget.

On June 27, 1976, an Air France flight carrying 248 passengers and a twelve-person crew left Tel Aviv for Paris with a stop in Athens. Shortly after leaving Athens, four Palestinian and German terrorists hijacked the plane and forced the pilot to fly to an airport in Entebbe, Uganda, where other Palestinian terrorists and Ugandan dictator Idi Amin, with dozens of Ugandan troops, were waiting to greet the hijackers as heroes. The terrorists herded the passengers into the airport terminal, and released all passengers except Israelis and other Jews—ninety-four of them—and the French crew. The terrorists demanded that Israel release forty Palestinian terrorists held in Israel, and that other countries release another thirteen terrorists held elsewhere. They threatened to kill the hostages unless their demands were met.

On the evening of July 3–4, four Israeli transport planes carrying Israeli commandos—most just young soldiers, all extraordinarily brave—flew more than 2,500 miles, at extremely low altitude to avoid radar detection, from Israel into the heart of Africa and landed quietly at the Entebbe airport. In a daring military operation, they killed the terrorists, neutralized the Ugandan troops protecting the terrorists, rescued the hostages, and destroyed the Ugandan army's Soviet MiGs at the terminal to prevent pursuit. Three hostages and the leader of the Israeli assault unit, Yoni Netanyahu, were killed in the operation, and an elderly Jewish woman hostage who'd been hospitalized was murdered by Ugandans after the raid. Yoni was the older brother of the future Israeli Prime Minister.

I had been following all available bits of news concerning the hostage-taking. The event was mind-boggling: One of Europe's largest airlines had inadequate security to prevent four terrorists from seizing control of the aircraft; it had been flown to one of Africa's largest countries, whose anti-Jewish dictator enthusiastically hosted other Palestinian terrorists awaiting the hijackers' arrival and greeted the hijackers with open arms, literally and figuratively, protecting them with Uganda's army. Israelis and other

Jews were segregated from others and remained hostage, and the non-Jews were freed; the Jews would be summarily executed, one by one, unless and until Israel and other countries released other terrorists. The world couldn't or wouldn't do anything about it.

People remember where they were when they learned President Kennedy was shot, and when the twin towers were hit. In the morning of July 4, 1976, I was on vacation, driving on Montauk Highway in Amagansett, New York, to bring back breakfast for Ruthie, who was with Jennie, and listening to the car radio. When I heard of the hostage rescue I made a U-turn, forgot about the food, and raced back to tell Ruthie the news. We were ecstatic, although saddened by the deaths of several hostages and a commando and injuries to others, including one commando seriously wounded from a bullet hitting his spine.

I often wondered what happened to that commando. Decades later, I would find out.

The hostage-taking and rescue stayed in my mind all day and night. Mid-sleep, I woke with an idea: a novel about the next series of Palestinian terrorist attacks, and about the next Entebbe-style Israeli operation. By dawn, the general shape of the book percolated in my mind. I called my old friend Jethro—we'd already written one unpublished manuscript and one published book, and two heads might be better than one.

We met a few days later in a Manhattan deli, and by the time we left we had outlined *The Aleph Solution*. The book was published within the year, widely praised by reviewers ("moves like a projectile," said the *New York Times*; "the most imaginative fictional coup of the century," gushed the *Washington Post*—a bit excessive but I didn't complain), translated into several languages, and generated a handsome paperback sale. Unfortunately, even as it has aged over the years, new readers tell me they are struck by the accuracy of some of the terrorist attacks it predicted.

I thought it would be fun to take the family to a game at Yankee Stadium. We drove past P.S. 31. It looked smaller than I'd remembered, and had prison-like bars on the windows. I found a parking space right in front of my old apartment building. I hadn't been back in many years.

One of the girls asked where the grass and trees were. We didn't have any, I answered.

The lot was still there, but was now a parking lot covered with asphalt. In the old days, near the spot we'd used as home plate, there had been an iron bar protruding nearly a foot out of the brick wall of one of the lot's surrounding buildings. The bar had some give to it. I used to yank it up and down while waiting for my turn at bat, and the iron would loosen tiny shavings of brick and make a slight grinding sound.

I left Ruthie and the children for a moment at the edge of the lot and walked inside to look around. The iron bar was still there, with the same slight give. I yanked it up and down, and it loosened some tiny bits of brick and made the same sound as decades earlier—a Bronx remembrance of things past. As I went back to the car and locked the doors, two kids who couldn't have been more than ten years old came up to me and said that for five dollars they'd make sure nobody slit my tires. I paid. It was cheaper than the parking lot.

About thirty years after I had moved from the Bronx, I received a xeroxed invitation to attend a reunion of "The Yankee Stadium Gang," signed by three names vaguely familiar to me. The reunion was held in a nondescript bar in lower Manhattan.

Several dozen people attended. The group was unstuffy; we had known each other before any of us had anything. Most hadn't seen each other for decades. You can tell your age in the faces of your friends. I had visualized seeing children's faces on grown-ups' bodies. But if these kids were now middle-aged, so I must be too. For a few short hours, we were young again and helped each other remember.

There had been one bully in the neighborhood. The last time I'd seen him was in a park, where he had taken away a toy my next-door-neighbor Guy and I were playing with. One of us had pulled a long thorn off a bush and jammed it into the bully's buttocks. Guy and I ran as fast as we could to escape retribution. When we got older and occasionally reminisced, we'd alternately blame each other, or take credit, for the assault. I hadn't seen the bully since then.

Until the reunion. Though everyone else was dressed casually, the bully showed up in an expensive suit, starched white shirt, and tie. He arrived in a limousine, as befitted one of Wall Street's top equities traders.

Chapter 6
Cases

As the years passed, I was fortunate enough to get most of my clients results that pleased them, and my civil litigation practice began to grow. I also continued to defend a fair number of criminal cases, and hired one, then two, then three associates.

Civil cases are different from criminal. In a criminal case, the government prosecutes someone for allegedly having committed a crime; conviction means a judge may sentence the defendant to jail, along with other punishment. In a civil case, someone (or some entity) is suing someone else for a perceived wrong, usually seeking money to redress the wrong, or a court order requiring the defendant to do (or not do) something. Jail and freedom are not at stake. When you're used to handling criminal cases, where the stakes are so high, the stakes in civil litigation, however important they may be, are different.

Many rules and procedures differentiate criminal from civil cases, but for me the biggest difference was the amount of evidence available to us. Lou's and my white-collar criminal cases were usually very difficult. The government often had a mountain of evidence and we had little, if any, which meant that trying the case was uphill, and working out a plea deal sometimes the best strategy.

In civil cases, I often have considerable evidence. A briefcase full of evidence, when you're used to having close to nothing, is a luxury that allows you to flesh out a narrative rather than tiptoeing and looking for a tiny opening in a prosecutor's case.

Much of the civil litigation that came to me at the beginning involved commercial disputes:

A YOUNG LAWYER BUILT a lucrative practice. As he aged, he elevated several of his associates to partnerships, without written agreements; he trusted them, and made sure they developed relationships with his clients. After enough years, the client relationships were now with the younger partners. They eventually banded together and told him his services at the firm—his firm, he thought—were no longer needed, although he had brought in the clients and built up the practice. He came to me to vindicate what he believed to be his rights. Loyalty and gratitude often play second fiddle when money is on the line.

A BROTHER AND SISTER were at each other's throats over their respective rights to their deceased parents' property. They had gotten along fine until their parents died and money was at stake. Each fought without giving an inch, going through multiple depositions, document discovery, court appearances, and the emotional and financial costs of full-bore legal warfare—until a jury was empaneled and sitting in the jury box, and the prospect of losing loomed for both. Then they settled.

A YOUNG COUPLE BOUGHT a brand-new house in the suburbs for two million dollars. The day after they moved in, the wife was strolling with her baby when a neighbor approached and asked whether she had bought the house. When the wife answered yes, the neighbor said she was amazed the builder had finally found a buyer. The young mother asked why.

The neighbor asked: Don't you know?

The neighbor explained that when construction of the house was nearly completed, the town had ordered the builder to stop construction because the house was impermissibly close to the boundary line with another neighbor. As a result, the builder had to physically remove the house from its foundation and reattach it onto a new foundation.

Neither their broker nor the builder had disclosed to the young buyers this unorthodox disassembling and reassembling of the house. When they found out the truth, they didn't want the house and wanted to rescind the purchase. The builder and broker told them to go fly a kite.

We sued the builder and brokerage firm to undo the transaction. Insurance company lawyers got into the fray, with no financial incentive to do anything but litigate and rack up fees. On the eve of trial, after two years of legal warfare, the builder grudgingly returned the purchase price to the couple and took back the house.

MANY YEARS AGO, AN experienced lawyer advised me, I thought jokingly, that when a friend or relative asks you to take on a case, you should say that you don't do that type of case but that you know a lawyer who does and that you will get that lawyer to take it at a reduced fee; then call that lawyer, give him $5,000 out of your own pocket and ask him to credit it privately to the friend's or relative's account. I was too much of a softy, and as a result wound up handling more than my fill of complimentary cases for friends and relatives, always with an emotional overlay and extra level of anxiety because of the personal connection.

As A CATEGORY, PROBABLY the most emotional cases are matrimonials. I have been involved behind the scenes in several. Many matrimonial disputes, when the marriage is truly over, are about money and vengeance, and many litigating spouses either try to hide money from their soon-to-be exes, or have done some financial finagling in business or taxes that the other spouse knows of and threatens to use as a weapon. In those situations, my background in litigating tax matters has been helpful in guiding matrimonial lawyers handling fights between spouses who really, really want to hurt each other.

MASTERS TEACH BY EXAMPLE, even to complete strangers. I had a case against a Fortune 500 company represented by a prominent Manhattan law firm whose preeminent lawyer was Simon Rifkind. He was legendary: a former federal judge, he was then in his early eighties, and there was no more highly regarded lawyer in New York City. One of his younger partners was my adversary. I had filed a motion seeking emergency relief. That kind of motion frequently involves fast-paced bang-bang litigation. We negotiated a compressed several-day schedule to exchange voluminous papers, haggling over every hour of the schedule. I agreed to serve my papers by 4:30 a.m. two days hence.

A few minutes before 4:30 that morning, having been up all night drafting and finalizing papers, I trudged wearily up the steps of my adversary's Park Avenue office building, to serve my papers on the other side. The lobby was deserted. I walked sleepily to the elevator bank. There, waiting for the same elevator, at the same ungodly hour, was octogenarian Simon Rifkind.

SOMETIMES THE LEGAL PROCESS is an inadequate mechanism for resolving disputes. A company I represented wanted to prevent a key employee from defecting to a competitor in violation of his contract, and we obtained an injunction prohibiting him. To enjoin a contractually bound employee from leaving for a competitor, a company is required by New York law to offer continued employment to the employee. In this case, after we got the injunction, the employee didn't bother appealing. Instead, he returned to work, and the floor in the company men's bathroom got soiled daily. The company let him leave.

As my practice grew, some of the cases involved the entertainment business and high-profile personalities:

I'VE REPRESENTED WILHELMINA MODELS in many litigations. A common problem in the modeling industry is models jumping from one agency to another without regard to contractual commitments. The most valuable assets of modeling agencies are their contracts, so we wound up suing many other model management companies that tried to poach Wilhelmina's models, and many models to get them to comply with their legal obligations.

Wilhelmina also represents performing artists. The agency signed a contract with the singer/performer Beyonce to be her exclusive representative in connection with commercial marketing activities—hair products, cosmetics, and the like. When Beyonce refused to pay Wilhelmina its commissions, we had to sue her. She was always too busy to appear for a deposition, until a judge finally ordered her to. She knows how to flick the on-off charm switch even on the other side of a deposition table, but not enough to prevent the judge from ordering her to pay Wilhelmina the million dollars she owed.

BILL MOYERS PRODUCED THE award-winning PBS series and best-selling book *The Power Of Myth*, co-featuring the mythologist Joseph Campbell. After Campbell died, a California law firm representing a production company that claimed the Moyers project violated its rights under its own contract with Campbell sent Moyers a draft of a lengthy legal complaint, threatening to sue Moyers in California unless he were to agree to its demands. Moyers lives in New York. We preempted the California lawsuit by seeking a judgment in a New York court that the claims asserted in the draft California complaint were meritless—thus permitting the issues to be determined a subway-ride away from Moyers rather than trans-coastally.

Representing Moyers is a humbling experience. Much of litigation is telling a story, and there aren't many better storytellers than he. When I began debriefing Moyers so that I could draft an affidavit for him reciting the factual background of the dispute—typically a task for lawyers—he offered to draft it himself, and produced a flawless and compelling narrative.

Moyers is not only a fine storyteller but a highly credible person. It soon became clear to me that simply getting him in a room with the moving force behind his adversary, Joseph Campbell's widow, without lawyers angling to drive the case into a courtroom to bask in Moyers's reflected glory, could cut the lawsuit short. So I arranged for Moyers to meet with Mrs. Campbell, and although I couldn't prevent the other lawyers from attending, my self-designated role was to keep lawyer-posturing to a minimum and let Moyers and Mrs. Campbell talk to each other. They did, and the claim went away.

I MET BARRY MANILOW decades ago, when you couldn't listen to the radio without hearing him sing "I Write The Songs." When a singer/performer/songwriter is as popular as Barry, people come from all directions trying to capitalize on his success—using his picture for commercial purposes without authorization, infringing his copyrights, falsely claiming he infringed theirs, claiming rights they don't have—a potpourri of hands trying to reach into his pockets. Barry is a man of peace and wisely tries to avoid litigation, but over the decades we've had to visit courtrooms to prevent people from ripping him off.

We had a string of hit litigation results over the decades. Barry would show his appreciation with center orchestra seats at his New York concerts. While the rest of the audience would hear his hits and sing along, I'd hear cases: songs that others had falsely claimed as theirs, or in which they falsely claimed some financial interest, or with which they misused his name and photos, or tried to cheat him in some other way.

One of his cases stands out as an object lesson of "Thou shall not bear false witness."

Barry and his long-time co-writer Bruce Sussman wrote a terrific musical called *Harmony*. They were trusting, and signed a contract giving production rights to a charlatan who'd misrepresented his background, his credentials, and his financial and professional ability to produce the musical. When the scope of the man's incompetence and dishonesty became clear, Barry and Bruce asked him to tear up the contract and return production rights to them. He refused. So we sued.

Barry and Bruce's contract with the producer contained an arbitration clause: Any disputes would be resolved in an informal out-of-court proceeding called an arbitration, conducted by three arbitrators, rather than in court with a judge and jury. Arbitrators are often lawyers, or people involved in the type of business involved in the dispute (here, one of the arbitrators was Sheldon Harnick, the lyricist of *Fiddler on the Roof*), temporarily donning another hat for a change of pace. They generally resolve cases with a brief verdict—you win, you lose—without explanation.

The arbitration lasted for several days but was really over soon after it began. The producer testified, under direct examination by his attorney, to routine background facts about himself. Among them was his educational background: that he'd gone to Yale.

No way. In preparing for the arbitration, we'd seen many dozens of emails and letters the producer had sent. They were rife with spelling and grammatical errors—not typos that lazy e-mailers don't correct, but really bad English. When the first day's session ended, we contacted Yale, and got a letter from the Registrar of the university stating that Yale had no record of the producer's having graduated from there.

The next day, confronted with the truth, the producer's lawyer offered versions of "the dog ate my homework": the testimony was "not untruthful"; his client misunderstood the question; we were engaging in "character assassination." But the fish was on the hook, and the more he squirmed the deeper the hook sank. Skillful cross-examination was not required.

Judges, juries, and arbitrators—and doubtlessly you—don't like it when people don't tell the truth. Lying about your background is particularly unwise when you're charged with having defrauded someone by having lied about your background. The arbitrators unanimously ruled that all rights to the production of *Harmony* reverted to Barry and Bruce. (After the arbitration, they renamed one of the characters—the most minor—"Sandor Frankelovich.")

DON KING, THE BOXING promoter, retained me when he was sued by one of the fighters he had under contract. We—mainly King, who is not shy—negotiated a settlement with the boxer and his lawyer. King is an experienced negotiator. He and I, and the boxer and his lawyer, were in a room with what was supposed to be the final draft of the settlement contract. I won't reveal the terms of the settlement, but let's say, hypothetically, King had agreed to pay $100,000. The draft settlement contract reflected that amount, but the other side had renegotiated him up to $150,000 and we penned in that amount. Seeing whether they could do it again, they upped their demand to $200,000.

King asked me to step outside the room with him, and to take the draft contract. He wrote out a check payable to the boxer for $150,000 and signed the draft reflecting a $150,000 settlement. He gave me the check and the signed contract, and left the building to fly back home to Florida. I returned alone to the room where the boxer and his lawyer were waiting. They asked where King was. I told them he was on his way back to Florida, but had left me a check for $150,000 and had signed the contract in that amount. I asked whether they wanted it. We promptly closed the deal at that figure.

KING'S PERSONA HAD PRACTICAL effect inside the courthouse. He was sitting next to me at counsel table during jury selection for one of his cases. We were facing the spectator gallery, where the prospective jurors sat and listened to the judge ask questions designed to elicit any reason why they could not fairly sit as jurors in the case. A young woman sitting in the front row kept smiling flirtatiously at King, licking her lips and rubbing her thighs against each other. After the questioning, the judge called the lawyers back to his robing room and asked if anyone objected to any of the prospective jurors. The opposing lawyer began describing what he'd seen her do; the judge said he'd seen it too, and she was disqualified.

I experienced King's influence among ordinary people during the lunch break. Jury selection had gone on longer than usual, and by the time we got downstairs to the courthouse cafeteria, it was closed and the workers were mopping up. But when they saw King, they reopened the grill and hovered around him, asking for autographs, urging us to sit down and serving us.

(I learned a hard lesson in the business of lawyering while representing King. During one case, I got jammed up with other matters and with King's permission brought in another lawyer, a friend of mine, to assist. At the end of the case, the lawyer-friend handed his business card to King and offered: If I can ever help you, give me a call.)

A CLIENT'S POPULARITY ALSO helped when I represented Cyndi Lauper, the singer-songwriter. Cyndi was sued, along with her agency, for canceling a series of concerts in Germany. The case was brought in New York City by the German promoter. The judge referred it to mediation—a process where a neutral third-party meets informally with the litigants and their lawyers to see whether a settlement can be reached. The promoter came to New York for the mediation. We denied any liability, and Cyndi was firm about it. After a day-long session of discussion, the mediator, who understood that Cyndi had in fact not committed any wrong against the promoter, turned to him and said, You know, among the things you should consider is that this case is going to be tried before a New York City jury, and Ms. Lauper is very popular here. The German promoter dropped the case against her, and worked out some arrangement with the agency that didn't cost Cyndi a penny.

I REPRESENTED AN INDEPENDENT record company named Profile Records for many years. Before rap music became popular, Profile had signed a long-term contract with a then-unknown group Run-DMC, which soon became the most popular rap group in the world. Major record companies flocked to the group's door, offering truckloads of money if Run-DMC could get out of their contract with Profile and record for them. The group repeatedly invented pretexts to try to extricate themselves from their Profile contract, claiming an assortment of alleged breaches of contract, to gain a richer contract with one of the majors. We had to beat back those claims whenever it was time for Run-DMC to deliver another album to Profile and they tried to get out of their contract.

The last time they tried, they sought an expedited court determination that their contract with Profile was over. Their lawyer and I appeared before a judge, who accepted my arguments, made short shrift of the group's position, and clearly indicated we were hitting a home run. Soon after leaving the courtroom, their lawyer called me, gave up, and said the group would deliver their latest album to Profile and cede other rights we wanted.

That afternoon and evening, we prepared the group's documents of surrender. The group showed up with their lawyers shortly after midnight to sign, accompanied by their manager, Russell Simmons, brother of Run DMC's "Run" and himself a multi-media business mogul/entrepreneur who was one of the original impressarios of hip-hop music. I made clear that after our successful morning in court, we were not in a negotiating mood. I had placed signature-ready copies of all the papers on the conference-room table, with pens. Russell sat at the table for the document-signing, removed a condom from his pocket, and put it on the table. He explained: "At least do it to us safely."

(Dotting and crossing the i's and t's of the documents carried into the early morning hours. When everything was finally signed, Russell asked my associate to accompany him downstairs to get a taxi. Cabbies don't always stop for black men, even very successful ones, at 3:00 a.m. in midtown Manhattan.)

THE MANAGER OF A popular music group had a written contract with the group. They didn't honor the contract, and he retained me to sue them. We entered into a contingency fee agreement: I'd get a percentage of any recovery, but nothing if there was no recovery. I learned a valuable lesson about remaining calm in stressful situations while the other person loses his temper. Shortly before my client was to receive a substantial settlement payment, of which I was entitled to a portion, he called and created a phony dispute. I methodically and without show of emotion addressed each of his gripes. The calmer I spoke, the more infuriated he got, until he ended the call by angrily slamming the phone down so hard it bounced off the cradle. I could hear him tell his secretary how he intended to skunk me out of my fee. I went to court and thwarted him.

LOU REED WAS A songwriter and performing artist. He owed his former manager a substantial amount of money but refused to pay. The manager obtained a court decision that Reed owed him a percentage of Reed's earnings. But Reed refused to disclose the amount of his earnings, so the manager couldn't collect anything. Frustrated, the manager hired me to take over the case.

We served legal papers demanding that Reed produce specific documents that would disclose his earnings. Reed refused. We asked the court to hold him in contempt; the court refused, but directed Reed to produce the documents by a specific date. Reed again didn't produce them. We filed another contempt motion; same court order, same refusal. We filed a third contempt motion, this time asking the court to imprison Reed unless he produced the documents by a specific date.

We appeared before the judge on the morning of a day when Reed was scheduled to perform before a large crowd in Milwaukee. The court was in Manhattan. The judge ordered Reed not to leave Manhattan until he produced the documents. Reed protested that he had to perform that night in Milwaukee. The judge said too bad. Reed produced the documents within a few hours, made it to Milwaukee that night, and my client collected in full.

THE CARS, A PLATINUM-SELLING (that means over a million copies of a single album) rock band, were sued by their former manager for commissions he claimed they owed him. He brought the case in arbitration before a single arbitrator, as his contract with the group required, rather than in court. The band knew they owed the manager a bit of money, but nowhere near the amount he claimed.

The arbitration went on for weeks. At the end, the arbitrator sent everyone his decision. It was one sentence, without explanation, and seemed to say that we'd lost, big-time.

When an arbitrator renders a decision, he loses jurisdiction—the legal power to take any further action. You can't go back and ask him to change his mind, as you can sometimes do with a judge. The only power the arbitrator retains is to clarify any ambiguity in his decision. So I submitted a set of papers to him arguing that his decision was ambiguous and requesting clarification in the Cars' favor.

In fact, I didn't think the arbitrator fully comprehended the financial consequences of what his decision seemed to say, and I thought that if he knew, he wouldn't want that result. So I argued that the one-sentence decision had an ambiguous phrase. Construed one way, we win: The manager would receive only the small amount the group acknowledged it owed him. Construed differently, the manager could spend the rest of his life surrounded by handmaidens on the Riviera. I gave the arbitrator detailed financial analyses demonstrating the two alternatives.

The manager's attorneys cried foul. They said the claim of ambiguity was nonsense—that we merely didn't like the decision, and that the arbitrator had no power to change it.

The arbitrator handed down a second decision. He said his first decision was ambiguous, awarded the manager a small amount, and the band went home happy.

Representing The Cars taught me a useful lesson. The leader of the group was a talented musician/songwriter named Ric Ocasek. I represented him in a second lawsuit. David Geffen, the Hollywood mogul, whom I'd never met, called me to say he was interested in signing Ric to Geffen's record label, and asked me to describe the lawsuit. I did, and ended by saying Ric's record company would never release him to sign with Geffen without litigation. Geffen didn't respond. Soon afterward, he signed Ric, having worked out a business resolution with Ric's prior record company. The lesson: To a carpenter, everything looks like a nail; to a litigator, problems are often seen through a narrow litigation lens. But there's a much wider world out there.

SOME PEOPLE'S BRAZENNESS KNOWS no limits.

I represented the blind singer Jose Feliciano, best known for his "Feliz Navidad." He had an oral agreement with his manager, terminable at will, and fired him. The manager claimed to have a written agreement signed by Jose and, against instructions, continued to book concerts for Jose and refused to return Jose's business records and other materials. We sued for a judicial determination that the "manager" was no longer the manager, enjoining him from acting on Jose's behalf, and directing him to return everything to Jose.

In defense, the manager presented a document which he claimed was a written agreement signed by Jose. The signature was an illegible chicken-scrawl. On the same page was the signature of a supposed witness to Jose's signing of the document. The manager named the attorney who, he claimed, had drafted the contract.

Jose denied having signed the document. He said he would never sign a document unless it had been read to him, and this document was never read to him. But beyond that: The "witness" to the chicken-scrawl said she had not witnessed Jose signing the document, that the signature wasn't hers, and that her name was misspelled; the lawyer who had allegedly drafted the document said he hadn't drafted it; and the manager's own address as stated on the "contract" was an address he hadn't moved into until two years after the date of the alleged agreement.

How could the manager have thought he'd get away with it? Who knows. In any event, when we uncovered (without much difficulty) proof that the document was bogus, he conceded that he was no longer Jose's manager, returned the materials, and slipped out of Jose's life.

Jose's manager must have been cloned from another one I met.

A young four-man band was sued by its former manager. The group had tried to shed the manager's contractual clutches by filing for bankruptcy, which normally extinguishes contracts of that sort.

The bankruptcy proceeding had followed a uniquely circuitous legal path. Eureka-like, the manager produced an amendment to his contract with the group, dated shortly before the bankruptcy filing, which was extraordinarily prescient: It had a clause stating that if the group were to file a bankruptcy proceeding that followed precisely that path, the bankruptcy would not extinguish the contract. Those circumstances, he argued, miraculously anticipated in the amendment, warranted holding the group to the contract despite the bankruptcy.

All the group's members denied having signed the amendment. I called for the manager to produce the original at his deposition. He didn't, only a copy—he said he'd lost the original. The signature of each member of the group appeared over a signature line on the last page, something like this:

Signature 1

Signature 2

Signature 3

Signature 4

The page looked fishy. At his depostion, I handed the manager a finely calibrated ruler and asked him to measure the exact size of the space between the left edge of each line, and the exact size of the corresponding space between the right edge of each line. The spacing was slightly askew. Of course, if the contract were legitimate, the lines would have been exactly parallel (like the lines above).

Plainly, the manager had xeroxed each person's signature line from other documents and created a composite of signatures on a fake document—carefully but not perfectly, with revealing misalignments. His lawyer understood the serious implications of the fraud. The case quickly disappeared.

A lawyer friend of mine had a comparable experience with brazenness. He represented the owner of a popular bar/restaurant in midtown Manhattan who hired an investigator to figure out why the business was losing money, suspecting employee skullduggery. The investigator sat undercover at the bar for days, and finally reported that he hadn't seen any wrongdoing. He told the owner that every dollar paid by customers to the bartenders went into the four cash registers behind the bar, and nobody was skimming cash. I only have three registers, the owner told him.

Sometimes a lawyer is luckiest with cases that slip away.

A partner in a large California law firm called on behalf of a company named MP3.com, Inc., asking me to serve as local counsel in federal court in Manhattan. The client had been sued by the country's largest record companies for massive copyright infringements over the internet through a then-new technology known as MP3.

The California firm sent me their draft answer to the complaint. I suggested numerous changes, all of which they rejected. They scheduled several meetings with me in New York and then cancelled each. It became clear that the firm had no interest in my views about how to defend the case, and I foresaw a disastrous result ahead, both for the client, because of the way the case was being defended, and for the law firm and perhaps the local firm when disaster struck. So I told the California lawyer that since they didn't want my lawyering but just my address, the client should get another New York lawyer instead of me, which they did.

MP3.com lost the case to the tune of over $53 million. Not long after that, MP3.com sued the California law firm for $175 million.

Some cases were dry and emotionless, businesspeople fighting over how much money goes or stays in which bank account. Others:

In the mid-sixties, a teenager from Jacksonville, Florida named Ronnie Van Zant formed a band with two high school buddies. They played in local clubs under different names, finally settling on "Lynyrd Skynyrd," a spoof on their gym teacher, Leonard Skinner. Ronnie's girlfriend, Judy, offered to support him if he wanted to pursue a music career full-time, and he did.

The group's popularity grew. In 1973, Ronnie married Judy and the band released their first album, *Pronounced 'Lĕh-'nérd 'Skin-'nérd*. In short order, they were playing to packed venues worldwide, sometimes with groups like the Rolling Stones, and millions of their records were sold. Ronnie was lead singer, front man, primary songwriter, and in charge.

In the fall of 1977, the band went on a fifty-six-city tour to promote their sixth album. Judy was home in Florida when the band and crew flew in a small chartered plane from Greenville, South Carolina, to Baton Rouge, Louisiana. She went out to dinner with a friend—the wife of one of Ronnie's band members—and their young daughters. When Judy returned from dinner, she turned on the TV and heard a news flash: The plane carrying Lynyrd Skynyrd had crashed in Mississippi, and there were multiple deaths and injuries. She called her friend and they waited until, finally, learning that Ronnie had been killed, along with the friend's husband and sister, and three others.

After the survivors recovered, Judy and the two surviving co-founders of the band made an oral commitment at a kitchen table—what they called a "blood oath"—that nobody would ever again perform as "Lynyrd Skynyrd." The two co-founders continued to perform, but under a different name.

Ten years later, the two surviving co-founders, with several other survivors of the crash, performed in some tribute shows to honor the original band. The shows were so successful that they decided to tour again as "Lynyrd Skynyrd." Judy did not approve—the blood oath that had been honored for a decade should continue forever, she said—but she was reluctant to sue. So the others simply began touring, using the name. In connection with the tour, a major record company, MCA, released an album of tribute tour performances, marketing it as "Lynyrd Skynyrd Live" in large, bold, highlighted letters across the top of the album cover, mentioning in smaller, meaningless letters near the bottom that the performers were only the 1987 tribute band.

Finally, Judy decided to try to stop the tour and suppress the misleading album—but how could she, after the tour had been booked, the band was already on the road, and the album about to be released?

Normally, a court doesn't order somebody to do or not do something until a case is over. But where an emergency exists, a court may issue a "preliminary injunction," ordering someone immediately to stop doing something, even while the case is pending. Because it is an extraordinary remedy, a plaintiff seeking a preliminary injunction has to satisfy rigorous legal requirements. Judy's delay in starting the lawsuit, and the band's having expended substantial money for the tour and actually having begun it, presented a serious obstacle to immediate relief.

Nevertheless, we sued, in federal court in Manhattan, and asked the court for several remedies, including a preliminary injunction against continuation of the tour. The chance of the court granting that remedy was remote, but there are different ways to skin a cat.

The judge held a prompt mini-trial on our request. We simply presented Judy's case in a straightforward way: Ronnie's having made Lynyrd Skynyrd a phenomenal success; the tragedy; Judy's compelling and sympathetic recital of Ronnie's success and sudden death; the blood oath; and the decade-long non-use of the name "Lynyrd Skynyrd." We figured that simply presenting the facts might impel the judge to protect her.

He did. Because of Judy's delay, he denied the emergency relief we'd requested, but he issued a written decision stating that he believed her testimony about the existence of the oral "blood oath," and forecasting that we were likely to win the case at a full trial. The ultimate handwriting on the wall was clear enough for the band members and their counsel to read, and they promptly agreed to severe written restrictions on uses of the name "Lynyrd Skynyrd," and substantial payments to Judy, including a hefty percentage of all proceeds from the tour and future revenues of the band. The judge also ordered MCA to put a prominent label on each album cover clearly disclosing that this was not the original Lynyrd Skynyrd but a new band. "Winning" comes in different flavors.

I could tell you about other cases, but the attorney-client privilege prevents me from giving details of several juicy ones, so you'd leave the page still hungry. For example: Claus von Bulow came to consult with me at the recommendation of Alan Dershowitz. In a case that attracted worldwide attention, von Bulow had been convicted of attempted murder of his socialite wife. Alan had argued the appeal, which was still pending, and suggested von Bulow meet with me concerning a strategic question involved in the case. After von Bulow recited the facts relevant to the question, I told him he was asking the wrong question, explained why, and answered the question he should have asked. He smiled broadly, immediately agreed, thanked me profusely, and left.

See what I mean about still being hungry?

(Note to any lawyer looking for a fight: Nothing in this book violates the attorney-client privilege, either for reasons clear on the face of what's written or for other reasons not worth writing about—this isn't a treatise on the privilege. So don't play "Gotcha.")

O pposing lawyers ranged from single practitioners to mega-firms, and ran the gamut from excellent to shoddy, pleasant to offensive. A haughty partner in a major multi-hundred-lawyer firm representing an adversary attended a deposition in my office, nose in the air at my down-to-earth suite. By the next time he came, the litigation wasn't going too well for him, and he flatteringly commented about some artwork on my wall. I knew I had him.

I'd bring my cases home with me—not just the papers, but mentally. I got satisfactory results for most clients, but I'd always think of things I could have done differently, mistakes I made even if the client didn't recognize them. I'd be having dinner with the family when Ruthie would suddenly ask "Where are you?" reminding me that at the dinner table, talking about math class trumps reverie about cases.

My practice didn't require much traveling, and I tried to get home every night.

A witness in a litigation was to be deposed in his temporary abode: a minimum security federal prison in Florida, home to white-collar low-risk inmates, many serving short sentences. I flew down early one morning to attend.

When I got off the plane, only one cab was available at the airport. Another traveler was also looking for a cab to the prison, so we shared a ride.

He began making small talk: How long are you down here for, he asked.

Only for the day, I answered; flying back home tonight.

You're lucky, he said. I got a week.

F or many years, Lou and I shared a suite of offices with another older lawyer, Bob Rosenthal. He was a quiet, unassuming man, practiced corporate law, and enjoyed hearing about Lou's and my cases. I didn't know his background until long after we'd been suite-sharing. He'd never talk about it, but gradually, very slowly, I learned.

Bob had enlisted in the Army the day after Pearl Harbor was attacked. He became one of America's most daring and accomplished pilots, flying the most dangerous missions. On his third mission, he'd led a bombardier group over Germany, and his was the only one of twelve planes to return, with two engines dead, a non-functional oxygen system, and a hole in one of the wings—but he had successfully bombed the target. He flew fifty-three bombing missions. His plane was shot down over Germany and he suffered several broken bones, but as soon as they were fixed he led another bomb squad over Berlin; this time his engine suffered a direct hit that set it on fire, but he still managed to bomb his target, and ordered his men to parachute out before he finally left the plane—last man out—seconds before it exploded. He was one of the Air Force's most decorated pilots, receiving the Distinguished Service Cross for extraordinary heroism, the Silver Star for gallantry in action, the Distinguished Flying Cross for heroism, a Purple Heart, the Distinguished Flying Cross from Great Britain, and the Croix de Guerre from France. His bombardier group, "Rosie's Riveters," became legendary in the Air Force. After the war, he served as a prosecutor in the Nuremberg trials.

Bob was a humble, self-effacing man, who never talked about himself unless I'd press him to. We'd often lunch together at an aptly named fish joint "Sloppy Louie's." He didn't just order from the waiters, but had an uncanny ability to speak with them as an equal and make them feel like kings. Talking with him, no matter how big the case I was working on or how famous the personality, helped keep my head screwed on straight.

My cases came from a variety of sources. Some were referred

by lawyers who did transactional (non-trial) work and referred their clients to me when litigation matters arose. Mostly, the referring lawyers only wanted a good result for their clients. Occasionally, a potential referring lawyer would tell me he was thinking of referring a client and asked if I would tack on an additional fee to the client and pay it over to the referring lawyer. After declining, I'd never hear from the client, and the lawyer would never refer anyone else.

Some of my clients were repeats: They'd found the result of our prior litigation satisfactory and came back when another lawsuit arose. Some matters came simply from people I knew, who thought of me when a legal problem developed. Some were referred by other trial lawyers who had a conflict of interest in representing a potential client, or had multiple clients in a trial or investigation and for one reason or another thought separate counsel for each would be best. Some clients were referred by former colleagues in Washington, sometimes because they practiced elsewhere and needed New York counsel.

That is how I became involved in representing former Philippine President Ferdinand Marcos and his first lady, Imelda.

In 1986, in the face of a popular uprising in the Philippines against their rule and life-threatening dangers of remaining at their palace, the Marcoses and an entourage of 122 aides and servants were flown by U.S. military carriers to Honolulu. The Marcoses were immediately confronted with a barrage of legal problems, including a federal grand jury investigation in Manhattan. They were indicted for racketeering, conspiracy, obstruction of justice, and other crimes. The heart of the charges was that they had plundered billions from the Philippine treasury and used the loot surreptitiously to purchase and improve valuable real estate properties in Manhattan, and defrauded American institutions out of enormous amounts of money for similar purposes.

Shortly after their arrival in Hawaii, the Marcoses hired a long-time friend of mine and former colleague in the U.S. Attorney's Office, Dick Hibey, to defend them against this onslaught of legal problems. Dick's office was in Washington D.C.

When the Marcoses were ultimately indicted in New York, they needed New York counsel, which was legally required and because an out-of-state lawyer is often better off working with a local lawyer familiar with local practices. With the Marcoses' permission, Dick asked me to be his co-counsel representing Ferdinand Marcos; for a variety of legal and strategic reasons, Imelda would retain separate counsel. I said sure. Dick told me there might be a problem getting paid because much of the Marcoses' wealth was tied up in litigation. I told him that I'd stay in the case, no matter what, for as long as he and the client wanted. Ferdinand Marcos faxed me authorization to represent him.

The morning of the Marcoses' scheduled arraignment in Manhattan federal court was tumultuous. Media representatives from around the world and interested onlookers surrounded the courthouse and filled the courtroom. Out of deference to her status and her physical vulnerability, Mrs. Marcos was permitted to wait in an anteroom off the main courtroom for her case to be called. President Marcos was still in Hawaii, too ill to travel to New York for arraignment.

The judge set bail at $5 million for Mrs. Marcos. She had to deposit that amount in court or would be remanded to jail pending trial. Mrs. Marcos protested, without avail, that she did not have that much money. The judge asked whether she could post her house as collateral, but Mrs. Marcos said she'd already pledged it as security for payment of her attorneys' fees, which elicited guffaws from the spectator section. Fortunately, that evening, a deus ex machina materialized: The billionairess Doris Duke agreed to post $5 million bail on Mrs. Marcos' behalf.

Dick advised the judge of President Marcos' dire medical condition and inability to be arraigned, even if the proceeding were to take place in Hawaii. But the prosecutors didn't believe it and wanted him in New York. The judge scheduled an evidentiary hearing to determine Marcos' physical condition. Before the hearing was held, Dick and I flew to Hawaii to confer with President Marcos. Because Marcos was under constant government surveillance in Hawaii, the only way to communicate with him without being overheard by government electronic eavesdropping was face to face.

Government agents, with hearing devices in their ears and wearing Dick Tracy-style trenchcoats, hovered outside the house. Dick and I sat at the dining room table, curtains drawn, with Marcos and several of his hangers-on. Dick introduced me, explained my role as co-counsel, and reviewed various matters with him. The former president listened, without responding. I was looking for any telltale indication of whether he was quietly listening and absorbing, or simply out-of-touch.

At the end of Dick's explanation I got my answer. President Marcos turned to me and said, Thank you for giving us the $5 million.

Here's a health tip from the Marcos case.

A bunch of the Marcoses' lawyers met one morning to discuss a long list of strategic and legal issues. One was a Phillipino lawyer, rail-thin, whip-smart, making astute legal observations, and close to ninety years old.

After several hours, the host lawyer announced it was time for lunch, and passed around a delivery menu from a local eatery, with a sheet of paper for everyone to write an order. When the menu and paper reached the Phillipino lawyer, he simply passed them to the lawyer next to him, without ordering. After the menu and paper had completed their journey around the table, someone commented that there was one order short, and asked the Phillipino what he'd like. "Nothing, thank you," he answered. "I only eat when I'm hungry."

To this day, when Ruthie suggests I lose a few pounds, I refer to the Phillipino lawyer and paraphrase: "I only eat when I want to."

Eventually, we arranged for doctors in various medical fields to examine President Marcos, and they concluded that he was not in medical condition to stand trial or even be arraigned or come to New York. At an evidentiary hearing before the court, we called four doctors with different specialties who had examined Marcos and who testified that his condition was grave and that his mental acuity had significantly deteriorated. The judge concluded that Marcos's condition was dire and dismissed the case against him.

But the prosecution of Imelda Marcos continued. Dick and I joined her defense team. Many lawyers had their hands in drafting motion papers on her behalf. They'd be finalized in California by her principal lawyer and then, to make sure deadlines were met, transmitted to me in duplicate for filing: one set by FedEx and another by personal delivery from an intern who'd fly in from California. We wanted to be sure not to miss a deadline, and if an accident were to occur, we wanted a back-up: The law and a judge can be unforgiving when deadlines aren't met. Not everyone can afford such service.

I met with Mrs. Marcos several times, enough to perceive that she did not overflow with humility and compassion. But before I could deeply immerse myself in her case and really get to know her, I met another front-page and extremely wealthy lady, and the course of my life changed.

Chapter 7
Defending "One Tough Bitch"

After years of handling tax fraud trials and investigations, I thought that the stories of human folly and greed I had come across would make interesting reading. I contacted a friend of mine, Bob Fink, whose practice was almost exclusively in that field. Bob was my age, and as I had become Lou Bender's protege, he was Boris Kostelanetz's. We had worked on several tax fraud cases together, as had Bender and Kostelanetz before us. I told him I had an idea for a book about the world of tax fraud.

My book agent was the head of the literary department at the William Morris Agency. He advised against my writing a book on tax fraud because, he said, its abrupt departure from my earlier books would result in loss of my readership. I told him that I hadn't published a book in six years and my readership was between tiny and smaller. In short order, Bob and I wrote *How To Defend Yourself Against the IRS*, praised by both a former IRS Commissioner and the lawyer in charge of the U.S. Justice Department Tax Division. The book described how some folks cheat and get caught, how the IRS selects people to audit, how to conduct audits, and what to do when the IRS wants your hide. It became, at least by my standards, a popular book.

In the fall of 1989, after the paperback version of the book had run its course, I had some thoughts about a sequel—a kind of *Son of How To Defend Yourself Against the IRS*—and wanted to discuss them with Bob. I met with him at a restaurant where he was having dinner with a friend of his, Jerry Feffer. Feffer was a lawyer in the midst of that year's trial of the century, defending Leona Helmsley in Manhattan federal court against criminal charges that she had cheated on taxes by using phony invoices to pay personal expenses with business funds.

Like most New Yorkers, I had been following the case in the newspapers. Everyone in New York City knew of Leona Helmsley. She was a piñata for the media, consistently vilified as arrogant, nasty, bullying, greedy, imperious, and mercurial; firing employees on a whim, stiffing vendors, abusing whomever she wished, however she wished, whenever she wished. Even Feffer, her lawyer, had told the jury that she was "one tough bitch." One businesswoman who had interacted with her put it this way: "Don't believe everything you've read about Leona. She's worse than that."

Her husband, Harry, a multi-billionaire, had been the premier developer, owner, and operator of real estate in New York City. He'd worked his way up from a twelve-dollars-a-week office boy. Now, his holdings were an inventory of some of New York City's most iconic buildings. He held the largest financial interest in the Empire State Building; owned or had major interests in others of New York's largest office buildings, including the Lincoln Building, the Graybar Building, the Helmsley Building, the Flatiron Building; owned major hotels in the city, including the Park Lane Hotel on Central Park South and the New York Helmsley on 42nd Street, and a major share of the Helmsley Palace Hotel on Madison

Avenue; and owned other fabulously successful residential buildings and other real estate throughout the city and in many states throughout the country.

Harry Helmsley had divorced his first wife, to whom he had been married for thirty-three years, and married Leona Helmsley in 1972. She ran the Helmsley hotels, and featured herself in a series of narcissistic ads: smiling broadly, dressed in an expensive evening gown and dripping in jewelry, standing on the palatial entryway staircase of the Helmsley Palace Hotel, arms spread in grandeur and proclaiming herself a queen: "The only palace in the world where the queen stands guard."

Newspaper articles about the ongoing trial reported allegations of her abusive behavior toward employees and numerous others who crossed her path. A book entitled *Queen of Mean*—a name that stuck—painted a devastating picture of her and was later made into a movie. One of her housekeepers testified that Mrs. Helmsley had told her, "We don't pay taxes. Only the little people pay taxes."

Feffer was bemoaning the difficulties of the case. He said she was basically charged with having had Helmsley businesses pay for renovating a Helmsley mansion in Connecticut through a scheme to charge personal expenses of the renovation to businesses the Helmsleys owned or controlled. There was an infinite sea of phony invoices he had to deal with, Feffer said, and the case was hopeless.

A few weeks after the dinner, Mrs. Helmsley was convicted on a raft of felonies.

In late December 1989, after her sentencing, I was home, working on some legal pleadings in the Imelda Marcos case, when the phone rang. Harvey Silverglate, a law school classmate, was calling. Over the years, he had developed a close relationship with Alan Dershowitz, whom both of us had met twenty-five years earlier in law school; we were first-year students when Alan began teaching at Harvard Law. Since then, Harvey had represented Alan in some personal matters.

Alan had just been retained by Leona Helmsley for the appeal from her conviction, and was assembling a legal team to work with him on the appeal and related legal problems. Over the years, Alan had referred several cases to me. He had written an effusive blurb for the cover of *How To Defend Yourself Against The IRS*, and now needed to bring someone onto the team who had experience in defending criminal tax fraud cases. He had asked Harvey to see whether I was interested.

I told Harvey I was, but that I had committed myself to the lawyer who brought me into the Marcos case, which would soon go to trial. I said I would speak with that lawyer and get back to Harvey soon. Imelda Marcos's case was extremely time-consuming. I knew that the Helmsley case would also require enormous time and effort, and with other commitments, I couldn't responsibly be involved with both Marcos and Helmsley.

I called Dick Hibey and reported the invitation I had received to join the team representing Leona Helmsley. I told him that I would like to accept, but that I had promised him I'd stay on the Marcos team for as long as Dick and the client wanted me to. He thanked me for remembering, but said that at that point, with Ferdinand Marcos now out of the case, Imelda had more than enough lawyers and he would be fine with my leaving the Marcos case and joining the Helmsley team. He said he would verify it with Mrs. Marcos.

So, in January 1990, I was in Harvey Silverglate's conference room in Boston, with Harvey and his partner Andy Good, Alan Dershowitz, Alan's brother Nat (also a lawyer, with whom Alan worked regularly), and several other lawyers and helpers, waiting to meet Leona Helmsley. In the several days before the meeting, I had read a bunch of documents to understand the outlines of her case.

A jury had convicted her of thirty-three felony counts centered around the tax fraud scheme. She had been sentenced to four years in prison, to be followed by three years' probation, plus fines and restitution totaling $9 million. In addition, a pending state court indictment brought by the New York State Attorney General charged her with 188 counts of tax-related state crimes arising out of the same transactions as her federal conviction. The federal trial record, including thousands of exhibits, was voluminous.

Mrs. Helmsley had been charged with her husband Harry and his two right-hand financial assistants. Harry Helmsley's wealth could not save him from the ravages of time and age. Shortly after his indictment, the case against him was dismissed when doctors chosen by both Harry and the government certified that his mental abilities had so degenerated that he was not competent to stand trial. His wife and his two financial underlings had stood trial without him, and all were convicted.

Though she was only meeting with her new legal team, Leona Helmsley walked into Harvey's conference room dressed to the nines and bedecked in jewelry. She had flown up to Boston in her private 727. With her were Harry, a security guard, the Helmsley organization's current chief financial officer, an assistant, and several large cartons filled with dozens of sandwiches freshly made and imported from the Park Lane Hotel, for all of us to have lunch.

Alan introduced the Helmsleys to the lawyers around the table and explained their roles. Nat Dershowitz, Harvey, Andy, and I would write different sections of the appellate brief, with Alan overseeing it and making the oral argument. I would be the lead lawyer in the upcoming state court trial. We also discussed the possibility of asking the federal trial judge for a new trial if we could come up with a basis for doing so.

I didn't say much. It was Alan's case and client; I was there to provide some tax fraud experience and plug up any other holes I could. This was a big case, she was a fascinating public figure, I was content to play whatever role would be helpful, and it was bound to be a heckuva ride.

It was unclear how much of the explanations Mrs. Helmsley understood. She protested that she hadn't done anything wrong and didn't know why she'd been convicted, and seemed intent on convincing us that she was innocent. She seemed similarly intent on making sure we were fed, and insisted we all partake in the sandwiches she had brought for us. Mrs. Helmsley told us that not being able to care for Harry frightened her more than anything.

Harry Helmsley sat quietly at the conference table with us. He occasionally made innocuous comments in an attempt to appear to be following what was being said, but plainly didn't comprehend what we were discussing.

After a few hours, the Helmsleys and their staff left. I considered mentioning that I was returning to New York and asking if I could hitch a flight, but I wasn't invited and my instinct was to maintain a healthy distance from her, particularly at this very early stage. I simply stayed behind with the other lawyers and discussed in more detail the three tasks that faced us—the appeal, the upcoming state court trial, and a possible new trial motion. I caught the last shuttle back to New York, and for the next two years became immersed in United States v. Helmsley.

The Appeal

In appealing from a conviction following trial, the object is to convince the appeals court that a material legal error was committed in the trial court—for example, the trial judge improperly excluded evidence helpful to the defendant, or improperly admitted damaging evidence, or improperly instructed the jury on the law, or the proof was insufficient to convict—something which could have resulted in an unfair conviction. If the appellate court is convinced that such an error occurred, it remands the case to the trial court for a new trial or, better, dismisses the case. The arguments are presented in an appellate "brief," which in this case would be anything but, followed by oral argument.

Appeals are vastly different from trials. In a trial, evidence is presented bit by bit, usually with a jury deciding the defendant's fate; witnesses testify and are cross-examined; exhibits are offered into evidence; lawyers for both sides make opening and closing arguments to the jury; the trial judge rules on evidentiary issues and at the conclusion of the case instructs the jury on the law; and ultimately, the jury gives a thumbs up or thumbs down. They don't have to justify their decision. They simply say, unanimously, guilty or not guilty, and that's it—no explanation necessary. If they ultimately can't agree, the "hung jury" is dismissed and there is a new trial. The trial can take whatever time is required—less than a day, or months. The Helmsley trial had lasted ten weeks.

Different lawyering skills are involved in trials and appeals. Trials involve presenting a client's narrative, or poking holes in the other side's narrative, ultimately to persuade laymen to accept your version of the facts. Jury trials often involve a bit of gamesmanship, sympathy, empathy, getting a jury to like you and your client, or other fuzzy subjective factors.

Appellate lawyering is a more intellectual exercise. The facts have been determined by a jury, and the appellate lawyer's job is to show presumably rational, unemotional judges that a legal error has occurred warranting reversal of a conviction or, better yet, dismissal of the charges.

On appeals, there are no witnesses and no juries, and the entire court proceeding typically lasts less than an hour, sometimes a few minutes. But many hours of lawyering precede that short court appearance. The appellate lawyer's "brief" is a statement of what the appeal is about: the case's procedural background, the facts, and the reasons why the defendant is entitled to reversal of the conviction. The appellate court does not make factual determinations—during the trial, a verbatim transcript is made of everything said in the courtroom, and following a conviction the appeals court is legally required to construe the evidence in the light most favorable to the prosecution.

Writing an appellate brief in a case like Helmsley is a substantial task, taking lengthy and intensive work. After the brief is filed, the government files an opposing brief, and the defendant files a reply. The appellate judges read the briefs before hearing oral argument.

In Leona Helmsley's case, we would scour "the record"—8,000 pages of trial transcript, all of the exhibits, and all of the pre-trial motions. Feffer sent me fourteen cartons of exhibits, accompanied by a seven-hundred-page description of the exhibits. Analyzing the exhibits would be a Herculean task. To help with that effort, we retained the accounting firm Arthur Andersen, which Feffer had used at trial and at the time was one of the "Big 8" accounting firms—an international firm that later dissolved under the pressure of its own criminal conviction in the Enron case.

We pursued two primary appellate arguments:

Years earlier, in an unrelated New York State grand jury investigation of sales tax fraud committed by major New York City jewelry stores, Mrs. Helmsley had admitted avoiding New York sales taxes by buying jewelry in New York City and having empty boxes shipped to her Connecticut home. She had testified under a grant of immunity: Nothing she said could be used against her. But the substance of her testimony had been leaked, resulting in a chain of events culminating in the criminal tax investigation that resulted in her tax fraud conviction. We argued that since the grant of immunity to Mrs. Helmsley prohibited use of her testimony in any respect, and since the leak of her immunized testimony led to her indictment and conviction, her conviction should be reversed.

Our second main appellate argument was that, in fact, Mrs. Helmsley not only had *not* cheated on her taxes, but had *over*paid her taxes and was entitled to a tax refund under arcane tax laws beyond anyone's ability to explain in readily understandable terms—so I'll take a pass on trying.

Much of what lawyers do is legal research and writing. "The law" is primarily contained in statutes (laws passed by legislatures) and cases (decisions by judges and published in thick books you've seen pictures of in movies, lining the shelves of law offices). Those physical books have since been largely replaced by computers. What used to be miles of law books are now available electronically—but that was not so in 1990.

We divided the legal arguments among ourselves. I had principal responsibility for writing the argument that the prosecution had simply failed to prove a case of tax evasion against Mrs. Helmsley. I'd pull books off the shelves and scour them for decisions that supported the arguments I was drafting. There is a way to do this, to trace the evolution and variations of a legal principle. The details of the process are not particularly exciting. The journey from one case to another, searching for the judicial nugget that best supports the legal argument you're making, is tedious and time-consuming, but a real high when you strike judicial gold—finding the case that clearly, or nearly, supports your argument, or even a phrase which, by your logical extension, does the trick.

Justice Oliver Wendell Holmes, Jr. wrote: "The life of the law has not been logic; it has been experience." Framing a legal argument often requires both. You have the best chance of success if you can convince the appellate judges that your argument makes good common sense, and also flows logically from decisions of other courts. The appellate lawyer searches the law books for support, going from case to case, to build a superstructure of judicial precedent on which to erect a particular argument. You've seen pictures—lawyers sitting at library tables, ties askew or off, surrounded by open books, rubbing their eyes in exhaustion.

Some of the search was interesting and some boring, exploring minutiae of hard-to-follow tax laws. But all of it was necessary, and Ruthie was always understanding when I'd call home to say I'd be eating a sandwich at the office for dinner that night because of the need to keep tracking down some point of law. I once saw a sketch of half-a-dozen lawyers sitting, bedraggled, ties off, shirt-sleeves rolled up, the morning sun beginning to rise outside the window, with large mounds of open books stacked in front of them, and one lawyer moans: "The answer's here somewhere." That was me.

We synthesized our arguments into what turned out to be a book-length brief. Drafts were written, circulated among all of us, rewritten, and re-rewritten many times before the final product went to press. Ultimately, fourteen lawyers' names appeared on our brief.

The State Court Case

While we were working on the appeal, the state court trial date was approaching. The state court judge had postponed the state trial during the federal trial, but would no longer hold the state court proceedings in abeyance simply because we were appealing the federal conviction.

Here, we caught a break. New York State law protects anyone from being prosecuted twice for the same offense—a "double jeopardy" law similar to the one in the federal Constitution. New York law also permits dismissal of a case "in the interests of justice." Feffer had filed a motion seeking to dismiss the State prosecution on both grounds. The judge hadn't yet ruled.

I thought we could improve the legal arguments supporting the motion. Because I had never tried a criminal case in state court and knew nothing of Judge Bradley, the presiding judge, I spent several hours in the back of his courtroom one day, simply sitting in the spectators' gallery, watching him conduct a variety of proceedings. I got a feel for how he might be persuaded to allow new counsel to file a substitute, new-and-improved set of motion papers.

At our next court appearance, I asked him for permission to do so, and he agreed. We filed a comprehensive motion attacking each of the 188 state court charges, particularizing how each charge violated the state's double jeopardy laws because each arose out of the same transactions on which the federal prosecution was based. We also expanded on the reasons that dismissal was warranted in the interests of justice, and added several other arguments.

I was Mrs. Helmsley's courtroom lawyer—the talker—throughout the state court case. Each appearance was scheduled for the morning, and the team's routine was the same. We would gather at the Park Lane Hotel with Mrs. Helmsley the night before, usually in a spacious conference room on an upper floor with grand views overlooking Central Park. Dinner would be served, either there or in the hotel restaurant. We would explain the status of the case and the nature of the next day's proceedings. Mrs. Helmsley would listen dutifully.

The extent to which she absorbed what we were explaining was uncertain. At one meeting, one of the accountants sat across the table from her, explaining, in non-technical language, a simple accounting concept involved in the case. Mrs. Helmsley looked in his general direction as he spoke, but seemed to be staring at the wall over his shoulder. When he finished and was waiting for her reaction, she turned to one of the waiters in the room, pointed to a dead light bulb on the wall, and asked, How long has that bulb been out? It was replaced immediately.

We were all given rooms at the Park Lane on the nights before court appearances. Ordering breakfast room service at a first-class hotel in New York City is not painful when all you have to do is sign the bill.

Promptly at 8:30 a.m., we would convene in the lobby of the hotel and walk outside to waiting limousines. Mrs. Helmsley, Alan, and I would ride to court in the lead car; the rest of the entourage followed. At the courthouse, a horde of paparazzi would be waiting, and as we got out of our car, camera shutters would click like crickets until we entered the courthouse.

The legal team and Mrs. Helmsley sat at the defense table; I'd address the judge; the prosecutor would respond; I'd respond to his response; the prosecutor and I would do some more back-and-forthing to the judge; and the next court date would be scheduled. The crickets would reappear after the morning's proceedings when Mrs. Helmsley, I, and the other lawyers walked the gauntlet from the courthouse to the cars.

Although the federal case against Harry Helmsley had been dismissed, proceedings concerning his mental competence were still pending in the state court. I sat in the back of the courtroom one day when his lawyer was arguing about his competence to stand trial. At the end of the argument, Judge Bradley beckoned to me to come up from the spectators' gallery to the bench with the prosecutor. He said that the state Attorney General's office had offered Mrs. Helmsley's prior lawyers a plea-bargain for her: If she would plead guilty to some counts, she'd receive a sentence concurrent with her federal sentence—that is, no extra jail time—plus payment of some additional taxes. The judge said he wanted me to know that the plea-bargain was still available.

The decision to accept a plea deal is always the client's, not the lawyer's. But I had previously discussed with Mrs. Helmsley the possibility of a plea agreement and she had firmly rejected the notion. I told that to Judge Bradley, who said the offer would disappear once trial began.

Seven weeks later, I orally argued before Judge Bradley and a packed courtroom that the state indictment should be dismissed. I argued how all of the 188 counts—each of which I addressed in turn—completely overlapped the federal crimes of which Mrs. Helmsley had already been convicted, and that basic principles protecting against double jeopardy required their dismissal.

I also argued, as we did in the federal appeal, that the prosecution was barred because it resulted from an improper leak of her immunized grand jury testimony in the years-ago sales tax investigation. Moreover, I argued, the interests of justice required dismissal: The Helmsleys had paid nearly $58 million in taxes in the years in question, and over one-third of a *billion* dollars—$342 million—in taxes over the past eight years. The amount involved in this prosecution was minor viewed in that context, and any taxes allegedly due had been paid when the investigation began. The Helmsleys had contributed millions to charities. The federal sentence had been extraordinarily harsh, Mrs. Helmsley had already lived for years under the strain of two prosecutions, and just as she deserved no special benefit because of her notoriety, she didn't deserve harsher treatment either.

Judge Bradley listened carefully. After lengthy arguments from both the prosecutor and me, he reserved decision. As we left the courthouse, I ignored the media's requests for a prediction. In the car, Mrs. Helmsley gave me a big kiss on the cheek.

A month later, we appeared again before Judge Bradley to hear his decision. In the interim, I had learned something about the prosecutor. Because my practice at this point was too time-consuming with the one associate I then had, I had taken out a "blind" help-wanted ad in the *New York Law Journal*—not identifying myself, but saying a single practitioner with a sophisticated litigation practice is seeking an associate. Among the responding attorneys was the Assistant Attorney General handling the Helmsley prosecution—the same lawyer appearing against me before Judge Bradley—emphasizing his credentials as the lead prosecutor of Leona Helmsley. He had no idea he was job hunting to the lawyer fighting him in the Helmsley case.

Judge Bradley's decision was the first good legal news for Leona Helmsley since the investigation of Harry and her had begun years ago. He handed us a written decision dismissing 180 of the 188 charges. When we left the courtroom, Mrs. Helmsley threw her arms around me in gratitude. I told her we still had to get rid of the eight remaining counts. And we did: The Appellate Division accepted our arguments and dismissed them all. The state court prosecution was over, and we had won.

Alan argued the appeal of Mrs. Helmsley's federal conviction in the U.S. Court of Appeals. That court has over twenty judges and hears cases in three-judge panels. The argument lasted about an hour, split evenly between both sides, and the judges reserved decision. There was no way to predict how they would rule, and no requirement that they rule by any deadline. Their written decision would be filed whenever they chose. Unlike a jury, which simply say "guilty" or "not guilty," appellate judges rule by filing written "opinions" explaining the legal grounds for their decisions.

Waiting for a jury to return a verdict is a time of enormous tension, but ends within a day or a few days when the verdict is finally delivered. In an appeal of a major case like U.S. v. Helmsley, with no deadline for decision, the tension lasts far longer.

Finally, nearly ten months after the case had been argued, the Court of Appeals filed its decision: Her conviction was affirmed.

Two of the three judges rejected all of our arguments. The third—the Chief Judge of the court—voted to dismiss nearly half the charges against her, and for her to be resentenced on the remaining counts. His dissent was based on the technical tax argument we had raised—that the Helmsleys had actually overpaid their taxes.

We had come close. But you don't get credit for persuading the Chief Judge when the two other judges disagree, and you can't pretend that losing two-to-one is a win—that's like a baseball player line-driving into a double-play and boasting he'd hit the ball hard. The noose was tightening.

Winning always beats losing. Clients think you're hot stuff when you win, and think you can keep doing it.

In the state court case, Judge Bradley had insisted that Mrs. Helmsley attend all court sessions. She offered flattering comments to me after each appearance.

I began to develop a close professional relationship with her soon after our introduction in Boston. In the beginning, Harvey was her main channel of communication with the team, as Alan was often involved in other things. But Harvey was in Boston, and it was easy for her to ask me to come up to her apartment on short notice. When she whistled, I went.

Although we were getting closer and having frequent contact, I kept my formal distance. She had a battery of outside lawyers handling a multitude of matters, and they easily slipped into "Leona" with her. To me, she was always "Mrs. Helmsley." As the years passed, we occasionally lapsed into a Laurel and Hardy routine:

She: "Don't you know my first name?"

Me: "Sure. It's Leona, Mrs. Helmsley."

I observed fairly early that she seemed to be a prisoner of her wealth. In the eighteen years that she wound up as my client, I met very few people she referred to as friends. She seemed to regard everyone with whom she interacted—maybe including me, though she never indicated so—as interested in her only as a means to possible access to some of her money. I thought she always perceived herself as a target, a mark.

She had piercing green eyes that could drill a hole through you, but she could smile and flutter her eyelids when the mood struck. She had a way of instantly ingratiating herself with other professionals she'd newly met. She would listen to them intently and react with apparent amazement at what was being said, as if to convey: Where have you been all these years while I have been suffering fools—you're the one I've been waiting for. Inevitably, the flatteree would think he'd struck gold, become over-friendly, start "Leona"ing her—and get fired. She made one lawyer-suitor feel so comfortable that he rested his feet on an ottoman in her living room and, when she suddenly glared at him, he removed his shoes and put his feet back up; he was toast. Someone else was always waiting in line to minister to her needs and compete for her affection and fees.

Her wariness of others extended across the broad range of people whose paths crossed hers. When Donald Trump suggested a business transaction involving her hotels, she told me: "I wouldn't trust him if his tongue was notarized." When she became suspicious about a housekeeper who cleaned her apartment, where extremely expensive jewelry was sometimes left around carelessly, she put a twenty-dollar bill on the staircase leading up to her pool to test whether the woman would return it.

She could be overly demanding, divorced from the lives of everyday people. At one of our pre-court all-hands dinner meetings in the Park Lane restaurant, she so abused a waiter that one of the lawyers privately gave him a large tip for his sufferance. She confessed, "Maybe I'm spoiled," but said that the best way to fly is to have your limo drive onto the airport tarmac and then to walk a few steps onto a private 727—the interior retrofitted into an elegant living room with rich paneling and plush furniture, plus, of course, a kitchen and bedroom. She ordered decks of playing cards with Harry's and her pictures on each card—the Queen of Hearts was Mrs. Helmsley in an evening gown; on the Jack of Diamonds she wore a less flamboyant outfit plus a tiara; Harry's face on all of the Kings; and so on for all fifty-two cards.

She was impervious to most public criticism. A highly critical book about her claimed that after each lap she swam in her pool, she'd order a housekeeper to feed her a shrimp; she told me that never happened because she avoids shrimp—too much cholesterol. She found laughable her former maid's testimony at trial that Mrs. Helmsley had boasted, "Only the little people pay taxes"; when I asked why she ran hotel ads in the *Times* but not the *Post*, she answered: "Only the little people read the *Post*."

She lived a life of supreme luxury. Her primary residence was the penthouse duplex in the Helmsley Park Lane Hotel. You'd take an elevator to the 46th floor, where security guards sat 24/7 outside her front door. The apartment had picture-perfect views of Manhattan—Central Park and both the East and Hudson rivers. From top to bottom, plush carpeting to gold-painted moldings, furniture, and wallpaper: everything was the most expensive money could buy.

On the second floor of the apartment was an indoor pool into which nobody but the Helmsleys would dip. Outside the pool was a wraparound rooftop deck with 360° take-your-breath-away views of Manhattan, extending as far as the eye could see. The roof also had a separate all-glass room. When we'd sit there while the criminal appeal was pending, she would have the curtains drawn on all four sides because of photographers overhead in helicopters.

Another of her homes, Dunnellen Hall—the primary scene of the alleged crime—was a palace: forty magnificent rolling acres in the most expensive area of Greenwich, Connecticut, surrounded by an iron gate and fence and guarded by security personnel and ferocious-looking German shepherds tethered to the fence; a long, winding driveway flanked by ornate lampposts and statues leading to a twenty-eight-room brick mansion, in front of which was a marble reflecting pool. A heavy oak door opened onto an always-shiny marble entryway, which led to an enormous living room; a grand staircase similar to the staircase in the Palace Hotel; and a series of sitting rooms, bedrooms, and assorted other barely used rooms. There were two extra-large swimming pools, indoor and out, and a tennis court. The court reminded me of an expression Ruthie's mother used: God gives nuts to squirrels with no teeth.

If Mrs. Helmsley wanted a change of scenery, she could take Harry to their hilltop estate in Scottsdale, Arizona, or their beachfront apartment in their Sandcastle Hotel in Sarasota, Florida.

The first time I was at Mrs. Helmsley's homes, after being struck by their uber luxury, they seemed to be a showcase of evidence: the rooftop dance floor over the indoor swimming pool in Greenwich, paid for by Helmsley businesses, was a large part of the criminal trial; several of the artifacts in both the Greenwich and Park Lane homes were evidence in the criminal trial—when I saw them, I visualized invoices and trial exhibits instead of grandeur.

She was not used to taking orders. When we prepared with her at the Park Lane for our first court appearance, she invited the gossip columnist Cindy Adams to attend. I explained that was a bad idea because it would destroy the attorney-client privilege and could result in our strategy being printed on the front page of the newspaper. She pooh-poohed the objection, and Cindy Adams stayed.

But I've digressed. We had won the State Court case, lost the appeal of her federal conviction, and now all that stood between Mrs. Helmsley and prison was a motion we made in federal court for a new trial, based on our claim of newly discovered evidence.

The New Trial Motion

The evidence that tax fraud had been committed was overwhelming. The question was whether Mrs. Helmsley had participated in the fraud—had she helped conceal from the Helmsleys' accountants, as they testified, the fact that payments made by Helmsley businesses were for personal expenses?

Most cases have at their heart a simple issue. Here, payments by Helmsley businesses for personal purposes were improperly deducted from the Helmsleys' business tax returns (decreasing the businesses' income taxes) and improperly not included as income on the Helmsleys' personal tax returns (decreasing their personal income taxes). The invoices used to accomplish this scheme were phony—some falsely described what the payments were for (for example, repair of business property in Manhattan rather than building the indoor pool and its overhead rooftop dance floor at Dunnellen Hall), and some had been altered (for example, changing an invoice for work at Dunnellen Hall to make the invoice appear to have been for work at one of the Manhattan business properties).

There is nothing illegal about a business paying for personal expenses. A businessman can pay for repair of his home by issuing a check from his business account—as long as the payment is ultimately treated correctly for tax purposes. So, if the check is not deducted as an expense of the business, and is reported as income on the businessman's personal income tax return, no tax fraud has been committed and no additional tax is owed. The responsibility of the taxpayer is simply to make sure that the payment is, ultimately, accurately reported to the IRS. If he fools his accountant and the personal payment is treated as a business expense, the businessman has committed tax fraud.

We asked the trial judge to grant Mrs. Helmsley a new trial on two grounds:

Harry Helmsley had used the same accounting firm for many years, paying them many millions of dollars. The government's theory in prosecuting Mrs. Helmsley was that she had duped the accountants, concealing from them the true nature of the checks. Several of the accountants testified at trial that the firm had been unaware that the Helmsleys' personal expenses had been paid by Helmsley businesses. But the Helmsley CFO gave us an internal ledger handwritten by one of the accountants treating the payments correctly—strongly suggesting that the accountants knew that Helmsley business checks had paid for personal expenses.

The accountants' knowing the true nature of the invoices would have undercut the prosecution's basic theory: that the accountants had been duped into believing personal expenses were for business. Mrs. Helmsley could be entitled to a new trial because the entire theory of the prosecution was bogus.

But the CFO told us he had told Feffer about the ledger and Feffer hadn't used it at trial. To obtain a new trial based on newly discovered evidence, a defendant has to prove that the evidence is indeed newly discovered—and the ledger was not. We argued, though, that not only did the evidence show that the accountants knew the true nature of the invoices, but the prosecutors knew or should have known that fact.

One way to try to skirt the requirement that newly discovered evidence be in fact newly discovered is to claim that the trial lawyer's failure to use the evidence was so professionally inexcusable as to have deprived the client of effective assistance of counsel. But here, both because Feffer was an experienced and highly credentialed tax fraud lawyer and because Mrs. Helmsley of all people could have hired any lawyer or army of lawyers she wanted, that claim would be highly problematical.

We also discovered that the prosecutors had failed to disclose evidence creating a motive for one of their accountant witnesses to lie—at the time he testified, he himself had been under investigation for unrelated criminal activity. But that argument could be attacked because the accountant's credibility had been impeached at trial in other ways.

Courts are generally skeptical when new lawyers come into a case and second-guess the original trial lawyer's strategy. New trial motions are not vehicles to retry a case—the defendant gets only one chance, at the trial, and that's it. Our motion would be a long-shot involving an amount of lawyering that most people cannot afford. "Equal justice under law" does not mean *exactly* equal justice.

A starting point in learning the origins of the fraud would be Harry Helmsley. Though Mrs. Helmsley always shielded Harry from stressful situations, she consented to let me speak with him about the invoices. He was standing in the pool in their Park Lane penthouse, a physical therapist massaging his arms; plainly frail; he walked in the pool toward me, with the therapist's help, very slowly. I asked him about the invoices and the renovations at the Helmsley's mansion. Much of what he said was incomprehensible, and his only intelligible responses were that he didn't understand what I was asking.

Since the evidence that *somebody* had committed tax fraud was overwhelming, I decided to have the Arthur Andersen firm conduct a detailed examination, which I oversaw, of the hundreds of invoices that had been introduced en masse at the trial to see whether any in particular implicated Mrs. Helmsley. According to the primary Arthur Andersen accountant, the defense had not done any such invoice-by-invoice analysis for the trial, even though the invoices formed the heart of the prosecution. I figured: Who knows, maybe if we can convince the trial judge that Mrs. Helmsley was actually innocent, he'll follow our legal path to give her a new trial. Many years earlier, I had argued to a federal judge, who was about to grant relief to an adversary over my objection, that the judge didn't have the power to do so because he lacked jurisdiction. The judge had leaned back in his chair, glowered at me, and responded, Oh, I have plenty of power.

Maybe that power could help us here if we could convince the judge that Mrs. Helmsley was innocent, or if we could at least plant a seed of doubt in his mind. He might then exercise his discretion and grant a new trial.

Mrs. Helmsley had approved hundreds of invoices, by initialing them. I wanted to determine whether any of them indicated that she was a knowing participant in the tax scheme, or only that she approved the purchases without concealing their personal nature.

The result: Numerous invoices to Helmsley businesses were unquestionably for personal expenses, but *none* showed on its face that it falsely described the nature of the payment, and dozens actually disclosed on their face that personal expenses were being charged to businesses—the very type of information Mrs. Helmsley was charged with having conspired to conceal. The reams of invoices, examined one by one, proved nothing against her. The devil was, indeed, in the details.

I prepared a comprehensive affidavit for submission to the court, attaching a thick set of exhibits, spelling all this out in detail—430 pages of invoices and analysis. We all recognized that Feffer had not established any of this at trial, even though the underlying exhibits were all introduced into evidence, but we hoped that this analysis might influence the judge's consideration of the new trial motion.

If we got a new trial, I believed we could win.

Our first courtroom appearance on the new trial motion was before Judge Thomas Griesa. I'd never appeared before him. When we were preparing, Alan said he'd had a case before Judge Griesa that had gone well.

We appeared before the judge for a scheduling conference. The prosecutor began, stating his position. Alan then rose to speak. He began:

Alan: "Your Honor, we don't dispute the——."

Judge (interrupting): "What is your name?"

Alan: "Alan Dershowitz. Sorry, your Honor. "

Judge: "I didn't hear you announce your name. I am not acquainted with you."

I was sitting next to Alan, and Andy next to me. Andy leaned over and whispered to me, "Uh-oh."

He was right. A month later, we appeared in court to argue the new trial motion. We got hammered.

Andy began. Then it was my turn. Then Alan's. Judge Griesa swatted away everything we said. He scoffed at every argument we made, cut us off mid-sentence, said our papers were shoddy and imprecise, our arguments were flawed, our submissions untimely, and our answers to his questions unresponsive. We could say nothing right.

All lawyers lose arguments. Here, though, the judge seemed not just unreceptive to everything we said and impatient with how we said it, but downright hostile. The entire tone of the proceeding contrasted sharply with another appearance I'd had before him a few weeks earlier.

That earlier appearance was to argue a motion we had made asking Judge Griesa to eliminate, for medical reasons, Mrs. Helmsley's prison sentence. An expert cardiologist—I'd retained the same expert who had examined Ferdinand Marcos in connection with his case—had concluded that the impact of Mrs. Helmsley's four-year sentence could be lethal for both Mr. and Mrs. Helmsley. I had argued to Judge Griesa, before a similarly packed courtroom, to eliminate her jail sentence. The judge had denied the motion, but had been respectful of its presentation.

Now, just a few weeks later, the same judge was completely dismissive both in tone and substance of everything we were arguing and how we were presenting our arguments. I couldn't understand why. Certainly, challenging a major conviction after a ten-week trial was a steep struggle. But that shouldn't have generated the apparent hostility, if not downright anger, our arguments were provoking.

The judge called a recess. When he left the courtroom, I predicted he'd come back and not simply deny the motion but have a guillotine. In fact, after court resumed, he made an astonishing disclosure.

During the recess, the judge said, his law clerk had reminded him of something he had forgotten. Last week, a letter intended for *Newsday*, written by Harvey, had been misdirected to the judge's office. I hadn't known of the letter. The judge now disclosed that his secretary had opened the envelope and that his law clerk had "looked through just enough to see what the nature of the letter was, and one of the things that it contained was an advice to *Newsday* that at this hearing, a bombshell would be dropped." The judge continued: "In an issue of *Newsday* which appeared, there was a discussion of the bombshell and some indication of something about invoices." The judge then said, "Somebody from *Newsday* came over and said, 'You got the letter by mistake,' and we said 'take it.' But I think it is quite apparent that there has been some attempt to fight this motion in the press." Although lawyers are free (with some limitations) to speak with the press about a case, judges generally don't like it.

The judge hadn't told us until now about the reading of this misdirected letter, and was obviously furious over Harvey's leak to *Newsday*. The letter totally took the steam out of our motion.

We had no choice but to plow ahead. In attacking our presentation, Judge Griesa had referred to a statement by the Court of Appeals, in its decision affirming Mrs. Helmsley's conviction, that the evidence against her had been overwhelming. This opened an opportunity, I thought, to demonstrate to him that our analysis of the invoices, which had not been before the Court of Appeals, showed the opposite. That analysis was the "bombshell" Harvey's misdirected letter had referred to, though the chance of the judge now being swayed by it was beyond remote.

In one last effort, after the judge had made his disclosure and was ready to rule, I stood again and asked: "If you give me ten minutes, I can prove to you that the heart of the prosecution against her, these invoices, not only don't show her guilt, but prove her innocence, and I beg you for that ten minutes."

The judge answered: No. He said the ten minutes would run into more than ten minutes; we'd had our chance; we had had enough time; and the evidence had been available at trial. "So I would like to have you sit down," he said.

I remained standing, resolved to try again to change his mind, but before I could respond the judge repeated: "Would you please sit down."

When a judge tells you to sit—twice—you sit. So I sat, and the judge dictated a decision denying our motion, denying Mrs. Helmsley bail pending appeal of his order, and ordering her to surrender on April 15—tax day—eight days later.

The jail gates were closing fast on Leona Helmsley. Our last hope was either a successful appeal from the denial of the motion, or a successful appeal from the denial of our motion for reduction of her sentence. We asked the Court of Appeals to accelerate our appeal from the denial of our motion to reduce Mrs. Helmsley's sentence, so they could consider it before her April 15 surrender. The court scheduled oral argument for April 14.

There was no chance that our appeal from denial of our motion for new trial would be heard before the surrender date. We had to draft a brief, and argument on the motion would be months away. But if we could file our brief within the next few days, and if our arguments were strong enough, we could ask the Court of Appeals to postpone her imprisonment until the court heard oral argument of the appeal—and attach our brief to show the Court of Appeals how strong our appellate arguments were. But time was short.

Six days before her scheduled surrender, I flew to Boston to work with the team and write an appellate brief seeking a new trial, hoping to write it in a few days and accompany it with a motion to postpone her surrender until the appeal was heard. The brief on her primary appeal had taken several months and thousands of hours to write. Now, we had a self-imposed deadline of a few days. I worked around the clock, with Harvey and Andy, in a tiny fraction of the time necessary for a first-rate job. Neither Alan nor his brother showed up to help.

After several days, Harvey, Andy, and I concluded that the brief we had been drafting was simply not good enough. This would be Mrs. Helmsley's last real chance to overturn her conviction— the brief had to be superb. We all could recognize superior legal work, and this one wasn't. Time had simply run out. I flew back to New York, disappointed in our inability to produce a quality product in a very short time.

The following day, April 13, I checked into the Park Lane Hotel and went up to Mrs. Helmsley's apartment. Two of her grandsons and several other people were there. Mrs. Helmsley showed me a letter Nat Dershowitz had asked her to sign, authorizing the Bureau of Prisons to release to him any information about her, including her medical condition.

She asked me whether she should sign it. I knew it was a trick question with no good answer. Mrs. Helmsley had grown disenchanted with Alan, believing he wasn't paying attention to her case, or to her, or giving her the legal services she was paying him for. But I thought this was exactly the wrong time for a crisis in representation—the day before Alan was scheduled to argue before the Court of Appeals for a reduction of her sentence. I said I didn't know anything about the Bureau of Prisons form, and tried to avoid answering. But she pressed me for an answer, yes or no. I said yes. It was the wrong answer, and she yelled at me angrily for advising her to allow the Dershowitzes access to such information.

Clearly, Mrs. Helmsley had been speaking with others over the weekend, and there was a lot of second-guessing going on. Another lawyer had told her that she would not be surrendering to prison in Danbury, Connecticut, a minimum security prison near her home and close to Harry in Greenwich, but to a more secure prison in Lexington, Kentucky. The reason: the prison in Lexington housed inmates with potential medical problems. She would be going to a worse prison, far from Harry, because of the unsuccessful motion we had made concerning her medical condition. Our strategy to reduce her sentence had backfired.

She exploded at me, the only lawyer there. How could we have done this to her. It was an uncontrolled outburst, and it prompted Harry to start yelling in a pathetic way at me also. He might have recognized my face, but had no idea who I was.

Shortly, Milton Gould came up to the apartment for what I

gathered was a scheduled meeting. Gould was an elder statesman in New York legal circles: a highly experienced trial lawyer, one of the deans of the city's legal establishment, and a co-founder of Shea & Gould, a large and powerful New York law firm. It was clear whom Mrs. Helmsley had spent the weekend consulting.

With Gould now speaking with Mrs. Helmsley, I went down to my room. Soon, Mrs. Helmsley's bodyguard came down and said that Mrs. Helmsley felt terrible that I had borne the brunt of her and Harry's anger. I told him to tell her not to worry about it, that I understood.

When Harvey and Andy checked into the hotel, I told them what had happened. We all went upstairs and Mrs. Helmsley again exploded, in a roomful of people. Much of what she had to say was an attack on Alan. She said we should have advised her to fire him a long time ago, said he'd not paid proper attention to the case, and made some other very pointed criticisms of him. I had been generally aware of smoldering anger Mrs. Helmsley had developed toward Alan, but not its depth; I'd been buried in lawyering, not focused on her growing resentment toward him.

Late that night, when Harvey, Andy, and I were still with Mrs. Helmsley, Alan called the apartment, looking for Harvey. Mrs. Helmsley asked for the phone and was about to excoriate him, but I cautioned her that Alan was going to argue on her behalf the next day for a reduction of her sentence, and attacking him now would be a mistake. She followed the advice and quietly handed the phone to Harvey.

On the morning of April 14, the day before Mrs. Helmsley was scheduled to report to prison, Alan argued before the Court of Appeals for reduction of her sentence. The judges reserved decision, but we all left the courtroom pessimistic about Mrs. Helmsley's chance of avoiding jail. As with all appeals, only the lawyers were required to appear in court, and Mrs. Helmsley remained in her apartment.

After the oral argument was over, a throng of reporters gathered outside the courthouse. Alan held a press conference; Harvey, Andy, and I took a car back to the Park Lane. Over lunch, we learned that the Court of Appeals had rejected our appeal. We went upstairs and told Mrs. Helmsley, then left her and returned to the restaurant. Alan and his brother eventually joined us.

While we were sitting there, Mrs. Helmsley phoned Alan and he left the table to take the call. When he returned, he said that she was very upset because of a statement that he had made during his courthouse press conference earlier that day: that Mrs. Helmsley was prepared to give up her hotels to house New York City's homeless in order to avoid her jail sentence.

We all went up to Mrs. Helmsley's apartment after lunch, and she lambasted Alan for his statement about the hotels and the homeless, screaming that it was completely unauthorized. She was livid, yelling at him so furiously the security guard and household help came into the living room to watch. He kept repeating to her that of course she would do that if she could avoid going to jail, and she kept screaming back that he had no right to say that, that's not what she would do, and that he was completely ignoring what she was saying. She then told him exactly what she thought of him, and none of it was good. She left no doubt about her opinions. I shall leave out the details of all the verbal daggers she flung at him; she let him know with crystal clarity, at an off-the-charts decibel level, in no uncertain terms and with the veins in her neck bulging and her face reddening, the extent of her deep dissatisfaction with him and his legal services.

Alan argued back about the excellent work he said he had done; but she let him know, loudly, fiercely, unequivocally, and in a verbal bloodletting, how deeply she disagreed. He told her we'd won the state court case. You, she shouted at him, didn't win anything—*he* did, pointing at me. Then she ordered him out of her apartment.

She didn't boot anyone else out, but all the other lawyers left with Alan. Before the door shut behind them, I had to decide whether to join them or remain behind. If I were to stay, she might then attack me and order me out as well. She was enraged.

In making important decisions, I'm generally cautious, mulling over the pluses and minuses of alternative actions. But here, there was no time for mulling. I had to decide in an instant what to do.

I stayed.

My choosing to stay was made instinctively, knowing that it would be the end of my relationships with people I had known for many years. But Leona Helmsley would shortly be going to jail, much of her criticism and anger was valid, and she couldn't be left adrift without legal help from someone who knew her case. Though she hadn't said it, I thought she wanted me to stay. So I did.

When the others left, the room suddenly became quiet. She, her bodyguard, Mr. Helmsley, his nurse, some household help, a grandson, and I remained. Mr. Helmsley, as usual, had remained quiet during the shouting match—impassive, expressionless, seated. As soon as the front door shut behind Alan and the others, Harry Helmsley lifted himself out of his chair, stood up as straight as he could, and lurched fitfully toward me, shaking, pointing his finger at my face, and angrily and haltingly saying to me, in as loud a voice as he could muster: You-know-the-way-out-same-way-you-came-in.

Mrs. Helmsley put an arm around him and calmed him down. He's okay, she told him. Mr. Helmsley let his arm drop; his face reflected befuddlement, and he let his nurse help him back to his chair.

Mrs. Helmsley would be flying to prison in Lexington, Kentucky the next day. She was going to leave soon for Dunnellen Hall to make some last-minute arrangements, and would fly by her private plane early the next morning to avoid reporters at the prison.

During the day, CNN had been calling my office, leaving messages asking me to appear that day opposite the always-in-the-spotlight lawyer Bill Kunstler, who was going to argue in favor of Mrs. Helmsley's lengthy jail sentence. I had avoided the press throughout the case, but because her imminent imprisonment had become top news, I asked Mrs. Helmsley whether she wanted me to appear. She asked me to ask her longtime publicity agent, who urged me to. So later that afternoon I appeared on CNN against Kunstler, who attacked her viciously and defended the sentence while I defended her and attacked the sentence. Mrs. Helmsley called, thanked me for publicly defending her, and then was gone. But first, she sent a letter to Alan, firing him.

Before daybreak the next morning, April 15, Leona Helmsley flew in her private plane to prison in Lexington, Kentucky, accompanied by her bodyguard. She arrived shortly after daybreak, before the paparazzi. Her bodyguard stayed in a motel room near the prison, where he would live throughout her stay in Lexington.

The last few weeks had been physically and emotionally exhausting. I had been an absentee husband and father, and encouraged Ruthie to take the children to Florida during their school break, saying I'd join them when the craziness ended.

On the morning Mrs. Helmsley flew to prison, I flew to Fort Lauderdale to join my family. I had barely arrived when the phone rang. It was Mrs. Helmsley.

She was frightened, and thought the guards were eavesdropping on our call. Though she was not a religious woman, her parents were Jewish and she was aware of her Jewishness. I knew a handful of Yiddish words and expressions. Because I had sprinkled them into conversation over the two years that we had known each other, she apparently thought I spoke Yiddish; she spoke Yiddish to me in that phone call, and from the few words I understood, and my sense of what she must be experiencing, she was expressing great fear and a feeling of being alone. She switched to English and asked if I would come to see her. I said yes. Following our conversation, I requested permission of the prison authorities to visit her the next day, and permission for a brief visit was granted.

My simply showing up was important to her. Right then, Leona Helmsley didn't need a fancy-Dan lawyer tossing around Latin legalisms or grinding out sophisticated legal arguments. She needed to know that someone was thinking of her, worried about her, and working on her case even while she was locked up far away. When I put down the phone and told Ruthie I'd have to leave her and the children again, she told me to make sure I was on the next plane to Lexington.

The quickest way to get there was a flight to Cincinnati; from there, a small propeller plane flies to Lexington. I don't like small planes. When I worked in Washington, a friend had induced me to fly in his propeller-driven two-seater. As we circled without instruments in a mass of clouds, unable to see out the window, I made a deal with the Lord that if we landed safely this would be my last such escapade. The plane to Lexington was only slightly bigger, and I breathed a sigh of relief when we landed.

I took a cab to the prison. After a short drive, we approached a stunning green hill, with a large building near the top. As we got closer, I could see that the building was a prison, which grew more awful the closer we got, particularly when we got close enough to see barbed wire surrounding the entire perimeter and armed guards patrolling.

I was told to wait for my client in a large meeting room where several other prisoners sat with their families. I went through a series of heavy steel doors; each would open only when the previous one clanged shut. After a short wait, the door on the far wall swung open, and a large female guard walked out and called to someone behind the wall.

Leona Helmsley appeared in the doorway, and the guard frisked her. I turned my eyes away, not wanting Mrs. Helmsley to see that I had seen. When I looked back up, she flashed a broad smile at me and struck the same nauseating "Queen of the Palace" advertisement pose, arms thrown back in glory. This time, however, she was wearing an oversized gray prison sweatshirt and sweatpants instead of being dressed in an evening gown dripping with diamonds. She wore no lipstick, no makeup, and was only a seventy-one-year-old woman in prison.

When the guard told her she could enter the room, she greeted me warmly and we sat down. After telling me how horrible this place was, Mrs. Helmsley asked if I had a dollar. She pointed to a popcorn vending machine in the corner of the room and said she'd been craving popcorn, and would I buy her a bag. I did, and told her that she owed me a buck when she got out. She wolfed down the popcorn and asked if her credit was good enough for another bag. It was.

She described her first day and night in prison. She was plainly fearful, barely able to sleep at night for fear of being attacked. Shortly before surrendering, she had received a letter from a neo-Nazi group named the Aryan Brotherhood which began "Dear Jew excrement," called her "the very worst of the foul, scurrilous, despicable sub-human creatures that Adolph Hitler strove so valiantly to eliminate from this earth," and threatened "to issue a cripple contract on you while you are in prison," "severely tear your anal sphincter," and "have your face horribly disfigured."

I tried to reassure her that she had no reason to fear for her safety while in jail, and that we'd do our best to get her transferred to Danbury as quickly as possible. I couldn't assure her of the result, but let her know that she was out of sight but not out of mind—we'd be working hard on her appeal seeking a new trial; no guarantees, but I thought we had a shot. Before we were finished speaking, the same burly female guard materialized from behind the wall, told us the visit was over, and took her away.

Mrs. Helmsley called me several times that weekend. She now wanted Gould to head the criminal defense team and me to work with him, and asked me to meet with him on Monday to explain the case. I said I would.

I met with Gould Monday morning. He introduced me to several lawyers from his firm who'd also be working on the case. He said he wanted me to help write the brief appealing from the denial of our new trial motion. Gould was plainly starting from square one. He knew nothing of the new trial motion.

Before we began, I said to him, By the way, I'm pretty sure that Mrs. Helmsley was not guilty. He looked at me as if I were a naif, and gave me an old schoolmaster's version of: "Now, now, let's not get carried away."

In fact, Gould knew very little about the case at all, except that Mrs. Helmsley had been convicted of tax fraud, lost her appeal, won her state court case, lost her federal new trial motion, lost her motion to eliminate her jail sentence, and was now in prison. He didn't know the basis of the new trial motion, didn't know of our invoices analysis, and didn't know that underlying all of these issues was Mrs. Helmsley's claim that she was in fact innocent. I gave him a lengthy overview of the case and told him I'd like to meet with him for an uninterrupted immersion in the details. Overviews are never sufficient in a major and complicated case; you've got to get down in the weeds and sift through the details. Gould agreed to meet with me again.

Mrs. Helmsley called often from Lexington. Because she'd been sent there as a result of medical issues, she was now being examined by prison doctors and transferred from one prison wing to another—all very unpleasant for someone used to giving orders and having every need and whim immediately satisfied.

Being obstreperous in prison is rarely a good idea, particularly when you're hoping for a discretionary transfer elsewhere. I flew to Lexington several times to calm her down, hoping that short-term obedience to the prison authorities and showing deference to them could help get her transferred. I explained the process and urged patience. There are simply times in life when most people need a hand held, figuratively and literally, and Leona Helmsley's prison stay in Kentucky was one of those times.

Life presents its own relativity. To Mrs. Helmsley, being transferred to prison in Danbury would be a godsend compared to Lexington: a minimum rather than medium security prison, and close to Harry. Who would have thought that the queen of the Helmsley Palace, bedecked in splendor in those *New York Times* ads, would so relish the prospect of being imprisoned in Danbury.

My visits to Lexington had occasional incongruity. On one visit, when I missed the last flight out of Kentucky, I spent the night at the Harley Hotel—a meld of "Harry" and "Lee"—one of a chain of Harleys owned by the Helmsleys throughout the country. I was sleeping in her hotel; she was sleeping in jail.

Her patience and the hand-holding paid off. After several weeks, she was transferred to Danbury Federal Prison, where she could be visited regularly by Harry. A personal benefit for me was that my visits involved a short drive, rather than an all-day trek via two planes.

We brought in Robert Bork to argue the appeal from the denial of our new trial motion. He was a former U.S. Solicitor General, which means he'd argued many times before the Supreme Court of the United States on behalf of the federal government's positions. He had also served as a federal appellate judge in Washington. His nomination five years earlier by President Reagan to fill a vacancy on the Supreme Court of the United States had been rejected by the Senate, creating a new verb in political vocabulary—being "borked." His academic brilliance, conservative credentials, and unquestionable legal gravitas would make him, we thought, an ideal advocate on the appeal.

Bork was a quick read. I travelled to his summer house in Bar Harbor, Maine, and met him with other members of the legal team. Bork, who had been demonized by the media during his unsuccessful confirmation hearing before the U.S. Senate in connection with his Supreme Court nomination, was a charming host—as gracious, warm, and hospitable in private as he was perceived to be cold and uncaring in his public appearances. More important, his intellectual firepower was evident. We met several times before the oral argument, and Bork was thoroughly prepared.

But that didn't help. Nearly four months after oral argument, the Court of Appeals upheld the denial of our new trial motion.

The judges surmised that Feffer may have chosen not to use the handwritten accounting ledger because he might have feared that if cornered, the accountants would have admitted knowing of the scheme and implicated either Mrs. Helmsley or one of her co-defendants as orchestrator of the fraud. As to the prosecution's not disclosing evidence that would have undercut the credibility of its star accountant-witness, the court ruled that the undisclosed evidence against him would have provided at most only a slightly enhanced basis for challenging his credibility, and would not have affected the jury's verdict.

Though Mrs. Helmsley had a right to seek further review by the U.S. Supreme Court, we all recognized that the chance of getting that court to review the case was infinitesimal. The string was up. Her four-year sentence, with time off for good behavior, would keep her in jail for thirty-two months.

Almost, but not quite.

Gould was a savvy, experienced lawyer. Shortly after coming into the case, he had asked for a conference with Judge Griesa. Though we'd previously made and lost a motion to eliminate her jail sentence, under the then-operative rules a defendant was permitted to make successive motions to reduce a sentence, even though the chance of succeeding on a second go-round wasn't great.

Gould explained to Griesa that he intended to file such a second motion, but asked Griesa to adjourn it for the time-being rather than rule on it. Gould recognized that Griesa was not about to change his mind so soon after having denied our first motion. Filing motions to reduce sentence were precluded after a certain time period, even if they were meritorious, and we didn't want to be jurisdictionally barred from having the judge reduce the sentence in the future. Gould told the judge he simply wanted the motion in place so that at a later point, if circumstances warranted, Griesa would not be barred from considering it.

Griesa granted Gould's request. Gould filed the motion, which was adjourned without any date. We waited, and simply let the motion sit, with Mrs. Helmsley in prison, pursuing the appeal on our new trial motion.

When we lost that appeal nearly eight months later, Gould returned to Griesa and asked him to act now and to reduce the sentence as a matter of judicial discretion. The Parole Commission had refused to release Mrs. Helmsley on parole. Griesa recommended to the Commission that it reopen her case and parole her after she'd served twenty months in prison. The Commission refused. Griesa then took the matter into his own hands, and reduced the sentence from four years to thirty months. With credit for good behavior, Leona Helmsley was released from prison after serving twenty-one months and eleven days.

A few months after Mrs. Helmsley's release from prison, Gould invited me for lunch at a penthouse dining club he belonged to. After regaling me with stories of celebrity clients he'd entertained there, he started talking about Leona Helmsley.

Soon after his involvement in her case, he reminded me, I had told him I thought she was not guilty. He'd thought—as he put it—I'd drunk the Kool-Aid. But now, he said, having studied the case—particularly the new trial motion, and how it demonstrated that someone had committed tax fraud but not Mrs. Helmsley—he was convinced I was right: The system hadn't worked, and an innocent woman had spent nearly two years in jail for nothing.

Chapter 8
Practicing Doesn't Make Perfect

After Mrs. Helmsley had been convicted, people could barely wait to sue her. She had been wounded; her time and attention were focused on her criminal case and avoiding jail; and lawsuits galore began confronting her. She used several different law firms to defend her. Some did all right, some didn't.

When she was in jail she began using Gould's firm for much of her civil litigation. But Gould was only one man and, expert and experienced as he was, others at his firm were actually doing the work. Her dissatisfaction with them reached a boiling point when one of them settled a case against her on what he thought were extraordinarily favorable terms. But he had overlooked a cardinal rule: Lawyers recommend; clients decide. Mrs. Helmsley was furious when she told me, on one of my visits to Danbury, that the lawyer had settled a case without her approval, and she asked why I didn't handle civil litigation.

I told her I did.

Why didn't you tell me? she asked.

Because you didn't ask, I answered.

You should've told me, she said. Call Gould's worker and tell him to send you the lawsuits he's handling for me. And don't be gentle with him.

When I left, I gently reported the conversation to Gould's partner. He said he understood and sent me his Helmsley litigation files. And that's how I more or less became Leona Helmsley's litigation lawyer for many years.

She was not enamored of paying bills, and sometimes had to be saved from her own worst instincts. I was with her one day when her accountant presented her with a check payable to the utility company that provided gas and electricity to Dunnellen Hall. She refused to sign—the bill was too high, she said—until we convinced her that if she didn't pay the bill, the utility company would in fact turn off her gas and electricity, and suing wouldn't help.

She had plenty of lawsuits.

The first civil case she retained me for was a lawsuit brought against the Helmsley interest in the Empire State Building. I'll explain later the ownership structure of the building. Simply put, the Helmsleys owned by far the largest financial interest in the building; the Malkin family controlled the second largest; and several thousand public investors owned much of the rest. One of those public investors brought a class action lawsuit against the Helmsley ownership entity and the Malkins, claiming fraud and seeking recovery of enormous damages. I filed papers arguing that the court should throw out all of the Helmsley-related claims. The court dismissed them all, while keeping the case alive against the Malkin defendants. Mrs. Helmsley was very pleased.

When you win, and especially when others don't, clients think you're a winner generally. Mrs. Helmsley did not shy away from disputes and wasn't afraid of being sued, so I wound up handling quite a few other cases for her. Some were a bit difficult; there's simply no encyclopedia of defenses for nonpayment of your electric bill.

SHE WAS FRIENDLY WITH the owners of an advertising agency, inviting them to her grand birthday parties at Dunnellen Hall and originally naming them successor trustees of a charitable trust she'd established. At Mrs. Helmsley's request, they placed and paid for full-page Helmsley Hotel newspaper ads costing $600,000. Mrs. Helmsley refused to pay. They sued.

MRS. HELMSLEY REFUSED To pay the company that serviced the hotels' elevators. They sued.

A BROKER FOR A Helmsley company claimed that Mrs. Helmsley had withheld a commission due him for the sale of a Helmsley property. He sued.

A MAID WHO WORKED at the Park Lane claimed she had been raped there, and blamed the hotel and Mrs. Helmsley for negligently hiring unsuitable employees and inadequately providing for her safety. She sued—for $50 million.

A MAN WITH DISABILITIES stayed at the Park Lane, and claimed the hotel was not in compliance with the federal Americans With Disabilities Act—not enough handicap-compliant guest rooms, insufficient handicap parking spaces, inadequate cut-curb entrances, and the like. He sued.

A FORMER GENERAL MANAGER of the New York Helmsley, without authorization, signed a long-term exclusive contract with a technology company to provide the hotel with in-room internet connections, videos on demand, and other entertainment options.

The hotel unilaterally terminated the contract. The company threatened to sue. The hotel's legal position was so weak that we settled before they sued.

I'd become an experienced civil litigation attorney, dealing with many attorneys of all stripes—working with and against them, and observing others from up close. Many of these lawyers have been smart, honest, practical, and interested primarily in obtaining the best results for their clients. I've crossed swords with many fine lawyers over the years, and often the lawyer with the best case wins, or the result is rationally related to the merits. There is a certain artistry and joy-in-combat when dealing with professionals.

And then there are the others.

I began practicing law as an idealist, fighting doggedly for justice—victory—for clients. But over the decades, I have had to explain to many clients that the letters etched in stone over so many courthouses spell "Courthouse," not "Palace of Justice." Here's how courts and lawyering frequently work:

Litigation is a wearing-down process; plus, it's costly. Often, the costs are excessive, either because of the legal process itself or because of the lawyers. The process is often full of waste that drains clients' money.

Much of this waste is absent in federal courts, but access to those courts is limited to cases where all the plaintiffs are citizens of different states from all the defendants, or where federal questions are involved, or other unique circumstances exist.

The primary state trial court in Manhattan is called New York State Supreme Court. "Supreme" is a misnomer; it is a trial court, with two primary levels of state appellate courts above it. Visit that courthouse any day you choose (except during the pandemic):

Courtrooms will be filled with lawyers waiting for hours—hours—to see a judge. The lawyers are often being paid for their time on an hourly basis, just sitting and waiting, reading newspapers, talking among themselves, or . . . waiting. They are being paid by clients to . . . wait. Since there are at least two sides to every case, the waiting comes in multiples. If you're the client, you're paying unless it's a contingency case.

Most of the issues being disputed every day in these wait-filled courtrooms are routine "discovery" disputes. In discovery, one lawyer sends another a demand that the other side produce documents, or submit to a deposition, or otherwise produce some preliminary matter. Stiff-necked lawyers often fail to agree on what is appropriate discovery even though the matter in dispute is clear, or is inconsequential, or at least not worth multiple lawyers' time fighting over the dispute. Never backing down to compromise with an obnoxious adversary is a lawyer's luxury paid for by the client.

So one lawyer prepares (at the client's expense) a motion asking the court to order the other side to produce the disputed discovery. The opposing lawyer then prepares papers in opposition. The first lawyer then prepares reply papers, responsive to the other lawyer's opposition. Both lawyers (often accompanied by associates) trudge to the courthouse. This preparation of papers, and the trek to the courthouse, and waiting to see the judge, and then getting to see the judge (if they are lucky), and then travelling back to the office—often over a picayune matter that mature professionals should have been able to resolve quickly themselves—involve costs for two (or more) sets of clients.

Sometimes the client insists on fighting over issues when the flame isn't worth the candle. When that happens, the lawyer should explain the cost/benefit implications of the client's wishes. If the client then persists, there's no choice but to follow unless it's a frivolous issue—but at least it's at the client's instructions rather than for the lawyer's benefit. Often, though, it's the lawyers who pick the fight.

In fact, sometimes the waiting lawyers never see a judge at all. Instead, they ultimately see a judge's law clerk. As a practical matter, the clerk decides the issue in dispute. He or she doesn't formally decide it, but "recommends" the decision, by meeting with the lawyers and then filling out a form titled "Order" and stacking it with similar forms, one atop the other as the day progresses. The clerk then gives this pile of forms to the judge to sign, or the judge's signature is simply stamped on the "Order." These clerks are not judges, but often wield the power of a judge. There is simply too much inefficiency in the system, and too many cases, to have a judge actually judge all of these issues.

Much of a litigator's life is spent with other lawyers. Though painting with too broad a brush is dangerous, I've observed some rascals—doubtlessly a small minority of the profession—and since knowing a bit about occasional rascality may help if you ever need a lawyer, here's an inside peak.

The standard method of lawyers' billing is on a time basis. That system is abused in numerous ways. Perhaps you also pay your plumber on an hourly basis, but at least you know how long he's worked, since he's doing it in your home. With a lawyer it's different. You have no way of knowing whether he (or she, though I'll be chivalrous) worked for two hours, or four or six, on a set of papers. You don't know whether he's rounded his time charges up. You don't know whether he's litigated an identical or similar issue in the past—and if you have an experienced lawyer, he may have—and has simply pulled from past files a set of papers he can use as a template. That's why a seasoned lawyer charging a high hourly rate is often less expensive than a newbie charging a far lower rate; the former has probably seen problems like yours before and can deal with it efficiently, without reinventing the wheel.

In law as in life, the shortest distance between two points is usually a straight line. But if he's being paid by the hour, the knave is occasionally tempted to zigzag. I've seen experienced lawyers charge clients not based on the amount of time actually incurred, but on the amount of time that "could have been" incurred. It's tempting for the impure: If he's spent days briefing exactly this issue in another case and needs to spend only an hour updating the research, padding "only" a few hours onto the bill can be rationalized by a dishonorable lawyer as a saving to the client. Those lawyers are like the Roman emperor who, when accused of pilfering from the coffers of the treasury, indignantly responded: When I consider the opportunities I had for plunder, I am amazed at my moderation.

You've of course heard the joke about the lawyer who dies and goes to heaven, where the Lord treats him like royalty: You must've lived a righteous life, since your billing records indicate you're seven hundred years old. How that sometimes works is via "minimal time entries": Every task is presumed to take at least a quarter of an hour, or maybe a tenth of an hour. So if you send your lawyer an email which takes him three seconds to read, or a longer one that takes a full minute, he jots down the "minimal time"; and by the time the day's over he's worked thirty hours and burned a hole in your pocket.

Time-based billing is not only susceptible to abuse, but minimizes the most important asset a good lawyer brings to any problem: thought and judgment. I've seen many lawyers' bills, with an array of billing categories: "correspondence," "drafting," "phone calls," "legal research," "emails," etc. But I've never seen a category labeled "thinking."

In Lou's and my tax fraud work, we'd bill on a flat fee basis.

We had enough experience to know roughly what would be involved in handling the case. Some clients preferred to be billed by the hour, probably fearing that we'd skimp on time, and would ask why the fee couldn't be time-based. Our answer was usually a variation of: When I'm in the shower thinking about your case, I don't want to have to fill out a timesheet, the ink will run.

There's often a thin line between lawyers who are incompetent, foolish, or downright dishonest. A suburbanite built a fence along his neighbor's property line that substantially exceeded the height permitted by the local zoning law. The fence gave the neighboring property a fortress-like look, but the offending homeowner refused to lower the fence and the town refused to compel him to. So we sued the offending neighbor and the town, forcing the town to force the offending neighbor to lower the fence. We prevailed and the fence was lowered, but the offender's lawyer filed yet another set of legal papers, asking that the innocent homeowner pay his client's legal fees even though it had been his client who had violated the code and had only complied as a result of our litigation. Hard to decide whether the lawyer was a fool, a cheat, or both, but of course the court rejected his request.

One of the most common money-wasters in legal practice is letter-writing last-word-ism. Lawyer 1 writes a detailed letter to Lawyer 2, complaining of sins committed by Lawyer 2's client. Lawyer 2 writes back, denying everything Lawyer 1 said, calling Lawyer 1's assertions frivolous, fictitious, nonsensical, and meritless, and claiming that Lawyer 1's client's conduct has been outrageous. Lawyer 1 writes back defending his previous letter, defending his client, and attacking Lawyer 2's letter as frivolous, fictitious, nonsensical, and meritless. Lawyer 2 writes back attacking everything in Lawyer 1's responsive letter and calling all of his assertions. . . . You get it. And all of this is paid for by clients 1 and

2, who often don't realize that the lawyer's letters serve no useful purpose whatsoever, and may not even know that the letters have been written. A client of mine calls them "nyah nyah" letters.

I usually respond to such letters by simply saying "I disagree." The "I disagree" letter sometimes precipitates another lengthy screed, repeating the litany of my client's sins and the letter-writer's client's virtues—all set forth, again, at length and at the expense of the author's client. Another simple response—this time, "My position is as previously stated."—often terminates the game.

Even lawyers on the same side sometimes fight each other. There's this apocryphal story:

Two court-appointed lawyers defending a highly publicized murder case in Washington constantly bickered with each other for the limelight during pre-trial proceedings. At the start of the trial, the judge, fed up by then with both lawyers, assigned specific roles to each: One would deliver the opening statement to the jury, the other would cross-examine prosecution witnesses, and so on. The first lawyer delivered the opening: "Ladies and gentlemen, the prosecution claims that my client was in Washington on the day in question, committing this murder. We will prove that not only is the charge false, but my client was in California on that day. Not only was he three thousand miles away from the murder scene, he was addressing a convention attended by hundreds of guests. And the entire convention, including his speech, was nationally televised at the very moment this heinous murder was being committed by someone else on the other side of the country."

The lawyer then sat down, turned to his co-counsel, and whispered: "Alright you sonofabitch, now prove it."

Then there is the use or (if you're a cynic) scam of lawyer

overload. My practice was solo for many years, and then with one or a few associates. Especially at the beginning, I'd usually do things myself: do research, go to court, argue motions, meet with clients, conduct depositions, prepare documents, conduct settlement discussions, the whole gamut. When help would be useful—at a trial, keeping track of exhibits and documents, needing legal research backup, and the like—I'd use an associate's assistance. That means that clients paid for my hours, and occasionally an associate's also, but only when needed. Later on, I found both a partner and an associate whose legal skills, judgment, and integrity were exemplary, and who could very ably run with cases themselves.

If multiple lawyers' clocks are running, the bills get larger. Any practicing lawyer has seen—many times—small armies of lawyers used unnecessarily for legal skirmishes that simply don't warrant the bodies. Law firms sometimes send a senior partner, junior partner, associate, and paralegal to court for a routine legal matter that should have been disposed of with a single phone call. If your lawyer goes to court with a helper, you may be paying both for a plumber and someone to hold his tool kit when he should be holding it himself.

Of course, if you're running a public company or have a very large case or one involving the lifeblood of your business, you can get involved in major litigation requiring an army of lawyers. But most of us don't run public companies. If you're in litigation, sleep with one eye open.

Not far removed from lawyer overload is the art of lawyer training at client expense. Young lawyers fresh out of law school know very little—often nothing—about actually practicing law: that is, achieving a good result for a client at a reasonable price. They're trained on the job. They accompany a more experienced lawyer to court, or to a deposition, where they learn by watching, often at the client's dollars-per-hour expense, unless the client is an experienced consumer of legal services.

Or the newly minted lawyer is given a research task. The object of the task should be to get the answer to a question, or to develop a legal argument in support of a client's position. Often, though, the task is carried out with the young lawyer's rather than the client's interest in mind—writing a legal exegesis that far exceeds the question presented in order to impress a partner, or veering off-stream into distant legal tributaries called "footnotes" that demonstrate the researcher's ostensible thoroughness rather than finding a practical answer or solution to the problem at hand. All of this is paid for, of course, by the client.

Recognizing these tactics can turn them to one's own advantage. I handled a litigation against a company that had insurance, and the carrier used an outside law firm. Insurance companies often keep tight reins on costs, but this firm was simply over-lawyering the case. We had sporadic settlement discussions that eventually made progress, but ultimately neither side budged from the remaining gap between us. I got a call directly from the insurance carrier's in-house lawyer, who was plainly fed up with his outside litigators and wanted to end the legal costs.

He proposed: Why don't we split the difference and end the case?

No, I answered. Your company should pay the entire spread.

But that's not fair, he said. Why are you insisting on it?

Because I know you'll pay it, I answered.

And they did.

P eople often ask how lawyers can fight each other vehemently in court and then socialize outside. Actually, it can be difficult—some of the lawyers you fight with inside the courtroom are people you'd also like to fight with outside. But often, the lawyer on the other side is simply a professional doing what lawyers are supposed to do—vigorously presenting a client's case. When you leave the courtroom, you take the boxing gloves off.

After verbally wrestling with each other in front of the judge or jury, you ask, what sort of banter goes on when you're talking to each other outside the courtroom? Nothing out of the ordinary. I was in a heated battle against an excellent lawyer who'd been brought up from Texas to represent the other side. We'd never met, but during a recess we were standing next to each other at adjoining urinals.

"You hear the one about the old man who went to a doctor because of problems urinating?" he asked me.

"No, I haven't."

"So the doctor asks him: 'How old are you?' The man says: 'Ninety-five.' The doctor says: 'You peed enough.'"

I was a slow learner about some of the practicalities of legal prac-tice. Seeking "justice" for clients—naively seeking to vindicate all the clients' rights and leaving no stone unturned—can deprive a client of the best result. I learned that lesson the hard way in a case involving one of the best-selling record albums of all time, "Bat Out of Hell."

That album, recorded by a singer with the unlikely performing name "Meatloaf," was released by CBS Records. By 1997, more than 25 million copies had been sold, and sales continue today. The album had been produced by three men who did business under the name "Cleveland Records," and who came to see me years later because they believed CBS' successor, SONY, had been underpaying their royalties for many years. SONY was stubborn, wealthy, and wouldn't budge. We sued.

We brought the case in Cleveland, Ohio, hometown of the

principal producer. The case dragged on for nearly five years. It was torture. SONY is an enormous conglomerate with a virtually bottomless pit of money, fully capable of paying hordes of lawyers to wear down less wealthy adversaries in litigation. The producers of the album couldn't afford to pay fees on an hourly basis, and asked me to take on the case for a contingency fee—a percentage of the recovery, with no payment if no recovery. I agreed. That meant that I, not the client, was paying for my time and running the risk of doing mountains of work for nothing.

The litigation was a stark example of combat by pre-trial discovery. I'd ask for documents and responses to questions; SONY would resist; we'd file papers in the Cleveland court asking that SONY be forced to comply; SONY would file papers against us; we'd argue the matter; the judge would order production of documents and responses; SONY would produce less than they should have; we'd demand more; they'd resist; we'd file more papers in court; and so on. As a matter of principle and making sure that my clients got all the pre-trial discovery they were entitled to, I was determined to obtain every shred of relevant information from SONY's files, even if it took a figurative lifetime. SONY's lawyers were quite content to do the discovery dance forever or until I'd cry "uncle" and recommend a cheap settlement.

Until, that is, I finally realized how foolish my strategy was. Belatedly, I wised up to the fact that SONY would use its financial resources to play the game until we were all old men. So instead of continuing to insist on my clients' right to obtain every piece of relevant paper in SONY's files, I simply advised the court we were ready for trial. We had enough documents to establish much of what we wanted to establish; perfection wasn't necessary. We prepared all the necessary papers for trial, assembled all the exhibits, got our trial witnesses ready, and let SONY know that a trial and judgment day were near.

On a late Friday afternoon, all my files were packed in FedEx cartons stacked for pickup and overnight delivery to Cleveland, and I was ready to leave for the airport to start the trial that Monday. But it wasn't necessary to go. SONY's lawyer, on the virtual steps of the courthouse, called me and, before the night was over, SONY agreed to pay over $6 million. Had I not simply decided to get the case to trial, imperfect as the documentation from SONY may have been, I'd probably still be battling SONY today to produce more documents.

In fact, SONY's tactic of stalling, and postponing the day of reckoning drip by drip, was not a novel tactic. Any active litigation lawyer has had to defend a client against difficult cases where the best tactic is to postpone and delay. This was certainly true in my handling of criminal cases, where so many clients had, shall we say, considerable evidence to confront. Clients often say they want their day in court, but sometimes the best strategy is to stay out of the courtroom for as long as legitimately possible.

On many occasions, I've had clients ill-advisedly pressure me to move their case forward, and all I could do was give my best advice even if the client didn't want to hear it: Let time pass; be patient; don't rush to get justice; you may not like the justice you get.

The client often asks what's to be gained by delay? I've answered many times with this story:

In olden Russia, the czar rode his horse into a tiny village. When one of the serfs did not bow down deeply enough, the czar instructed his lieutenants to lop off the serf's head. The serf pleaded: "Dear sir, please spare me, and if you return to this spot next year I promise that your horse will be able to sing an aria in flawless Russian." The czar agreed, threatened to lop off the serf's head in a year if the promise were not fulfilled, and rode off. The serf's friends were aghast at the promise: "Think what will happen to you in a year, when the czar and his horse return!" The serf answered: "Don't worry. In a year the czar may be dead. Or I may be dead. Or maybe the horse will have learned to sing an aria in flawless Russian."

The client usually gets the point, and demands for "justice" slither into acquiescence with letting time pass.

The passage of time can help a client in the most unforeseeable, and sometimes tragic, ways. In the late 1990s, a businessman being investigated by the New York State tax authorities came to see me. His tax sins had been substantial and brazen, and it didn't take a superlawyer to foresee that if the investigators followed some fairly glaring leads, the client's life would become very unpleasant. Still, one never, or rarely, knows, and so we chose, within the bounds of law, not to cooperate, and waited. The investigation dragged on.

The tax authorities maintained the investigative records of his case in the World Trade Center. On 9/11, the records were destroyed. The client was never prosecuted.

Lessons in the practicalities of law come in all shapes and sizes. I had a case in a small town in Tennessee named Murfreesboro. We were doing fine. The judge had issued several rulings in our favor, and the opposition was in disarray. They fired successive sets of lawyers, and we were on a roll.

Until, that is, the opposing party finally wised up and picked the law firm of Murfree and Murfree. Murfree and Murfree's roots in Murfreesboro, as you might infer, go back many decades. The senior partner used to be County Executive and held other positions in Rutherford County, where Murfreesboro is located. Judges in the court where our case was pending are elected, and this happened to be an election year. The judge handling our case was up for reelection, and indications were he might lose his seat. Well, Murfree and Murfree convinced that judge in Murfreesboro to reverse an earlier important decision he'd made in our favor. I had sufficient vision—20/20 wasn't required—to read the handwriting on the wall, and we settled.

(Postscript: The judge lost the election anyway, having nothing to do with my case. A newspaper article shortly before the election, reporting the judge's having been accused by a grocery clerk of threatening to "cut your ass," may not have been helpful to his campaign.)

Different rules apply to different situations. Often, it's useful to get a lawyer's advice in writing. But I met a hedge fund manager who instructs lawyers to advise him orally rather than in writing—that way, the lawyers concentrate on giving useful advice rather than crafting impressive memos.

Beware of being a hand-me-down. As my practice was beginning to grow, I met an elder statesman of the bar who told me there are two important skills a lawyer must learn. The first, he said, is that when you're hoping to land a client, convince him you are the best lawyer in town for the case. The second is that after you've landed the client, convince him that your associate is the best lawyer in town for it.

Some of the opportunities for perfidy in lawyering leave no fingerprints—for example, judgment calls about whether to recommend a lawsuit or not. If there's a lawsuit, the lawyer makes money; no lawsuit, no fee.

I was involved behind the scenes in a matrimonial dispute in which the wife consulted a headline-grabbing matrimonial lawyer, unloaded her complaints about her husband, and the lawyer responded with various versions of "how horrible he is." The husband consulted a different class of matrimonial lawyer; when he unloaded his gripes about his wife, the lawyer saw two sides to the story, questioned whether divorce was really in the husband's (or wife's or children's) best interests, explained ways to deal with the issues that constantly separated the spouses—all with the result that the couple reconciled and, last I heard, are still married. Neither lawyer got to make money off the couple's problems but the husband's lawyer did what lawyers are supposed to do: counsel, and give advice that is in the client's, not the lawyer's, best interest.

I've seen both types of lawyers in numerous business disputes. Business partners fighting over money often bring their own unique anger and personal animus to squabbles between themselves. As a young lawyer, I'd mount my legal steed, grab the law's various lances, and race off to joust. These days, having learned through experience the financial and emotional costs of litigation, I explore whether there is a practical, quick, and relatively painless solution. Finding one is easier if the lawyer on the other side has the same agenda.

Watch out also for lawyers who speak in technical jargon, punctuated occasionally by a Latin-sounding phrase or two. Though intricacies in law surely exist, most of the concepts are explicable in everyday English, with small, common, eminently understandable words. If you've got a lawyer talking in a language you don't quite understand, ask him or her to rephrase it. If you still don't understand, walk out and find someone who speaks your language.

Simply because someone has a law degree doesn't mean he or she can deal with any legal problem; if you've got a rash, see a dermatologist. Beware of the lawyer who lets you think he can navigate whatever issue you've got. Any honest lawyer realizes that some cases aren't his or her cup of tea. An asymmetrically buxom woman came to see me. She'd had breast implants, but one of them had burst and she wanted to sue the doctor. I know my limits, and recommended another lawyer she might want to consult.

Don't be overly impressed by plaques on the wall. Like many professionals, lawyers can be a self-congratulatory fraternity. In an impressive glossy-print announcement, "The National Association of Distinguished Counsel" notified me that I had been selected as a "Member of the Nation's Top One Percent"—the best lawyers in the country. I could accept the honor by sending them $300, for which they'd also send me a commemorative "Top One Percent" plaque emblazoned with my name. Another $300 would get me a custom-crafted gold eagle perched majestically on a walnut pedestal, announcing my one-percentageness in gold lettering.

A few months later another invitation arrived. An organization announcing "Best Attorneys in America" requested "The honor of your membership in our organization as a lifetime charter member," limited to the "Top 100 attorneys in New York." I could accept by paying a one-time fee of $1,000.

I received another potential listing of supposedly the best lawyers in town, appearing in a separate magazine, in a newspaper supplement, on the web, and elsewhere. Selection is, ahem, merit-based "using a patented multiphase selection process." Or you can buy yourself onto a top spot on Lawyers.com in any legal specialty for a fee, with discounts occasionally available.

But if you really want to attract potential clients: Having you or your firm featured as a terrific lawyer in a photo covering one-ninth of a page in the *New York Times* best lawyers supplement costs $3,150, or $8,600 for a third of a page. The chintzier superlawyers can advertise their status on an assortment of plaques, or on cufflinks, baseball caps, wine glasses, umbrellas, window decals, coasters, and, most importantly, money clips—all for sale if you're lucky enough to have been selected. Or if you're feeling flush and want to blow your own horn via your full-page picture in *Delta*

Sky magazine, it's yours for a mere $24,995—or a two-page spread for $45,991.

A national institute of criminal defense attorneys notified me that I'd been nominated as one of the ten best criminal lawyers in the country. All I had to do was fill out a form, send in $275, and I'd get an engraved plaque. I hadn't handled a criminal case in over twenty years—since Mrs. Helmsley's. I am one of the ten best criminal lawyers in the country like I am an astronaut.

A lawyer best serves a client's needs by explaining honestly the ins and outs of the legal process and the unpredictability of the outcome and of the pathway to that outcome—even though the client often wants to hear how entitled to win he or she is, and how that's what's ultimately going to happen. Litigation is an unpredictable process, with unpredictable costs, unpredictable twists in the road, and unpredictable outcomes. The honest lawyer isn't one who outlines for the prospective client precisely what course the case will take; one never knows. The honest lawyer explains the vagaries of the process: If this happens then that is likely or unlikely to happen, but this and that aren't certainties, and litigation is a bramblebush whose ultimate paths and end result are often impossible to call. The client's sense of justice frequently bears no relationship to the end result.

Often, clients ask the natural questions: How long will the case take, how much will it cost, and will I win? My answer is often: Those are excellent questions, but the truthful answer is that it's like asking how long is a piece of string. You've got to see how the case unfolds, and let me explain a few of the different scenarios— none of which can be completely controlled—and the results those different scenarios may lead to. Clients usually appreciate that.

For others, it leaves them with a sense of uncertainty, and it's not what they want to hear. But the legal process is rife with uncertainty. Generally, the only certainty in litigation is uncertainty and that it will be expensive. The honest answer is to tell it like it is.

What often distinguishes the honest lawyer from the scoundrel is willingness to say "no" to the client. A client consulting with a lawyer over a perceived wrong is often very vulnerable: he's sure he's a victim, and wants "justice" or, worse, revenge. The thirst for either makes the client easy pickings: He often wants to hear agreement with his position, and a shared sense of outrage, from the lawyer. Many lawyers know how to feed that beast, and take advantage of it.

Some folks think they've got a good case when, truthfully, they don't. Man goes to a lawyer, says a neighbor drove him into a forest, tied him to a tall oak tree, and robbed him—and he says he's got evidence to prove it. Lawyer says show me the evidence. Man invites lawyer into his car, drives to a forest, parks, walks the lawyer into the forest, stops in front of a tall oak tree, points to it, and says: "There's the tree."

Being honest with a client isn't difficult. An example: Someone in a manufacturing business discovered that his partner had been cheating him. He was, of course, outraged, and wanted to sue; the cost didn't matter, he said, this was a matter of principle. Suing over a matter of principle often has an unhappy ending. Principles eventually take a back seat to costs—but after the costs have been incurred. I suggested, as I often do, that the client imagine himself several years from now, looking backward toward now. If he sued, would he think, years later, that that had been the smart thing to do?

I explained the judicial process: what I'd have to do to enforce the client's rights; what the other side could do; the years that would likely pass before "justice" would be done; the different variations of "justice"; the legal fees that would be incurred over those years, along with the emotional and psychological energy that the client would spend. I told the client I'd start a litigation if he wished, but the better part of wisdom would be for him to sit down with his partner, work out a separation, and do business without him; don't strive for vengeance, but for an acceptable result for yourself. The client's fury gradually subsided, he agreed, I helped him in the process, and he is now doing quite successfully in business by himself.

I'm sometimes reminded of a story my father told me when I was in law school. When he was in the clothing business, he found out that a manufacturer of his garments had been stealing. He brought a lawsuit by himself—"pro se," in lawyer-speak—for $500. After prolonged aggravation in the lawsuit, he went to see an honest lawyer, who told him, only partly in jest: Give the man you're suing $5,000 to go away.

Some people like to sue. A very rich person can sue someone without being concerned about the cost, to score a point or show he can't be pushed around. And the other person, if he too is rich, sues back, or, in legalese, counterclaims. All of this to no useful end—two richly groomed poodles barking at each other, until some other diversion captures their attention and they scamper away to other pastimes.

There are times, of course, when suing is a wise or necessary recourse. An independent record producer came to see me. He had delivered master recordings by two unknown performers to a major record company; the record had turned out to be a hit, but the record company simply wouldn't pay the producer his royalties. The record company's reason was spurious. In reality, it may have thought the producer, an inexperienced young man from Harlem working out of his apartment, would simply go away.

The producer's decision to sue seemed correct, as sales of the record had been substantial and there was no legitimate reason he hadn't been paid. So we sued, claiming back royalties and that the record company's complete refusal to pay royalties had resulted in its forfeiting all rights to the master recordings, which we further claimed had therefore reverted to the producer, and the record company should be ordered to give him all of its profits. Within days of our starting the lawsuit, the record company sent a large check for back royalties. The producer was thrilled but we weren't satisfied. I wrote a letter to the record company, demanding interest. A sizeable second check, for interest, arrived within days. The client was very happy.

Often, people who start unwise lawsuits eventually regret them. A company I've represented in several cases fired its president after discovering his self-dealing. Being fired meant the president was ineligible for his year-end bonus, part of which he'd already received in advance. Rather than keeping what he'd gotten and slinking off into another career, the ex-president sued the company, claiming he'd been unfairly terminated. That resulted in our doing some internal sleuthing and discovering the ex-president's other financial chicanery, including tens of thousands of dollars in made-up expenses and shortchanging of the company's clients. We counterclaimed, seeking recovery of money the ex-president had pilfered and the early partial bonus he'd been paid. As the likely outcome became starker, the ex-president offered to end the case with a mutual walkaway—both sides dropping their claims and leaving each other alone. But that result was no longer acceptable to my client. We insisted on money back from the ex-president, and got it.

Leona Helmsley had a similar experience while she was in

prison. A lawyer had been overcharging her and, when she refused to pay his latest bill, sued her. She disputed the claim and counter-claimed, seeking the return of excessive fees she'd previously paid him. The upshot: The lawyer agreed to pay $10,000 to a charity selected by Mrs. Helmsley, in exchange for both sides dropping their claims.

For sure, there are times you're in litigation whether you like it or not: Someone sues you. You can try to end it early, by paying money you owe, or you don't owe, or getting the case dismissed. There are times when you've got no choice but to litigate fiercely: the lawsuit is one that affects the continuing life of the business, or threatens the business in some material way. But litigants often look back and say: Why didn't I end this at the beginning, before I spent all that money and suffered that aggravation and diversion from running the business?

Many lawsuits are settled when both parties get tired of paying their lawyers. Had they foreseen fee-fatigue at the beginning and been able to cast aside the feeling of having been wronged, they'd have saved money, time, and sleepless nights, and the lawyers would have been paid less. Wonder why lawyers sometimes don't encourage early resolution of disputes?

Suing or deciding not to sue are not always the only alterna-tives when there is a legal dispute that can't be amicably resolved. The opposite of "don't sue" is not necessarily "sue aggressively." Suing more aggressively than the situation or wisdom dictates can produce disastrous results. Here's a somewhat morbid example.

Leona Helmsley fired me several times (more about that later). During one of those hiatuses, she got some questionable counsel.

Her only child, a son, had died of a heart attack at age forty. He and Harry Helmsley were interred in a mausoleum in the Bronx. She wanted to sue the cemetery because of new construc-tion being done by the cemetery near the mausoleum.

Her new lawyer went full steam ahead. He filed a complaint that began with a description of the history of mausoleums, beginning with—I'm not making this up—"a splendid tomb at Halicarnassus, around 353 B.C.," built for the burial of King Mausolus. Following this historical narrative, the complaint claimed that when the Helmsleys bought their cemetery plot, "the lot had a wide open view on the Northwest side," and the Helmsleys had not expected that any other large burial sites would be built there. Despite that expectation, the cemetery was constructing another large mausoleum which, the complaint said, "will block forever the once open view to the Northwest" from the Helmsley mausoleum.

Inherent in suing a cemetery over a burial place, one would think, is the need for a bit of sensitivity. If such a lawsuit were to be brought—*if*—it ought to be brought in as low-key and delicate a manner as possible. Not here. Instead, Mrs. Helmsley's complaint did not merely seek to have the cemetery honor what the complaint said was her expectation—not even a claim that there had been any such agreement with the cemetery—but her legal pleading was a diatribe against the cemetery owners, accusing them of a "willful and contemptible violation" of a so-called "fiduciary duty" and seeking $150 million in alleged but unspecified damages—all resulting in extraordinarily embarrassing press, including the entire front page of the *New York Post* featuring the headline "Tomb With A View" and a two-full-pages-with-pictures article inside.

One of my reconciliation calls from Mrs. Helmsley came on the day of the "Tomb With A View" headline. She was accustomed to hostile and demeaning press, but this was so highly personal. She'd not anticipated that the lawsuit could result in such humiliating reporting, and her public relations agent urged her to end the embarrassment immediately. She called me as if we'd had no gap in our relationship. My directive was to replace the lawyer who'd brought the case for her, and to end it quickly and quietly. I did, in a meeting with the cemetery's principals and lawyers, where everyone was practical and no one's objective was impressing a client or protracting the lawsuit.

Of course, not all cases have successful results, and not all clients are satisfied. In the early days, my older partner, Lou, had a client charged with tax evasion. The case against him was ironclad, but he chose to go to trial rather than work out a plea bargain. He was convicted and sentenced to jail.

The client switched lawyers and claimed on appeal that he was entitled to a new trial because Lou, he said, had mishandled the case. His argument was rejected. So he sued Lou, and for good measure threw me into the case as a defendant, though I'd had nothing to do with his case and had never said more than "hello" to him. Lou and I, though we'd surely not won all of our cases, had never been subjected to an attack on our lawyering, and had practiced for years without insurance for malpractice claims. So I was our lawyer. The former client's claim against us was dismissed. The collateral damage was expensive, though—I've carried malpractice insurance ever since, and the premiums aren't cheap.

Being sued by someone I'd never met, in connection with a matter I'd not been involved in, was one case among many of human nastiness and treachery.

After Lou retired, I set up my own practice in a new office, and hired an architect to design the office space. He obtained construction bids from various contractors, and I hired the one he recommended. The contractor was a disaster, and I wondered why the architect had recommended him.

I found out a few years later. The architect was indicted for taking kickbacks from contractors—he would select and recommend that his clients hire the contractor who'd offer him a kickback. That explained why he'd recommended such an inept contractor to me. But that was not the worst of the architect's chutzpah. He hired a lawyer after the investigation began, and the lawyer advised him to plead guilty. The architect wanted a second opinion. So he asked one of his victims for legal advice—me.

Starting a battle you're not prepared to finish is a fool's errand. I represented Brooke Shields and her mother Teri in several matters. In one, a lawyer who didn't look more than one step down the road sued Brooke in federal court on behalf of the Italian clothing designer Valentino, claiming Brooke and Teri had reneged on an alleged agreement that Brooke would wear Valentino's costumes in one of her movies. Brooke is of course one of America's sweethearts, and the tactic underlying the lawsuit was doubtlessly to generate publicity for the lawyer and designer and get some quick and easy settlement money, figuring that Brooke would be loath to engage in public battle and quick to pay money not owed in order to avoid the expense, noise, distraction, and assorted other unpleasantries of litigation.

But they figured wrong. Brooke and Teri denied Valentino's claim, and we demanded he travel from Italy to New York to face a deposition. His lawyer argued that since Valentino was a resident of Italy, we should have to travel there for his deposition. Very often, lawsuits are resolved on such matters of convenience—who has to go where, who has to pay for this or that, whose life is going to be more discombobulated and by how much money. I asked the judge to compel Valentino to come to Manhattan—he had sued here, and he's got to litigate here. The judge agreed, and ordered Valentino to appear in Manhattan. He promptly dropped the case.

Here's a sidebar about Brooke and Teri, since you may have read gossip about their relationship. Brooke is a smart lady who began her career at eleven months as the cute baby on Ivory soap packaging. Teri was an alcoholic ("Once an alcoholic always an alcoholic," she told me.) and the archetypical stage mom, controlling Brooke's life until Brooke married and became her own woman. Brooke's final declaration of independence occurred late one night in my office, under the watchful eyes of both me, representing Teri, and a gentlemanly practical lawyer representing Brooke (one lawyer representing both Teri and Brooke would have been a prescription for disaster). Neither he nor I was showing off for anyone. What could have been a messy fight over assets turned into an amicable resolution—we calmly discussed who in fairness should get what, and that's what happened. In a private moment, I explained to Brooke that her mother had always only intended good for her, and I think Brooke ultimately realized that. Teri was then able to function as a loving grandmother to Brooke's children, and she and Brooke remained close until Teri's death.

Lawyers sometimes do things that make no sense. The Nation of Islam was looking for a fight. The group wanted to hold a religious rally at the Javits Convention Center in Manhattan. When they applied for the booking, their representatives concealed from the Center who they were, claiming simply that they represented a group selling hair care products and wanted to rent space. When the Center found out the true nature of the event—a rally featuring Louis Farrakhan, the anti-Semitic pro-Hitler Nation of Islam leader—they declined to rent the space on the day requested by the group; there were other portions of the Center being used that day by other groups and there would be real security problems at a Nation of Islam rally. Their last rally had drawn a crowd of thirty thousand at Madison Square Garden. The Center offered other dates consistent with security concerns, when the Center would not be packed with other groups.

The Nation of Islam sued the Center, claiming racial discrimination because the proposed alternative dates did not include "Savior's Day," the group's religious holiday. The court held a trial to determine the facts. The Center retained me to defend it.

At trial, the Nation of Islam's lawyer got crushed by ignoring the most basic fact. When the group had initially sought space for its "hair care product" event, the date they'd applied for wasn't "Savior's Day." That fact was established both by the Center's documentation and witnesses. The judge dismissed the Nation of Islam's claim.

Bravado may pay off in some lines of work and play, but I've never felt comfortable with it and don't think it works in a courtroom. To me, being straightforward and honest pays the highest dividend, even if from time to time those characteristics are not rewarded. Judges and juries are generally not influenced by blowhards.

Bluster not only isn't a winner in most courtrooms, it often masks insecurity. A lawyer I casually knew used me as a sounding board. He was a partner in a not-so-good firm and always seemed full of himself. He received an offer to join a better firm with an improved financial package, but was hesitant to accept: What if, he mused, I can't perform up to their standards and they decide they've made a mistake? He turned down the offer.

The best lawyers, though they show confidence in their positions, understand the opposition's arguments and the weaknesses and strengths of their own. Good lawyering doesn't usually require fancy footwork, but just good old-fashioned blocking and tackling: knowing the facts, assembling the evidence, knowing the law, applying (very important) a good dose of judgment, and presenting what you've got in an honest, straightforward way, without histrionics. One advantage of the profession is that it doesn't require hand-eye coordination, so the skills don't start leaving you at an early age but develop with experience.

You've heard the old saw: If you don't have the facts, pound the law; if you don't have the law, pound the facts; but if you don't have either, pound the table. Table-pounding is overrated. If you don't have the facts and you don't have the law, maybe you shouldn't be in the courtroom.

Lawyers sometimes become enthralled with the sounds of their own voices. Early on, an experienced trial lawyer taught me: There's a reason for seats at the lawyers' tables; when the judge buys your argument, sit down and shut up. In appellate courts, when the appellant (the side appealing) gets pilloried and it's the other lawyer's turn, a judge will sometimes say "You may be brief." That's code for don't waste our time, you've won, say you've got nothing to add to your brief. In learning the ropes, I watched a lawyer get that signal but proceed nevertheless to pontificate about why his side should win, prompting one of the judges to pelt him with hard arguments his adversary hadn't even made.

Judges have ways of puncturing blowhards' balloons. My adversary in federal court in Manhattan was a lawyer enthralled by the sound of his own voice and the rightness of his cause. We were before Judge Inzer Wyatt, a courtly gentleman from Alabama who'd served on the bench for decades, spoke with a slight southern drawl, and brooked no nonsense. Before the trial started, my opposing lawyer described the relief he intended to ask for after winning the case. Judge Wyatt politely cut him off: "Sir, you've got to catch the rabbit before you can taste the rabbit soup."

I'm rarely satisfied with how I've done in court. I can't count the number of times I've walked out of a courtroom thinking I should or shouldn't have said this or that, or argued a better way, or done something different—no matter how prepared I may have been. I've often gone to sleep self-criticizing what I'd done that day in court, telling myself what I should have done instead, and mentally bopping myself on the back of the head.

I was trying a case with a fine lawyer one day, and while we were talking outside the courtroom she told me that she sometimes dreams she is back in law school and is completely unprepared for her final exams: She'd forgotten to study for them. I told her that I have the same dream, but in mine I haven't even bought the textbook or attended any of the classes.

That's because you're usually in federal court, she responded.

M y grandmother, in her later years, would occasionally take trips with my mother. When they'd return, my grandmother and I had a routine inside joke: After telling me how the trip went, she would add: "But I still didn't find the store." I'd ask: "What store?" and she'd answer: "The store that sells common sense."

Many lawyers never find that store either.

THE HELMSLEYS WERE THE controlling general partners in the partnership that owned the Helmsley Palace Hotel. Harry Helmsley had developed the property. When he became ill, a group of limited partners began an arbitration against the Helmsley entity, seeking to oust Mrs. Helmsley from control of the hotel. I represented Mrs. Helmsley when her partners subpoenaed her to testify.

The partners' complaint against Mrs. Helmsley was that she had mismanaged the hotel through her imperious and overbearing manner. When I accompanied her into the arbitration room, the arbitrators and lawyers were seated around a table, with bottles of water and paper cups with coffee in front of them. When Mrs. Helmsley sat down, the lawyer representing the Helmsley interests excused himself dramatically from the room for a moment, reentered with coffee in a fancy porcelain cup and saucer he'd brought for the occasion, and proudly placed it in front of her.

I HAD A CASE in which Madonna was a witness. I was unable to attend her deposition, and asked an associate—a lawyer with considerable experience—to appear instead. As he was leaving for the deposition, he asked, seriously: Do you mind if I ask for her autograph? I told him Under No Circumstances, and began looking for a new associate.

IT'S NOT ONLY LAWYERS who can't find the common sense store. A man who had been indicted for tax evasion came to see me for possible representation. The indictment was plain vanilla—it simply alleged the years and amounts of evasion but provided no details. I asked what the case was about, and he said he had no idea. This was very odd, since most tax evasion cases go through several layers of governmental review in which the taxpayer generally learns about the case. But this fellow said he couldn't fathom what his indictment was about.

He owned a small business, he said, reported all of his income, and documented all of his expenses. His business and personal tax returns, he said, were perfectly clean. He'd had a lawyer during the investigation, who, he said, had been equally befuddled about what the IRS was suspicious about. Maybe this was the dream case for a tax fraud lawyer: a perfectly innocent taxpayer, clean as the driven snow, and an IRS investigation gone wild.

After my lengthy grilling of him, our meeting was over and I still had no idea of the basis for the indictment. As he was about to leave, though, a thought seemed suddenly to strike him.

Maybe it was the prostitutes, he said. Maybe I shouldn't have put them on the payroll as salaried employees.

Winning can sometimes be bad for business—short-term. Through a common acquaintance, the Attorney General of Oregon retained me to represent the Oregon state broadcasting agency in a federal lawsuit brought against it in New York City by a German TV production company. The German company produced a television program titled *Soccer Made In Germany* consisting of taped excerpts of soccer games between European teams, and claimed that Oregon's public TV program *Soccer from Germany* infringed the German company's rights. We asked the court to dismiss the case on grounds of improper "venue"—the place where a lawsuit may permissibly be brought. The court agreed: All of Oregon's witnesses resided in Oregon, all of its records were there, requiring an Oregon agency to defend the case in New York would be a hardship, and issues we had raised under Oregon law would be better addressed by an Oregon court. The New York court transferred the case to a federal court in Oregon, and my services were no longer needed.

Litigation lawyers fight each other every day. Often, they leave their weaponry in the courtroom and are cordial and honorable with each other; often, not. Anyone in the field has experienced both:

Early in my practice, I had scheduled a vacation in California in the midst of a fiercely fought lawsuit in Manhattan. I sent a letter to the opposing lawyer, giving him the dates when I'd be on the other side of the country and suggesting dates for depositions after my return. He didn't respond. When my plane landed in California, my secretary called: The lawyer had hand-delivered to my office an "Order To Show Cause"—a method of accelerating the date a motion gets heard—returnable three days later, right in the middle of my vacation. No judge had yet been assigned to the case, so there was no guarantee that if I simply sent a letter to the clerk's office explaining that I was on vacation three thousand miles away, nothing bad would happen to the client's case. That was the end of that year's vacation; I had to fly back immediately to prepare papers and appear in court. Lessons like that are very inconvenient.

Yet there are lawyers of exactly the opposite stripe. After Lou retired, I hired a wonderful lawyer named Stuart Abrams, who became my partner several years later. We were involved in a lengthy legal battle involving many millions of dollars; our adversary was a lawyer who fought hard but honestly. I was overseas when the opposition broached settlement. Stuart and I spoke by phone to assess the opposition's offer and formulate a recommendation to our client. A series of faxed offers and counter-offers followed, with Stuart and me conferring long-distance at each stage. At a critical point in the negotiations, I called Stuart from a phone booth in Turkey (my cell phone hadn't yet been invented).

The lawyers on the other side made a mistake, he told me.

What was it?

They misfaxed—this was in pre-email days, too—to our fax number, a recommendation to their client.

And? I asked, already knowing the answer.

I called and told them, he answered. As soon as I saw that the fax cover sheet had their client's name on it, I put the fax in the shredder without reading it and told the other lawyer of his mistake.

Chapter 9

Consigliere, Sort Of

Often, lawyers romance their clients. They socialize, invite for dinner, entertain, vacation with, and seek other ways to develop the relationships. It's good for business, and nothing's wrong with it.

I've had the luxury of not having to do that. My clients were usually one-shot cases; after all, how many times can you get indicted for tax evasion, or break up with your business partner, or have your copyrights infringed? And if it happened again and we'd had a good result the first time, the client would come back, social friend or not. My clients were more interested in results than friendship; the only courtship they were interested in was in the courtroom. Winning was good, not winning not-so-good.

Same with lawyers who referred cases to me. All they wanted (except for the few who wanted referral fees, who never reappeared after being rebuffed) was a win for their clients. I didn't have a corporate or finance department or the like that might lead them to fear they'd lose a client by referring one to me for litigation. The client was theirs; only the case was mine. No need to worry that I'd violate the lawyer/businessperson precept "Thou Shalt Not Covet Thy Referrer's Client." I usually got satisfactory results, so the phone rang.

Getting too close to a client could be costly. I won a litigation for a client. Shortly afterward, he asked me to negotiate a contract with his employer, and asked what it would cost. I told him I don't do employment contract work, but he persisted and, since he had no lawyer and had come directly to me, I reluctantly agreed, and said I'd leave our fee arrangement to him: I wouldn't send him a bill, but at the end of the transaction, he could send me whatever check he thought was appropriate and I would send him a receipted bill—no questions asked, no bill to be sent until he sent me a check. His contract negotiation turned difficult and time-consuming, and he was pleased with the result. I didn't send him a bill, and waited for the check. He sent me a bottle of champagne and a thank-you note.

Keeping a healthy professional distance from clients allowed me a great luxury: Instead of nights out wining and dining in a hunt for business, I could come home at a decent hour—except when I was on trial and there were no decent hours—and have dinner with Ruthie and the children. Like many parents, I wanted to give them what I hadn't had—a father in the house, a dinner-time eating together as a family, and helping out with their home-work afterwards. It may not sound like much, but to me it was the old Mastercard commercial: Priceless.

I'd often get home late—very late when I was on trial—or in a different mental zone if a client's emergency was brewing. My esti-mated time of arrival was frequently unpredictable, but Ruthie would somehow manage to stretch out the cooking long enough to be right on time for my arrival. I'd push the day's work out of mind and listen to the children's and Ruthie's day. I confess, sometimes I'd appear to be listening but my mind would be wrestling with tomorrow's problems. Ruthie could usually sense when I was mentally wandering, and pulled me back down to earth. Being at dinner with the family, physically and (as much as possible) mentally, was important.

I've known many lawyers who stay out late with clients, rarely see their children, sometimes develop drinking or drug problems, ultimately are estranged from their spouse and family—but are wildly successful in their profession, raking in enormous income and rising to the supposed top of the profession. Hostility and orneriness become part of their personality; they equate nastiness with toughness, and become devoid of emotion. But there's no such thing as a free lunch in the organization of your life. I've been lucky enough to have done well enough in my law practice, have a wonderful wife, and, of course, my children always do whatever I tell them. Don't yours?

Some lawyers want to be stars—to see their name in the press, appear on TV, be recognizable, walk with a swagger. To me, there is something appealing about the ordinary. I recall visiting someone dear to me in the hospital one day, and hearing the commuter train I usually take come rumbling past. How nice it would be, I thought, if everything were back to normal and I was on that train, back in my usual routine, without having to worry about issues of health. There is, I'm told, what the Japanese regard as a happy story: Once upon a time there was a grandfather, a father, and a grandson. The grandfather died. Years later, the father died. Years later, the grandson died.

Gotta keep things in perspective.

Because my cases came from different sources, I wasn't reliant on any one person. Not being beholden to anyone for your livelihood is, of course, better than its opposite. Independence is good, dependence not. Very simple.

The nature of my practice changed when Leona Helmsley got out of prison.

After she got out, Mrs. Helmsley devoted herself to Harry. The illnesses that ended the criminal prosecutions against him were not feigned; he had become a very sick man. Mrs. Helmsley made sure he had the best twenty-four-hour care, ate the right foods, and joined at the lunch and dinner table even when it was difficult for him to do so.

She hired nurses to tend to his every need, keeping him elegantly dressed and looking distinguished, but he was now an empty shell and becoming more so every day. Steps became difficult for him to take. He and Mrs. Helmsley still travelled together to their various homes, driving in stretch limousines to Dunnellen Hall, or flying to their hotel in Florida or their home in Arizona in their private plane, but it was like a flying hospital.

She tried to strike a delicate balance: on the one hand, shielding Harry from exposure to others who would be shocked by his condition, while also maintaining the trappings of normalcy—the normalcy of the ultra-rich. She threw Harry a birthday bash at their mountaintop mansion in Arizona and invited a circle of their business associates—"friends" doesn't quite fit them—including two men who'd been Harry's right-hand men in his heyday. Harry sat next to them, old friends who'd made their fortunes together, Harry smiling faintly, perhaps sensing some connection, but giving no real indication he had any idea who they were, or where or who he was.

Toward the end of Harry's life, Mrs. Helmsley was constantly alone—surrounded by Harry's caregivers and her employees but basically by herself. I spent many days alone with her in her Park Lane penthouse, sitting in the gilt living room or in the den, with the late afternoon sun fading into evening and New York City lighting up magnificently below. Around her were pictures of Harry and herself in younger, happier times. We'd talk not only about legal and business matters but about people, and her thoughts about them were rarely positive. With all her wealth, she was basically a lonely lady, surrounded by household help and a dying husband when I'd leave. Often, it was never time to leave—she relished the company, even though it was just a lawyer who had come into her life a few years earlier. At least I was somebody.

She had everything. She had nothing.

Harry Helmsley died in 1997. He left Mrs. Helmsley all of his real estate, money, other assets, and alone. When he died, the focus of her life had suddenly disappeared.

I never met a true friend of hers. She had one brother, Alvin; her two sisters were deceased. Harry had no children. Her late son, who'd been married three times, left four children. They and her brother had their own lives.

She, alone, now owned the Helmsley fortune—the hotels, the buildings, the money, everything. Though she maintained a luxurious office at the Helmsley Building on Park Avenue and 45th Street, she presided over the empire from the Park Lane Hotel, ruling from her apartment and from the table she reserved for herself in the restaurant on the second floor, next to the grand floor-to-ceiling windows overlooking Central Park, with a bird's-eye view of everyone entering and leaving the restaurant.

Mrs. Helmsley ran her empire on a shoestring. Her chief financial officer, Abe Wolf, had joined the Helmsley organization in the late eighties and managed all Helmsley financial affairs; her in-house counsel, Harold Meriam, had been hired shortly before Abe and dealt with internal legal matters, farming out more specialized legal work when Mrs. Helmsley didn't assign it herself.

But there was never any question about who was in charge. There was no second-in-command.

Into this vacuum came John Codey. Shortly after Harry's death, Codey, who had briefly met Mrs. Helmsley once before, wrote her a condolence note which led to a meeting. She grew dependent on him for advice and companionship. Soon, ostensibly to relieve the pressures on her because of the burdens that came with her substantial holdings, Codey advised her to hire a real estate investment banking firm he knew. He and the firm recommended she sell $2.5 billion in real estate properties, for which the firm received many millions in commissions, and Codey received 10 percent of those commissions.

Codey, who was married and had three children, began taking Mrs. Helmsley to social events, and speculation swirled that they were romantically involved. He joined Mrs. Helmsley daily for lunch, discussing business and anything else that popped into their minds, often for hours. Resting at her feet was always her Maltese dog, Trouble—a gift from Codey.

They were sometimes joined by others—security guards, general managers, accountants, lawyers, and assorted employees. Her favorite waiter would tell her what the chef suggested he prepare specially for her, and Codey would order from the wine list. I don't know anything about wines, but the ones he picked were always expensive. When I joined them, my drink was water. Lunch would last for many hours, and the wine they drank flowed freely. Mrs. Helmsley would order the dog fancy food off the menu.

I first met Codey at one of the lavish birthday parties Mrs. Helmsley threw for herself at Dunnellen Hall. The parties would typically begin with hors d'oeuvres and drinks served around the outdoor swimming pool—where no one was ever invited to swim. Business acquaintances, advisors, some employees, her small family, and lucky sycophants would mingle with each other, waiting to seize the lucky moment when they could approach the hostess to marvel at how radiant she looked. I'd later litigate against several of the guests—Mrs. Helmsley would sue them, or they her. Others wound up fired. But on birthday party day, everything was hunky-dory.

Dinner would then be served—outdoor seating at a dozen tables—on one of the nearby grand open lawns on the estate. It was at one of those tables that I met Codey. He was a Kentuckian, spoke with remnants of a southern drawl, and was introduced to me as a business advisor with a background in real estate. Mrs. Helmsley called Ruthie and me over to her table and invited us to sit with her. Mrs. Helmsley's feet were bare and resting on an empty chair. Codey was massaging her toes.

Mrs. Helmsley developed a dependent relationship with Codey—skillfully managed, I always thought, by him. Frequently, she would call me, at any hour (3:00 a.m. didn't matter to her), to say she'd been trying to reach him but couldn't, and asked whether I knew where he was. I never did. Nor did I ever really understand their relationship. She was a wealthy widow, he a married man. Their personal relationship was none of my business. I'm just a country lawyer from the Bronx.

Though Codey swooped in to fill the void left by Harry's death, Mrs. Helmsley was street-smart enough to realize that she and the multi-billion dollar fortune now hers were vulnerable to predators. Despite her great wealth, or perhaps because of it, in view of her suspicious nature, she had nobody to turn to—no old friend, no trusted relative, no decades-long trusted advisor. She knew she needed protection. And I was there.

She began inviting me into legal and business areas in which I had no expertise, discussing with me her real estate holdings, her hotels, her thousand-plus employees, her few right-hand people, and a host of other matters, for which I was uniquely unqualified to give advice. The more I'd tell her I had no knowledge or experience in those areas, the more she'd consult with me about them. I'd tell her of my limitations and that I should stick to my knitting, and she'd insist on my roaming into her other fields.

Abe, Harold, and Codey became more involved in the day-to-day management of the empire. Since many aspects of running the businesses involved legal issues, they too began involving me more and more, and my role evolved into that of an advisor to them as well. This had a fortunate consequence. I began reading a mass of real estate agreements I'd never previously seen, and noticed that several of them had provisions that would, on Mrs. Helmsley's death, severely restrict her estate's ability to sell its interests. I pointed out the damaging language to Harold, Abe, and Codey, and they agreed. Nobody had focused on the provisions despite the increasing evidence of Mrs. Helmsley's mortality and the staggering amounts she had spent on lawyers and other professionals.

I recommended that Mrs. Helmsley retain outside real estate counsel to review the same documents I'd been reading, to see whether I was wrong, and she did. The expert agreed with my read. We retained him to review all of the contracts governing dozens of Mrs. Helmsley's real estate interests. Many contained the same infirmity. The result was some legal legerdemain—a series of perfectly legitimate internal transfers of her interests—that ultimately saved her estate countless millions of dollars.

My relationship with Mrs. Helmsley was not without its potholes, and if I'd become her "go to" lawyer, it was consigliere interruptus.

Firings in the Helmsley organization were a *spécialité de la maison*. There was always internal palace intrigue which I steered clear of but which occasionally nicked me. I'd sometimes give advice she didn't want to hear, which was not a phenomenon she had grown accustomed to. None of my firings was confrontational; she simply didn't take my calls for awhile, and another lawyer would send me her instructions to transfer files. Then she'd call me about some new problem, as if there had never been any hiatus in our dealings.

The first time she fired me, I was blindsided. I was at Dunnellen Hall with an investigator she had hired to work on a case I'd been handling. The meeting was odd: She directed all her comments to the investigator and ignored everything I said, as if I were invisible and inaudible. At the end of the meeting, she suggested to the investigator another meeting the following morning, then turned to me and said: Your presence won't be necessary.

I stayed behind after the investigator left and asked her: What's up? She said I knew, turned, and left me alone in the living room. I left the house with no idea where the lightning bolt had come from. My best hunch was that there'd been some internal back-stabbing at headquarters, and the shiv had lodged in my back.

Mrs. Helmsley sent an emissary to retrieve the files in the case I was handling with the investigator, and didn't answer my phone calls for several weeks. Then one day, poof, she called to ask my opinion about someone who displeased her.

Another time she got mad at me: A former manager of the Park Lane Hotel sued Mrs. Helmsley for firing him because he was gay. She retained another lawyer to defend the case. He couldn't get it dismissed or settled. When the case reached the point of going to trial, Mrs. Helmsley asked me to take it over. At the time, my mother was seriously ill and I would regularly receive emergency calls requiring me to drop whatever I was doing and immediately drive her to the hospital. Single-mindedly immersing myself in Mrs. Helmsley's case for the several weeks needed for preparation and trial would be impossible. I had to decline.

So she hired another lawyer. The jury returned an $11 million verdict against Mrs. Helmsley. She was not sympathetic to my having declined to try the case for her, and cut off communications for several weeks.

There were a few other firings—I didn't know why, but following the evaporation of whatever stimulus had caused her to cut off contact, she'd eventually call me as if nothing had happened. The callback would occur when she needed protection from someone trying to fleece her.

One of her would-be fleecers was a real estate operator who ingratiated himself with her. When he sensed the time was right, pretending to be looking out for her best interests, he introduced her to a friend of his who, he said, had the experience to function as chief executive officer of the Helmsley organization—a position that had never existed. Abe and I had met this man a few times, and warned Mrs. Helmsley about him; he seemed sleazier than most who tried to insinuate themselves into her life. But Mrs. Helmsley thought the man was a savior.

She finally listened when: There was a fashion show for men's clothing in the ballroom of the Park Lane. The real estate operator bought several suits there for close to $10,000, and charged them to Mrs. Helmsley's account. Abe saw the charge, reported it to me, and we told Mrs. Helmsley. That was the end of the real estate operator. He sent a letter apologizing for what he called a "misunderstanding," but couldn't undo the stench.

As she got older, Mrs. Helmsley became an even riper target for lawsuits. She was a convicted felon, and was also preoccupied with a panoply of pressing problems that come with owning a multi-billion-dollar empire. She'd often resist appearing for depositions, and many plaintiffs' lawyers believed that simply suing and pressing for her deposition would generate a big payday. Some of them were right: she had the financial wherewithal to simply sign a settlement check if she didn't want to testify.

Among the cases she asked me to handle, some were highly personal.

An optometrist named Patrick Ward had developed a relationship with Mrs. Helmsley—how personal, I had no idea, but apparently very. She hired him for an executive position in the Helmsley organization. Then she fired him. They entered into a settlement agreement. It contained a "confidentiality clause" prohibiting both of them from disclosing the agreement's terms or making any public statement about each other.

Shortly after she signed the agreement, with the proverbial ink not yet dry on the page, the *Wall Street Journal* ran a lengthy front-page article headlined "Palace Intrigue/Courting the Queen Led to a Big Position With Leona Helmsley/The Optometrist Checked In But Didn't Check Out/Hotel Empire Is at Stake/'I Don't Trust Men Any More'." The article was based on an extensive interview given by Mrs. Helmsley and Codey four days after the Ward settlement agreement had been signed, and reported that Mrs. Helmsley had hired Ward at an annual salary of $400,000 for a newly created high executive position in the Helmsley organization. As Ward's star had risen in Mrs. Helmsley's life, Codey's had fallen. He did some sleuthing, and told her that Ward was gay. That ended Ward's relationship with Mrs. Helmsley. They had then entered into the settlement agreement.

After Ward read the article, he sued Mrs. Helmsley for violating the settlement agreement's confidentiality provision. He claimed damage to his reputation. His legal complaint, attaching the settlement agreement, contained quite a story:

Ward was forty-five years old and lived in Florida. Mrs. Helmsley was in her eighties. To induce him to move to New York, Mrs. Helmsley had agreed to sell to Ward, for $1 million, sixty cooperative apartments worth tens of millions of dollars—in essence, a tens-of-millions-of-dollars gift. The transaction had closed. Codey had been having an affair with Mrs. Helmsley, had made disparaging comments about Ward to her, had told her that Ward was gay, and Mrs. Helmsley wanted to rescind the sale. She and Ward had entered into the settlement agreement, in which Ward had relinquished his rights to fifty-nine of the apartments in exchange for $1 million. Ward now sued to recover those apartments for a pittance.

Mrs. Helmsley still hadn't forgiven me for not handling her earlier case against the Park Lane manager, and she retained another lawyer to represent her against Ward. She refused to appear for her deposition. As a result, the court ruled that she was liable for financial damages to Ward, but still required Ward to quantify his damages—that is, prove how many dollars in damages he'd supposedly suffered as a result of the article. Ward then piled some more claims on: that Mrs. Helmsley had threatened to use her money to "professionally and personally destroy him," "tear him apart," "drag him through the press," and "ruin him"; his apartment had been broken into; he had received anonymous threatening phone calls making homophobic remarks; and—the capstone—he had received a bullet in the mail accompanied by a copy of his Helmsley employee life insurance policy with the accidental death clause highlighted.

Mrs. Helmsley—as though there'd been no hiccup in our relationship—called to ask me to take over the case, and I did. I argued to the court that Ward hadn't proved any damage to his reputation; that he was required to appear in court but hadn't; and some other stuff you might consider "legal technicalities"—but they worked. The judge dismissed the case and I was back in Mrs. Helmsley's good graces.

In late 2001, Mrs. Helmsley found a topic for which I had absolutely zero qualifications. She called me from the magnificent luxury beachfront hotel she owned in Sarasota, Florida, and asked me to fly down to discuss her will with her, face-to-face.

I arrived early the following day, and we met in her spacious apartment—glass doors opening from a living room to a bound-less vista of sand, ocean, and sun. She was seated with several assistants and her dog.

After some small talk, she told me she wanted me to draft a will for her. I told her we should discuss this privately. She told me not to worry about the others being there, that the assistants would remain. I explained to her that if her assistants remained, our conversation could be disclosed to others and would not be privileged, but she insisted they stay—and they listened intently to our conversation.

Mrs. Helmsley had signed many wills over the years—over a dozen. She wanted me to draft a new one for her. She handed me a file which contained her most recent will, several older ones, mis-cellaneous drafts of wills, and a hodgepodge of will-related letters from a gaggle of attorneys.

I had never drafted a will. "T&E" law—Trusts and Estates—is a specialized branch of law. Lawyers who concentrate in that field draft wills and trusts, and help administer wills after the testator (that is, the person who signs the will) dies. No lawyer without experience in that field should draft a will concerning an estate as large and complex as Leona Helmsley's.

I told that to her. I said that as flattered as I was that she would entrust me with that responsibility, it would be malpractice for me to draft her will, and I would be doing her a disservice. I said there are lawyers who do that kind of work for a living, and she should use one of them. I said I'd be happy to read it and review it with her, but could not take the responsibility of drafting it; she needed an expert in the field.

She asked if I could find one for her.

The question startled me. Leona Helmsley could hire any T&E

lawyer in the country—they'd all jump at the chance. A quick glance at the papers she handed me showed that she had already employed several of New York's most prominent law firms for her estate matters.

Yes, I answered, I can find a good T&E lawyer for you.

Then, she switched back to me drafting it despite my telling her that I wasn't qualified. She told me that I was qualified and was being modest. I told her that any modesty in that area was deserved, as I truly knew nothing and had no experience in such matters. She said she had no one else to trust. Finally, I told her that if she wished, I would take responsibility for a new will for her, but only in conjunction with a qualified T&E lawyer. She could discuss with me what disposition of her estate she wanted; I would make sure a competent T&E lawyer drafted a will reflecting her wishes, and would review other will-related issues with that lawyer and discuss them with her. She could choose not to interact with anyone but me, which I advised against, but in any event I would ultimately be responsible for making sure the will said exactly what she wanted, would review it with her, and would oversee its proper execution. She said that would be fine. I told her I'd be happy to step out of the picture after finding her a specialist, but she said no.

She asked me to read the most recent will in her file while I was there, and I went into another room to read in quiet. The will provided for several relatively small (for her) bequests, and the "residuary estate"—that is, what remained after those bequests (and some expenses), nearly the entire Helmsley fortune—was to go to The Leona M. and Harry B. Helmsley Charitable Trust. The name had a vaguely familiar ring to it.

Several years earlier, following Harry's death, Mrs. Helmsley had invited me to a meeting at the Park Lane in one of those large suites we'd used years earlier for our pre-court prep sessions. The purpose of the meeting was to discuss a charitable foundation she wanted to set up. Over a dozen people were there. The talk was general. There was no charitable trust lawyer present; no expert at all. It was simply an unfocused conversation, nothing more specific than that the foundation would do good works. Mrs. Helmsley would fund it and decide where the money went. The group's role was vague: she spoke about us advising her, and running the foundation if something were to happen to her. Most of the time was spent on unrelated chitchat.

The document setting up the charitable trust was also in the files she handed me. I read it, and saw that I was one of the people named as "successor trustees." Mrs. Helmsley was the sole trustee—the person who decided what charitable organizations to give the Trust's money to, and how much. But when she died, the successor trustees—including me—would decide. She'd never told me that she'd selected me for that role.

In addition to bequests and assorted other matters, her will designated several executors. Executors of a will are the people that the testator—here, Mrs. Helmsley—entrusts to make sure that the will's provisions are carried out after the testator dies.

After I finished reading the will, I rejoined Mrs. Helmsley—she still insisted her assistants remain there—and explained in simple language what the will said. She told me she had changed her mind about whom she wanted to leave money to and who she wanted to serve as her executors. To my surprise, she asked me to be one. She told me what else she wanted in the will and repeated that she wanted her residuary estate—billions of dollars—to go to the charitable trust.

I told her I would have a will drafted with the terms she wanted. She asked me to do it quickly, as she was dissatisfied with the provisions in her existing will and couldn't be sure what tomorrow might bring. I flew back to New York that night, and began the first step in a new line of professional work that would

My mom with her protégé.

My dad.

Me (top) in the Bronx lot with my pal Guy.

THE WHITE HOUSE

WASHINGTON

Hi Mom!

The first letter I sent from the White House. I found it saved among my mother's belongings thirty-seven years later.

Effervescent young lawyer meets
demure young fashion designer/model.
They are living happily ever after.

SANDOR FRANK   MY TERRY   GARRY GROSS   JUDGE EDW GREENFIELD   BROOKE SHIELDS

Courtroom artist's sketch of me with Brooke Shields. Brooke's on the right.

MANHATTAN LAWYER ■ NOV. 15 – NOV. 21, 1988

Use of Marcos Grand Jury After Indictment Blasted

BY ELLIOT PINSLEY

Prominent defense attorneys are sharply critical of the federal government's continued use of a grand jury to gather evidence against deposed Philippine President Ferdinand Marcos and his wife Imelda, even though the panel has already returned racketeering charges against them.

The Marcoses were indicted nearly a month ago by a grand jury which accused them of embezzling more than $100 million from the Philippine government and investing the money in prime Manhattan real estate. Yet prosecutors are still pressing for enforcement of four subpoenas issued by the same grand jury.

The government says its investigation is continuing, and therefore, it has a right to obtain fingerprints, voice and hand-

Marcos defense counsel Sandor Frankel argued that grand jury subpoenas were no longer enforceable against his client.

grand jury cannot be used by a prosecutor to help prepare his case for trial."

I was humming along contentedly on the Ferdinand and Imelda Marcos trial team when I got a call to join the Leona Helmsley team. When it rains, it pours.

THE NEW YORK TIMES METROPOLITAN FRIDAY, FEBRUARY 23, 1990

In State Supreme Court, sitting between Leona Helmsley and the prosecutor, listening to him respond to my arguments seeking dismissal of the State criminal case against her. (We won.) *Courtesy of the New York Times.*

New York Post: Don Halasy

QUEEN & HER CONSORT: *Leona links arms with lawyers Alan Dershowitz (left) and Sandor Frankel (right) at state Supreme Court, where yesterday they urged dismissing indictment.*

LEONA: LEAK LED TO DELUGE

By MIKE PEARL
and RANSDELL PIERSON

Leona Helmsley's lawyers yesterday alleged that The Post broke the Helmsley tax scandal in 1986 only after state investigators leaked secret information about the hotel queen's involvement in an unrelated tax scam.

Defense attorney Sandor Frankel demanded a hearing on the alleged leak, arguing it justifies dismissal of a 188-count state indictment of Helmsley for tax evasion and business fraud.

Frankel said state officials slipped reporters secret minutes of Helmsley's 1985 testimony to a state grand jury empaneled to investigate a scheme by which Fifth Avenue jewelers helped wealthy customers escape sales tax.

Helmsley was never indicted in the case, but testified under immunity she had bought at least $485,000 worth of gems from Van Cleef & Arpels without realizing she had not been been charged $38,000 in sales tax.

The Post, The New York Times and United Press International disclosed the grand-jury probe a year later, in November 1986, after a lawyer for the jeweler identified Helmsley in court papers as a frequent beneficiary of the sales-tax scam.

But yesterday, Frankel in-sisted state prosecutors were the ones who tattled to the press.

He told state Supreme Court Justice John Bradley that the defense intended to subpoena at least three reporters who "have acknowledged to us that the source of their articles came from law-enforcement officers."

Frankel said "new evidence clearly and unquestionably shows that this entire prosecution — the whole kit and caboodle" was an outgrowth of the alleged leak.

After the hearing, outside the courtroom, Helmsley exulted over Frankel's performance.

"It's a bombshell, isn't it?" a grinning Leona, dressed in a white sweater with black hearts, told reporters.

But state prosecutor Alfredo Mendez was less impressed. He scoffed at Frankel's claim, saying there had been no leak.

Two of the three reporters cited by Helmsley attorneys said yesterday their accounts of the jewelry scam were obtained through depositions filed in Manhattan Supreme Court.

The civil-case documents were part of the public record and were later confirmed by law-enforcement sources.

Furthermore, Mendez said, the jewelry scam was totally unrelated to The Post's subsequent 16-month investigation of Leona and Harry Helmsley's $5 billion real-estate holdings.

The Post series, which began on Dec. 2, 1986, revealed that the Helmsleys disguised millions of dollars in renovations to their Greenwich, Conn., mansion as business expenses.

When the Helmsleys were indicted by state and federal grand juries in April 1988, prosecutors said their first knowledge of the Helmsleys' home-renovation scheme came from The Post series.

Mrs. Helmsley was convicted by a federal jury last August on 33 felony counts of tax evasion and mail fraud and was sentenced to four years in prison.

She remains free pending appeal. Her husband was deemed mentally unfit to stand trial in federal court. A hearing on his competency in the state case is scheduled for March 29.

Leaving the courthouse with Leona Helmsley. *Courtesy of the New York Post.*

Popular recording artists receive gold records (for 500,000 sales) or platinum (for 1,000,000), and sometimes give duplicates in appreciation.

The Edgar from the Mystery Writers of America for *Beyond A Reasonable Doubt*.

A relaxed moment with Leona Helmsley.

With Israeli President Shimon Peres.

With President Peres' successor, President Reuven Rivlin.

The first time I met Natan Sharansky, in my office.

From the right: Natan Sharansky, President Shimon Peres, Prime Minister
Benjamin Netanyahu, Hebrew University President Menahem Ben-Sasson,
Ruthie, and me.

Opening of the Jerusalem Press Club at its Helmsley House.

My camera's-eye view of one of the dozens of tunnels terrorists built in the Gaza Strip to invade Israel—this one more than thirty feet deep and over a mile long. Construction of the tunnels often begins undetected in a Gaza mosque, house, or school; the terrorists' plan is to emerge with weaponry in Israel and annihilate or kidnap the unsuspecting civilian population.

The *Globes*, one of the many Israeli newspapers reporting our work, featured a front-page story with a two-page spread inside. The front-page headline quotes my answer to the reporter's question: "Leona Helmsley would have thought about our investments in Israel: Why didn't I do them myself?" The inside headline asks: "If somebody gave you 5 billion dollars and told you to do good things, what would you have done?" *Courtesy of the Globes.*

Our gang celebrates its newest member, who's a bit ambivalent about the bris.

ultimately result, years later, in my overseeing the disposition of a multi-billion dollar empire and directing its money to the public good.

I've often wondered why she involved me in her estate. She knew that if I had a forte, this wasn't it. Perhaps when you meet someone in dire circumstances, when her guard is down and she has no pretensions, a certain intimacy develops. You have unique access to that person on a level most don't. After several years of working closely with her on her criminal case, and visits to her in Kentucky and Connecticut prisons, she recognized I'd seen her at her most vulnerable. After her release, I'd simply done my job and stayed removed from the jockeying for position that seemed a constant among those around her. Maybe that's why she started stuffing my plate with non-litigation legal and business matters.

I'd like to think she involved me in her estate simply because she trusted me—trusting people was not a character trait she had in abundance—but that may be falsely self-flattering. Maybe it was the little things: She once told me she'd noticed that when the legal team handling her criminal case would have dinner at the Park Lane on the evenings before court appearances, I'd always order an inexpensive dish while others (she remembered who) ordered lobster or filet mignon. She might have just figured I was honest—totally, or relatively, or maybe. The simpler explanation may be that she trusted nobody else, and I was the least undesirable of all the imperfect alternatives.

W hen I got back to New York, I called a former college classmate of mine who was a trusts and estates lawyer, and explained the situation. If he wanted to participate, he'd be the responsible technician. Of course, he jumped at the opportunity. I told him the

ground rules: I would discuss with Mrs. Helmsley the disposition
she wanted for her vast assets, and he'd draft the will and any
appropriate revisions to the trust instrument to make sure they
delivered what she wanted. He and I would consider alternative
estate planning strategies, which I'd then discuss with Mrs.
Helmsley.

When the will was ready, I went to Mrs. Helmsley's apartment
and reviewed it with her, leaving a copy for her to read by herself.
She had some questions; I answered them and made changes she
requested; and she told me she was ready to sign. I met with her in
her Park Lane apartment, accompanied by a lawyer and assistant
from my office and the T&E lawyer I'd involved, and oversaw
Leona Helmsley's execution of a will directing the disposition of
billions of dollars in assets. I watched her sign every page. It was a
unique experience for a T&E novice.

I helped draft several later wills and trust documents for Mrs.
Helmsley in the same manner, each replacing all previous ones. On
the occasions when she fired me, she'd instruct me to turn over her
"wills" file to another lawyer, who would draft a superseding will.
After I'd return to her good graces, she'd have me prepare another
will and trust instrument to replace those that had replaced the
earlier ones I'd drafted.

The last time this happened, I used a different T&E draftsman
from the previous one. I'd had an unpleasant lawyers-can-be-the-
worst-clients experience with him. Another lawyer had sued him
for $300,000 over a dispute involving a fee on a case they'd worked
on together. He asked me to represent him, and I treated the case
like an important piece of litigation: depositions, document discovery, numerous motions and court appearances, and then a full-
blown trial. We won.

It had been expensive for me. I hadn't asked for any fee while
the case was pending. I'd invested hundreds of my and my

associates' hours. After the verdict, I suggested that it would be appropriate for him to reimburse me for the salaries I'd paid the lawyers who'd worked on the case. He asked how much time they'd spent, and I gave him their time records and told him their salaries and my out-of-pocket costs. He said it was too much money, told me what he'd be willing to pay, and said he needed a year to pay it. I agreed to whatever he requested, and never spoke with him again.

After my reinstatement in Mrs. Helmsley's good graces following the "Tomb With A View" episode, she returned her estate files to me—incomplete and shockingly disorganized, given the magnitude of her wealth. She told me that she wanted a new will drafted, plus an amendment to the document establishing her charitable trust. This time I enlisted the assistance of Tom, a T&E specialist at a large Manhattan law firm.

"Tom" isn't his real name. You'll see later why I'm sparing him through a pseudonym.

We went through the same procedure: Mrs. Helmsley met with me privately and told me what she now wanted in her will and trust; I shared the information with Tom; we drafted a will and trust document to reflect her wishes; and on July 15, 2005, I oversaw her sign the documents and initial each page in front of three witnesses from my office and me, in her plush living room on the 46th floor of the Park Lane Hotel. They were it: The last will and trust documents Mrs. Helmsley ever signed. As life and death turned out, they ultimately determined the disposition of the Helmsley billions.

The ultra-rich take a certain lifestyle for granted. I was sitting in the Park Lane restaurant one afternoon with Mrs. Helmsley when she told me she wanted to buy Codey some sweaters and scarves for Christmas from Paul Stuart, an expensive clothing store on Madison Avenue. I said she couldn't go wrong there. She said that's what she'd do—but kept sitting.

Then, she said to me: Call them.

I asked: Call who?

She said: The store.

I asked whether she wanted to see what she was buying before buying it. She said of course she did, I should call the store and tell them to bring over a suitcase with choices. I told her that's not how people shop. She said that's how she shops, and again asked me—told me—to call. So I did, figuring they'd say that's not how people shop.

I called. Hello, I said. I'm calling for Leona Helmsley, she's in the restaurant at the Park Lane Hotel and would like to buy some sweaters and scarves. Could you bring over a suitcase with a bunch of choices? The voice on the other end asked what size and said, Of course, we'll be right over.

Indeed, he came, with a suitcase full of sweaters and scarves. Mrs. Helmsley picked a few she liked, asked what I thought—I said they were lovely—and told the salesman she wanted those.

An awkward silence followed. Finally, the salesman asked: And will that be by credit card?

Mrs. Helmsley said she didn't have a credit card or any money with her. She turned to a waiter standing a few feet away: Do you have a credit card I can use? He said he didn't own a credit card.

To the rescue, I took out my card and gave it to the salesman. He charged the merchandise against the card, returned the card to me, carefully wrapped two sweaters and a scarf in a gift box, thanked Mrs. Helmsley, and left.

She asked if she'd made a good choice. I said yes.

The next day, I told Abe, the company's CFO, what had

happened. He suggested I itemize the charge as a personal expense of Mrs. Helmsley on my next bill, and I'd be reimbursed.

Mrs. Helmsley, Codey, and a security guard were riding down Fifth Avenue in her limo, heading for lunch, when the car's engine caught fire. They scrambled out and took a cab the rest of the way. After that, Codey arranged for Mrs. Helmsley to travel with two limos: The one she was riding in, and a backup following it, just in case.

Ruthie and I went to the Four Seasons, an expensive midtown restaurant (no longer in business), on a double date with Mrs. Helmsley and Codey. One of the owners knew she was coming, met us at the entrance, and escorted us to a table near the pool in the center of the room, making sure enough gawkers could see that Leona Helmsley was in the house.

He gave us menus, and said he'd like to bring Mrs. Helmsley something special they'd prepared for her. The waiter then came over with a ritzy appetizer he split for the four of us. It was far too fancy for my taste but I forced it down, thinking how nice that the owners concocted something special as a gift for her.

At the end of the meal, the waiter put the bill in the middle of the table. Since neither Mrs. Helmsley nor Codey reached for it, I did. Getting stuck with the bill wouldn't have been painful until I saw a charge of over $200 for the special culinary gift the owner had concocted for Mrs. Helmsley.

(Another lesson in meals-for-the-rich-can-be-expensive: A lawyer hustling for Mrs. Helmsley's business invited her for lunch at

Le Bernadin, one of Manhattan's most expensive restaurants. To his chagrin, Mrs. Helmsley asked me to accompany them. Lunch was *price fixe* at $51 per person, not including tax and tip—back when $51 was $51. The owner of the restaurant personally came to take her order, and she said all she wanted was a cup of soup. The owner explained that only *price fixe* was available, and he'd have to charge her that much for a cup of soup. She replied: Bring me a cup of soup. He did. The soup cost $51.)

W hen Mrs. Helmsley was in her eighties, she began to suffer physical infirmities that come with age. Though whatever expert medical care she needed was readily available, she was stubborn and would follow her own medical self-advice. Her physical condition began to worsen. She had difficulty signing her name to the ceaseless flood of documents that required signature; she was beginning to lose motor function.

Codey suggested to her that she sign a power of attorney in his favor. A "power of attorney" is a document in which a person gives someone else the legal authority to sign a person's name. In the wrong hands, a power of attorney can be an instrument of mass financial destruction.

At first, Mrs. Helmsley declined to sign. But as her condition worsened and she realized the need for someone to have authorization to sign her name, she agreed to Codey's suggestion, trusting that I would always keep the original in my possession and never relinquish it to Codey or anyone else, just showing it when necessary to implement its purpose. So, near the end of her life, she did not sign documents—Codey signed her name, pursuant to the power of attorney, with me retaining the original. It never left my possession.

In mid-August 2007, I visited Mrs. Helmsley in a private room at a hospital in Greenwich, Connecticut to which she had contributed $10 million. She was very weak and close to the end, but still able to communicate. She plainly needed sleep more than company, so I stayed for only a short time. As I got up to leave, her head was resting at an awkward angle on the pillow. I gently eased her head onto the center of the pillow.

"Are you comfortable?" I asked.

"I make a living," she answered with a smile.

I touched her cheek lightly and left the room. Those were the last words I ever heard her speak. A few days later, an ambulance returned her to Dunnellen Hall. She soon slipped into a coma, and the inevitable was near.

I met Codey, Abe, and Harold at Dunnellen Hall the day before she died. They showed me a press release the Helmsleys' longtime press agent had prepared, announcing her death, and asked me to rewrite it. I did. Writing an announcement of the death of someone you've known closely for eighteen years, while she is still alive in a room next door, feels very macabre.

In less than twenty-four hours, the release became timely.

Chapter 10

Gathering Billions

On August 20, 2007, at about 4:00 a.m., the phone rang. David Panzirer, one of Mrs. Helmsley's grandsons, was calling to tell me his grandmother had died. I expressed condolences, lay awake for an hour, couldn't sleep, and got ready for the office.

Codey took charge of funeral arrangements. He contacted a temple in Manhattan to arrange for a funeral service. They asked for a quarter-of-a-million dollars to do so, and Codey asked what I thought. I told him Mrs. Helmsley would have our heads if we paid that, and he agreed. So the service was held at a funeral chapel on Madison Avenue.

The sidewalk along the entire block was thick with cameramen and reporters. Police cordoned off most of the street. I waded through a sea of journalists to get into and out of the chapel. Having television personalities thrust microphones in front of you and ask for a comment can stroke the ego, but the dignified response seemed just to plow quietly through and remember: this is a funeral; somebody died.

Following her "Tomb With A View" fiasco, Mrs. Helmsley had built another mausoleum in a different cemetery, and transferred the remains of Harry and her son there. She also removed from the first mausoleum the stained-glass windows of New York City's skyline and had them installed in the new mausoleum, along with the finest crypts and expensive finishings throughout the interior surfaces, all waiting for her. As for the first mausoleum: There is a secondary market for used mausoleums.

I had retained, in a bank safety deposit box, possession of the latest will she'd signed under my supervision, from the day she signed it. Over two years had passed since then, and I had no idea whether she had signed another will in the interim superseding this one.

The will named five executors—her brother Alvin Rosenthal, two of her grandsons (David Panzirer and his half-brother Walter), Codey, and me. I contacted each of them soon after the funeral, and scheduled a meeting in the Helmsley organization's conference room in the Helmsley Building at 230 Park Avenue. I invited Tom, the T&E lawyer I had worked with on the will, to attend.

At the meeting, I distributed copies of the will to everyone and described its substantive provisions: bequests of $5 million to Alvin plus a $10 million trust fund; $5 million to David plus a $5 million trust fund; $5 million to Walter plus a $5 million trust fund; and a specific disinheritance of her two other grandchildren, "for reasons known to them," which she never publicly disclosed. As a condition for her two grandsons' entitlement to their trusts, the will required them to visit the mausoleum annually and sign a sign-in book kept there. She also left $100,000 for her chaffeur, but nothing to anyone else.

The outside of the mausoleum is a tourist attraction at the cemetery. The grandsons and I have keys to enter.

Mrs. Helmsley also left $3 million in trust for maintenance of the mausoleum and other family cemetery plots, and $12 million to a trust for her dog Trouble. After expenses, the balance of the estate was left to the charitable trust Mrs. Helmsley had discussed years earlier at our meeting in the Park Lane. The Trust document appointed as trustees the same five executors named in her will, including me.

Here I was, along with four others as inexperienced and at sea as me in such matters, in charge of an enormous estate. Alvin was eighty years old, long ago retired and, before that, had no significant business background; David worked as a real estate agent in New York City; Walter had been a paramedic, firefighter, and law enforcement officer in South Dakota, where he lived; and Codey had a real estate background before latching on to Mrs. Helmsley. We're suddenly in charge of an estate worth billions; we didn't even know how many. What does one do?

The five of us had a series of lengthy meetings over the next several weeks. Each of us was now a fiduciary of the estate: required to act in its best interests, to carry out the will's directives, to take possession and control of all of the estate's assets, and to make sure none of the estate's assets fell through the cracks. Each executor was entitled to his own counsel, paid by the estate, to guide him in fulfilling his duties. The three relatives jointly picked a lawyer; Codey picked his own; and I stayed with Tom.

Before a will has any legal validity, it must be "offered for probate"—in Manhattan, submitted to the Surrogate's Court (presided over by two "Surrogates," or judges of that court) for a Surrogate to approve it as being the decedent's legally enforceable last will. A court's doing so empowers the will's named executors to act on behalf of the estate and to enforce the will's provisions. Before the will is approved by the court as valid, the Surrogate may temporarily appoint a will's designated executors as "preliminary executors."

Although I had no idea whether Mrs. Helmsley had signed a more recent will than the one in my possession, if she had done so it would have named executors and directed disposition of her property in ways unknown to me. And if she had, I had no way of knowing whether it had been during the last few months of her life when her mental faculties had diminished and someone may have taken advantage of her. I knew firsthand that she had been competent when she signed the will I had overseen and for an appreciable time afterwards. It was important to make sure that the will I had was offered for probate as quickly as possible, so if someone showed up with a later will signed during Mrs. Helmsley's final days, the executors named in the will that I had prepared could retain control over the estate's assets until a court determined the validity of any later will.

When it had become clear that Mrs. Helmsley was near death, Tom and I had drafted a petition offering Mrs. Helmsley's will for probate, to make sure we could act quickly following her death and nobody could improperly seize control of her assets. A few days after Mrs. Helmsley's death, we filed the petition in court, including the will, and the court immediately issued an order appointing as preliminary executors the five people named in the will. No later will ever materialized.

When we filed the will it immediately became a public document, and the press pounced on it instantaneously. The will's provisions—its bequests, its disinheritances, the executors, the dog trust, and the charitable uses to which nearly the entire estate would be put—became front-page news in New York City and internationally.

I received a barrage of phone calls from media and ignored them all, but the media's appetite was insatiable. They were particularly fixated on the $12 million trust Mrs. Helmsley had established "to provide for the maintenance and welfare of Trouble at the highest standards of care." That bequest to her dog received worldwide media attention. The *New York Daily News* devoted its entire front page to a picture of Mrs. Helmsley holding Trouble (captioned "Leona Helmsley and her pooch") alongside a headline that blared "LEONA'S DOG GETS 12M! But she leaves two grandkids NOTHING in will," accompanied by lengthy inside stories headlined "HELMSLEY BONE-ANZA" and "LEONA'S DOG GETS HER PAWS ON $12 MILLION IN WILL, BUT THE GRANDKIDS GO BEGGING." On the same day, the *New York Post's* front page ran a different picture of Mrs. Helmsley holding Trouble, and the headline "RICH BITCH. No, not Leona—her dog just inherited 12 million," and featured two full inside pages describing the will's provisions.

Our job as executors wasn't to evaluate the will's wisdom but to carry out its mandates: have the will probated, collect all of the estate's assets, invest and manage those assets until they were distributed in accordance with the will's provisions, distribute the specific bequests as directed, pay the estate's taxes and debts, comply with the multitude of the will's other provisions, and transfer the "residuary estate"—that is, everything else, which was over 99 percent of the estate—to the charitable trust. But before we could do so, the Surrogate had to determine that the will was in fact Mrs. Helmsley's last will, that it was legally enforceable, and that we were therefore entitled to act as her executors. In the meantime, we were legally empowered to begin carrying out the will's dictates and to act on the estate's behalf.

A stumbling block lay in front of us.

The two disinherited grandchildren filed an "Objection to Probate" in the Surrogate's Court, claiming that when Mrs. Helmsley had signed her will over two years before dying, she "was not of sound mind and did not have the capacity to make a will." If in fact Mrs. Helmsley lacked "testamentary capacity"—that is, the legally required mental ability—to make the will, her prior will would become operative. And if that will were successfully attacked, the previous one would become operative—and so on, peeling back one will after another. If no will were to be sustained, each of Mrs. Helmsley's four grandchildren, including the disinherited two, would be entitled by law to divide the entire estate equally among themselves—substantially over $1 billion (you've read that right) apiece.

The dangers of such a challenge to the will were not merely that we could lose, though I had no question concerning her mental capacity at the time she signed the will: I had been there, spoken with her, interacted with her regularly, and she was unquestionably mentally competent when she signed it. I'd be the primary witness, and had no qualms about testifying to her mental capacity. But I'd learned through many years of lawyering that the only thing predictable in a courtroom is unpredictability.

Moreover, even though our case would be extremely strong, the costs to the estate in a will contest would be substantial—the financial costs of litigation, the media frenzy and public spectacle that such a litigation would involve, and the delay in achieving the clear purpose Mrs. Helmsley had intended for her fortune: use of the money for charitable purposes. I'd had enough experience to realize the delays, financial costs, turmoil, and other tolls of such high-stakes and high-profile litigation, and that getting rid of the two disinherited grandchildren's objections expeditiously and economically would be a good idea. The other executors reached the same conclusion.

So we negotiated and settled with the two disinherited grandchildren, giving them a total of $6 million, funded in part by Mrs. Helmsley's brother and two other grandchildren agreeing to reduce their own trusts by a total of $2 million.

In fact, the actual cost of the settlement to the estate was zero.

Through the who-would-believe-it hocus-pocus of the Internal Revenue Code, quick resolution of the will challenge allowed the estate to obtain certain tax deductions that would have been precluded merely by the passage of time during a will contest. In other words, the disinherited grandchildren got their settlement and it didn't cost the estate a penny.

Mrs. Helmsley's estate was massive—in our rough preliminary estimate, worth over $5 billion when she died, before the financial world collapsed in 2008.

Harry Helmsley had been a real estate genius, and had left his entire fortune to Mrs. Helmsley. The real estate empire was enormous: holdings in eighty-four properties, including an immense stake in the Empire State Building and ownership of several other of the most iconic buildings in New York City. She also owned municipal bonds worth over $2 billion, plus personal property galore—jewelry, furniture, artwork, and just plain money.

Part of the estate—a small part, though mammoth by the standards of any mere mortal—was Mrs. Helmsley's personal property.

I knew a bit about her jewelry. I'd seen her wear it, and she'd told me about the birthday earrings Harry had bought her. He'd come to her one day with three boxes from the pricey jewelry store Van Cleef and Arpels, whose Manhattan flagship store was right around the corner from the Park Lane. Harry said he'd picked out the three loveliest pairs of diamond earrings in the store and wanted to see them on her so he could choose. She had opened each box and modeled the earrings, and Harry had admired how stunning each of them looked on her. Finally, he told her he couldn't decide, she looked magnificent in each, and she should keep all three pairs. She did. She told me that story many times.

Leona Helmsley had much more jewelry and other stuff. She had two safe deposit boxes at a Manhattan bank. I went there with a few witnesses, including two security guards, and, because we couldn't find the keys, had the boxes drilled open. Inside were wads of cash and an assortment of diamonds. The bank's cash-counting machines finally stopped whirring at $1,290,758. She also had 299 gold coins in rolls of twenties; I wondered what had happened to the 300th.

Mrs. Helmsley had forty-seven safe deposit boxes in her basement at Dunnellen Hall, plus two Mosley safes. I stood and watched a locksmith drill open each box and safe. They were all empty.

One of the security guards at the house told me there was another safe, hidden off Harry's den. I asked the locksmith to drill that safe open in the presence of several witnesses, and it had stacks of hundred-dollar bills and jewelry. I'd brought a suitcase to the house just in case, and put all the cash and jewelry in; wrapped masking tape around the suitcase and had two witnesses sign the overlap in the tape; had a security guard put a combination lock on the suitcase with instructions not to tell me the combination; and drove home with the filled suitcase in the trunk of my car, to keep it overnight because the banks were then closed.

The following day, I took the suitcase with me on my commuter train into Manhattan. I took a taxi to the bank, where I met the same witnesses who had signed the tape and knew the lock's combination; had them verify that the tape was intact and the lock unopened; removed the cash—in front of everyone; and the counting machine this time stopped at $534,800. I put the jewelry in a vault.

I hadn't even considered the what-ifs: What if I'd been followed leaving Dunnellen Hall, or got a flat tire, or had a burglary that night and the suitcase had been stolen, or something had happened on the train ride the next morning or on my taxi ride to the bank? And what if one of those things happened and I was robbed but nobody believed I'd been robbed? Thank goodness, I must've just seemed like someone shlepping around a suitcase.

All told, we auctioned off Mrs. Helmsley's jewelry, furniture, artwork, decorative pieces, dinnerware, and other tchotchokes for nearly $14 million.

And then, of course, there was the big stuff: the real estate and bonds.

The biggest real estate transactions I'd ever been involved in were buying and selling my homes. Liquidating—that is, selling—billions of dollars-worth of real estate, bonds, and other high-priced assets is very different. You don't just hire a real estate broker and personal banker, set a price, and say "sell," or put some ads on the internet and choose the highest bidder. The process is involved, the stakes are enormous, everything is much different, and you have to hire experts in different fields.

If we made a mistake, the financial consequences could be severe. None of Mrs. Helmsley's money or other property was ours; we were simply entrusted, by her and by law, with handling it properly. We'd be financially liable if we screwed up.

To guide us, we interviewed a militia of experts—real estate brokers, lawyers, appraisers, bankers, financial advisors, investment bankers, and assorted others. Group by group, they all paraded into the Helmsley boardroom and described their experience and expertise—a continuum of mavens, none of whom came cheap. We heard fees quoted in dollars, percentages, and basis points (hundredths of a percent). I was no longer the lawyer hoping to get and please clients. I was now a client, to be pleased and smiled at. Suddenly, from being just me, I was the cat's meow. Having big shots from major banks, real estate firms, and others try obsequiously to curry my favor is nothing I was used to. I had experience kowtowing, but not being kowtowed to.

Shortly after Mrs. Helmsley died, I got a better understanding of the they're-just-using-me streak in her personality. Ruthie and I were in the Hamptons the weekend after the will was filed. The New York City press had already run large articles about it, including the names of the executors. As we pulled up to a road-side restaurant for lunch, a law school classmate and his wife, whom I'd bumped into once or twice over the past forty years, spotted us.

"Sandy," the wife yelled, racing over and giving me a big hug. "Great to see you. I've been reading all about you. We should get together."

But back to the task at hand. Our job was to sell the estate's assets, pay out the few bequests the will had made, and get the money to the charitable trust.

Mrs. Helmsley had been a very conservative investor. She owned no publicly traded stocks. Other than real estate, her only investments were over $2 billion in municipal bonds, primarily a subset of municipal bonds that are "pre-refunded." Never mind what that means—her $2 billion were a meaningful part of the universe of all such bonds.

Municipal bonds can be a suitable investment for a taxpayer. Even though they generate a smaller return than taxable bonds or other investments, they can ultimately yield a greater after-tax return because their return is tax-free. But the ultimate beneficiary of the estate was now the tax-exempt charitable trust. The lower yield of a tax-free municipal bond is not suitable for a charitable trust, as it derives no offsetting benefit from the bond's tax-free status.

Concluding that the bonds should therefore be sold was not difficult. But selling them was problematic. The estate's extensive holdings in pre-refunded municipal bonds were known within the municipal bond investment world; everyone had easy access to Mrs. Helmsley's will and could see that it required expeditious sale of the estate's assets; and selling such a high percentage of all such bonds could drive down the price on the next batch. These were not ideal conditions in which to sell.

We interviewed numerous investment firms eager to help us out—for a generous fee; selected the firm with people and a disposition plan that seemed best suited to guide us through these treacherous financial shoals; and through a gradual sale of the bonds that avoided our driving down the price of our remaining bonds by flooding the market, managed to distribute over $2 billion in proceeds to the charitable trust soon after the will was admitted to probate. We were playing with expensive chips: Sale of the municipal bonds and distribution to the charitable trust increased the return on those assets by $2 million dollars per month—that was just the *increase*.

Sale of Mrs. Helmsley's real estate portfolio—hotels, office buildings, apartment houses, warehouses, and other properties in seventeen states and the District of Columbia—presented a sea of challenges. She had owned (and therefore the estate—which meant me and my co-executors as fiduciaries—now owned) many valuable properties in their entirety: the Park Lane Hotel, the New York Helmsley Hotel, the Sandcastle Hotel, and others. But her ownership interests in most of the properties, including the Empire State Building, One Grand Central Plaza, and an inventory of some other of the most valuable commercial and residential real estate in New York City and elsewhere, were owned through a maze of corporations, partnerships, and limited liability companies, involving a dizzying entanglement of ownership arrangements, some involving hundreds of partners.

She had owned more than one interest in some properties; certain of her interests leased properties from other interests; ownerships of most properties were governed by highly convoluted agreements and amendments; many of the agreements had complexities built onto other complexities; many had restrictions on selling or transferring interests without consents of other partners; many gave other partners a right of first refusal on sales of interests, or had buy-sell and other pretzel-like provisions that provided a feast and good living for real estate professionals. Confusing enough?

No, there's more. Many of the properties were subject to interlocking ownerships. She'd been partners with numerous people in one transaction, several (but not all) of whom were partners (with others) in different properties—all entailing analysis of the potential impact that the sale of an interest in one property could have on another. It was a billionaire's version of whac-a-mole: hit one target, and another pops up somewhere else. In a nutshell: Selling these properties for the highest possible price was challenging. It took many years.

As if these layers of complexity weren't enough: All of our real estate partners were aware of the will's requirement that the executors sell all of the estate's interests in all of the properties, and that we do so "as promptly as they shall determine to be reasonably practical without adversely affecting the value realizable on the sale." We were playing poker with our cards showing. Moreover, experts told us that because of the limited marketability and non-controlling interests we held in various of the properties, we should anticipate a 30 percent reduction from actual value: In other words, selling our interest alone would give us 30 percent less than if the entire property were sold and we were to receive our proportionate share of the sale price. But we had no right to force our partners to sell the entire properties.

This was very difficult, head-spinning stuff. Nothing in my background prepared me for it. All of a sudden, instead of litigating discrete cases in a forum I'd become somewhat adept in— courtrooms—and being able to analyze a case down to its bones, I was faced with dozens of kaleidoscopes in fields—real estate and finance—where I was a novice and the people on the other side of

the table were experts. My co-executors brought no more expertise in those areas than I did.

So instead of fighting the battles myself, or ourselves, I became
the counterpart of what I'd been doing for decades: interviewing
real estate experts, lawyers, and others to seek their counsel. It
reminded me of a law school classmate I'd recently bumped into.
He worked in-house at a corporation. The last time we'd met,
years earlier, he described how hard he worked—long hours, late
nights, tiresome document-drafting, endless problems, constant
tension. He'd since become general counsel at the company. I asked
what he now does as the legal department's top dog.

"I point," he said.

It was a turnaround from do-it-yourselfer to using my judgment in hiring the best-in-class to assist. But in the final analysis,
the financial responsibility and liability would be mine, and the
fees would be theirs. I'd—we'd—better pick right.

We assembled a team of experts, and I tried to think like a lawyer in fields unfamiliar to me and develop expertise in disciplines
I'd never had to plow. We created contractual arguments to give us
legal power; insisted on rights that Mrs. Helmsley hadn't exercised
for years; and created a ton's-worth of leverage from a pound's-
worth of substance wherever we could. All of the proceeds from
sales of our interests would be transferred to the charitable trust
for charitable purposes, but our real estate partners couldn't have
cared less. Money and legal leverage was all that counted. In their
dealings with us, charity began at home.

We were in a "zero sum" game. Partners in these real estate
holdings were interested in squeezing us, getting our interests for a
song. And soon it was 2008, when the real estate market in New
York City and countrywide cratered, financial resources dried up,
and the United States entered its most serious financial crisis since
the Great Depression.

I asked Tom, my lawyer, what my legal obligation was under these circumstances. After all, I'd never been in charge of a multi-billion dollar estate, and figured there must be some guidelines.

He recommended that we sell all the real estate as quickly as possible, despite the horrendous real estate and economic conditions. The will required us to sell, he said, and we'd get no gold stars for waiting. If we waited and the market collapsed even further before we sold, we could be criticized and penalized; and if we waited for more optimal market conditions and got better prices, nobody would applaud. Sell quickly, he said—that's what most executors would do. And if the estate got tens of millions of dollars less, he said, or a few hundred million dollars less, what difference would that make in the context of an estate worth billions?

Tom's advice didn't sit right with me. If the money were mine, I wouldn't sell into a plummeting market, and Mrs. Helmsley hadn't named me an executor to engage in a self-motivated sale of the properties Harry and she had nurtured for over half-a-century. The other executors felt the same. So we waited, hired experts to help us analyze the market, and sold properties in an orderly, deliberate, and, I think, prudent way instead of at the market's bottom. Though hard to measure precisely, our doing so saved the estate, and therefore charitable organizations we'd later fund, an enormous bundle of money.

Liquidating a multi-billion dollar estate comes with significant risks. Each executor is liable for any negligence or wrongdoing, either his own or a co-executor's; we were vulnerable to claims that we sold assets too soon or too late, or too cheaply, or through an improper process, or to a buyer who couldn't close the deal; we'd be liable if we couldn't keep the hotels functioning before they were sold, or if we made improvident investments, or retained the wrong people to advise us; and for a variety of other nightmare scenarios. Our exposure for missteps would be astronomical, given the values of the properties we were entrusted with handling—enough to bankrupt all of us many, many times over.

Perhaps you've heard of "E and O" insurance: Businesses often obtain "errors and omissions" policies paid for by their companies to protect them in case of lawsuits charging wrongdoing or negligence. Executors of estates often obtain similar insurance, paid by the estate, to protect against those risks. We got quotes from several insurance companies, but the prices were off-the-wall: For coverage equal to only 10 percent of the value of the estate, premiums ranged from $6.6 million to $12.4 million per year. Moreover, the insurance companies weren't charitable institutions: they carved out categories of possible coverage that whittled down what they would insure against for that much money.

Neither I nor the other executors could see flushing tens of millions of the estate's dollars down an insurance company drain—the cost could total over $100 million during the life of the estate—even though the estate and not the executors would be paying the premiums. No rules dictated that conclusion; only the sense that burdening the estate with that size expense didn't feel right. So we managed the estate without any insurance coverage for us. If we blundered, we'd be walking around clothed in barrels. It reminded me of having practiced law with Lou Bender without malpractice insurance until some nutcase sued us, except this time a mistake could be catastrophic. Anyway, that's what we did.

W e hired a real estate consulting firm to help us navigate some preliminary issues: evaluating all the real estate, analyzing the present market, opining on which properties to sell and when, advising us whether to invest in capital improvements or other upgrades before marketing each property, whether to package certain properties together, whether to convert some properties to other uses, how to prioritize sales, selecting brokers, advising on risks of delaying sales, analyzing the state of the real estate cycle, counseling on terms of sales, and a multitude of other issues.

We decided to test the waters with the Park Lane Hotel, the crown jewel of the Helmsley hotel empire: a majestic 587-room hotel built by Harry, directly across the street from Central Park. We chose it as the first property to market not only because it was extremely valuable but because Mrs. Helmsley had been its sole owner, so a sale wouldn't involve other owners pulling and tugging for their own interests. We interviewed New York City's top real estate brokerage firms before selecting one.

Selling the Park Lane isn't like selling your home.

First, there were enormous tax consequences. We got expert tax advice, too complicated (again) to recount here but resulting in income tax savings of potentially more than $200 million, plus state and local transfer tax savings of many tens of millions of dollars more. And you think you pay high taxes?

Next, though the Helmsleys had operated the Park Lane as a hotel, a developer might want to convert part of the hotel into condominium units. That would involve creating higher ceilings, adding floors to the top of the building, downsizing some of the lower floors to comply with zoning laws, and doing plenty of this and plenty of that, all involving legal, structural, and engineering analyses. This required more experts. We avoided hiring unnecessary experts, but expertise was necessary. This was not child's play.

After studies and analyses that would bring you to tears or sleep, the brokers produced an "offering memorandum"—a glossy book about the hotel, to be given to prospective buyers, with breathtaking prints of the hotel, market analyses of comparative properties, discussion of development opportunities, financial data, and the other details you probably asked for the last time you bought a property for hundreds of millions of dollars.

When you're selling an enormously valuable property such as the Park Lane, you don't set an asking price, you let the market set the price. We held a first round of bids and winnowed the contenders into a second round. The finalists were not simply folks who offered the most money, though that surely mattered a heap. Some people offer oodles of money without having the wherewithal to actually pay it. The bids couldn't have any mortgage contingency: If you don't have the money, don't bother.

We ultimately picked the most favorable bidder and began to negotiate sales documents. If you ever have trouble sleeping, ask to see those documents.

That was all happening by the last quarter of 2008. But by then the financial world had collapsed, and the high bidder's financial ability evaporated. We ended negotiations and took the Park Lane off the market. We could have made a quick sale for half a billion dollars, but in the world of big-time real estate, and since it will be a long time before any more land is created across the street from the southern border of Central Park, that wasn't enough.

Actually, we couldn't really take it off the market. We stopped actively marketing it, but the real estate world knew of the will's requirement that we sell, and knew that the Park Lane's off-market status was temporary. Phone calls and letters kept sporadically rolling in, and we just said no.

I experienced spurts of popularity. I'm a handshake person, but some folks now greeted me with hugs. Lawyers I hadn't spoken to in years called like old friends to say they had clients who'd be ideal purchasers of the hotel. Lawyers I'd never met sent me letters out of the blue, congratulating me on my fine work and asking if they could be of assistance. A lawyer in the music business who had referred several cases to me called to ask if Mrs. Helmsley owned any music copyrights he could help us sell.

Some enthusiasts seemed to think that an invitation for lunch could result in an inside track on one of the most valuable properties in Manhattan; I maintained my routine of a salad at my desk for lunch. One real estate developer I'd never met or spoken with talked his way past security guards in my building and announced to my office receptionist that he was here for our (nonexistent) appointment. A real estate broker I'd met years ago contacted me to say he had a great idea for the Park Lane—convert it into condominium units—as if that was an idea nobody else could possibly have thought of. The list goes on. . . .

The combination of big money and high visibility lured people to attack. Soon after Mrs. Helmsley died, I was contacted by a potpourri of strangers claiming entitlement to some of the money. All eventually went away except a woman I'd never met or heard of who claimed Mrs. Helmsley had promised her scads of money. Now, she wanted it. I took the same tack with her that I'd taken with the others: a polite "no" followed by ignoring follow-ups—why feed the flames?

That didn't work this time. The woman filed a $25 million dollar lawsuit against me and several other executors, pro se (fancy Latin for representing herself, without a lawyer), for not honoring what she claimed was Mrs. Helmsley's promise to her. The court threw out her case, but the lady was not deterred. She filed a second lawsuit seeking the same amount against me and this time added one other executor. The court also threw out that case. She then lowered her expectations and sued two of the other executors in small claims court, for $5,000 each. The court tossed that case. But the lady kept pressing us for money, sending me dozens of emails (which I have ignored) over many years, and she may never stop.

There were others like her, blissfully imagining a magic land where easy dollars drop from the sky. When their demand letters arrived, I put them in my "Nuts" file.

Half a year after Mrs. Helmsley's death, Tom, my lawyer, called to meet with me. He had recently become less accessible, but I hadn't complained. When he arrived at my office, he told me he was switching law firms and hoped I would continue to use him as my lawyer.

I asked why he was switching. He said his old firm had asked him to leave because they had discovered that over the past five years, he had charged, as expenses to his clients, $5,000 in personal car services used by his family. He said the firm was investigating his other expenses, but assured me there were no other false charges. All of his other clients were moving with him to his new firm, he said, and he hoped I would too.

I did not want to be represented by a lawyer who had cheated clients, but wanted to discharge him gently (after verifying that he hadn't cheated the estate). How? He wanted as few people as possible to learn about his situation. I told him that even if I were to agree to his continuing to represent me, I would owe a duty to my co-executors to tell them the situation, since eventually this behavior would reach the lawyers' grievance committee and become publicized, and the Trust could be tarnished by Tom's representing me. He said he'd rather not have me tell the others, and we agreed he'd resign from representing me. I retained another lawyer.

I didn't see or hear of Tom for several years, until one morning the *New York Law Journal* published a decision of the Appellate Division, the appeals court that oversees charges of lawyer misconduct, suspending Tom from practicing law for one year for improperly charging clients $50,000 in personal car-service rides for himself and his family for over a decade. Plainly, there'd been many more cockroaches in the kitchen.

Having withdrawn the Park Lane, we held off marketing the New York Helmsley and other hotel properties. In the meantime, we had to run the hotels and attempt to make money from their operations, rather than simply closing them down and waiting for the economy to turn.

Overseeing the operations of five New York City hotels was a challenge and an education. My co-executors knew no more than I did about running first-class hotels, or any class of hotels. The hotels employed 1,200 people, all of whom knew their jobs were in jeopardy because we would be selling the hotels. I'd managed my law firm of four others, tops, but this job was of a completely different order of magnitude. We entered into retention agreements with hundreds of employees, guaranteeing them salary and severance if they'd stay until the hotels were sold to make sure the hotels could operate profitably until we sold. What did I know about retention agreements with hotel employees? More after the first hundred than at the beginning.

Retaining employees was just the tip of the iceberg of what had to be done. Maintaining the reputation of first-class hotels so they can continue to attract guests willing to pay top rates required dealing with a river of other issues: reviewing budgets, maintaining performance, overseeing operations, making sure that the hotels remained A+ physically, and on and on. At the Park Lane, we evaluated renovation options and ultimately refurbished the lobby and upper floors—new wallpaper (selecting among high-end versus inexpensive), carpeting (ditto), bathroom upgrades (showerheads, sinks, faucets, rods, switches, toilet seats—there really are quite a few parts to a bathroom, and if they taught bathroomology at Harvard Law, I missed the course), electrical work, new mattresses and bedframes, communications equipment, buying new furniture or reupholstering the old, lamps, draperies, hallway upgrades—you name it.

We made improvements to the hotel's facade. In everything, we weighed cost against potential return: whether the financial outlays would be recouped through increased room rates and ultimate sale of the hotel.

We converted Mrs. Helmsley's penthouse duplex apartment into one of New York's highest-priced suites. We had to evaluate the poor financial performance of the magnificent second floor restaurant overlooking Central Park, where Mrs. Helmsley had held court for years, and shortened its hours of operations to minimize the financial bleeding. At the New York Helmsley, we oversaw a multi-million-dollar lobby renovation, and the renovation of 345 hotel rooms and the fitness center. I was as equipped to oversee all this as the man in the moon.

We had to be like Caesar's wife. The hotels (and all the estate's other assets) were the estate's, not ours. We had no more right than you did to its benefits. We owned and controlled the assets as fiduciaries, not as individuals. We instructed the managers of all Helmsley hotels—in writing—that no executor, and no family member of any executor, was permitted to use any hotel or hotel facility. We couldn't simply pay to use the hotels, we couldn't use them at all—not even a bottle of water. That way there could be no hidden discounts or benefits from employees seeking to please us. Mrs. Helmsley's executor-grandson Walter, when he'd come to New York for estate meetings from his home in South Dakota, could use a single room at one of the New York Helmsley hotels, which would be more economical that renting a room in another hotel. There was no other exception.

We dealt with issues you don't think about when checking into a hotel. The Park Lane had an agreement with The Leading Hotels Of The World, an international listing of the world's premier luxury hotels. To maintain our status, the organization insisted that the hotel undertake renovations that would have cost $27 million. We chose not to re-up.

The hotel workers' union was everywhere. The union even kept its eye on the thread count of new sheets, since a higher count could make each sheet slightly heavier and therefore require more strenuous lifting by the cleaning ladies. I was not used to such stuff. The number of threads on a sheet had never, ever crossed my mind. If I had to write legal papers, I wrote them, period, no matter how heavy the paper.

We didn't make major renovations at the other hotels because the costs wouldn't be worth the benefits—but even those decisions required extensive review of the hotels' operations. Though we hired expert hotel consultants to help, ultimately the decisions were ours. Lots of issues, lots of decisions, lots of money. After all, what in the world did I know about running hotels? About the same as the other executors knew. I learned as I went.

There was the occasional emergency. One afternoon, Harold and Abe, the estate's lawyer and accountant, rushed to my office frantically and reported that in an hour, the *New York Post* would be publishing an article devastating to the Helmsley name. The Iranian mission to the United Nations had booked a two-hundred-person banquet room at the New York Helmsley Hotel, one block from the UN, to be held in a week. Iran's anti-Semitic lunatic President Mahmoud Ahmadinejad was going to be the featured speaker. An organization named United Against Nuclear Iran had found out about the event and tipped off the *Post*.

None of the executors, and neither Harold nor Abe, had known of the booking. All I knew about it was that in an hour the *Post* would blast us across the front page. After a flurry of calls on phones held against both ears, I found out that an employee in the meetings department of the hotel had been approached two months earlier and routinely booked the reservation—without thinking that it might be controversial and that getting permission of, or at least notifying, corporate headquarters might be prudent.

Though the executors normally acted as a unit and not alone, time didn't permit convening everyone. The other executors knew of the situation and that I was dealing with it under enormous time pressure. Once I learned the facts, the decisions were not difficult. First, I told the hotel's general manager to cancel the event immediately and return the $20,000 deposit to the Iranian government. He did, posthaste. Second, I had to deal with the *Post*'s imminent story, which might still run despite the cancellation.

Instead of calling the *Post*, I called the head of the organization that had fed them the story. I said I was calling to thank him, and that my colleagues and I shared his organization's view of Ahmadinejad; told him we were grateful that he had called the booking to our attention because the employee who had allowed the engagement hadn't bothered notifying any of her bosses; and told him we'd canceled the booking and were returning the deposit. He thanked me for the thanks, and offered to notify the *Post* of the story's finale. I accepted the offer.

The following day, the *Post* ran a four-column headline "A'jad gets heave-ho from Helmsley Hotel," with a story describing how neither the Iranian mission nor Ahmadinejad was welcome at any Helmsley facility.

When Mrs. Helmsley signed her will, her brother Alvin was seventy-eight and had some medical problems. Over two years passed before she died, and then Alvin also began showing the deteriorations inevitable with age. Two of the other executors, David and Walter, were his nephews, with a natural family allegiance. I had to perform a balancing act. On the one hand, Alvin was Mrs. Helmsley's brother, and some deference seemed to be morally owed. On the other hand, I had been picked by Mrs. Helmsley to act as an executor of her estate and as a trustee of her charitable trust, and had a legal obligation, and a moral obligation to her, to do my best to ensure that the estate and the trust were administered competently. I had neither the luxury nor the legal right to be overly solicitous of Alvin simply because he was Mrs. Helmsley's brother.

As his deterioration progressed, I finally had to convince him and his wife—and a lawyer they retained—that it was time for him to step down as both an executor and a trustee. When my persuasive powers failed, I did what I know how to do: I drafted legal papers asking the court to remove Alvin, and let him know the papers were ready. It was an unpleasant duty, but a duty nonetheless. When he learned I had drafted the papers, Alvin resigned as an executor without my having to file them, and soon after resigned as a trustee. We were now down to four.

Four years after we withdrew the Park Lane from sale, the world had changed. The country was emerging from the Great Recession;

Lehman Bros., AIG, and other debacles were receding in the rear-view mirror; capital—money—was now available for investment; and the New York City real estate market had rebounded sharply.

During the intervening years, we had been actively involved with the hotel. We hired special zoning counsel and investigated alternate usage scenarios with the New York City Board of Standards and Appeals; we implemented technical changes in the Park Lane's corporate structure that saved the estate significant amounts of money; we oversaw the hotel's operations, making sure its hundreds of employees serviced clients instead of looking for new jobs; we dealt with a variety of union problems; we fielded and considered a steady patter of unsolicited offers from bidders who incorrectly sniffed that we were hungry sellers.

Finally, we again put the hotel on the market. Interest was tremendous. The ultimate buyer paid $660 million and assumed liabilities of an additional $45 million for a total sale value of over $705 million. This amount exceeded the hotel's initial appraised value, before the financial tsunami, by over $105 million—and far exceeded the highest bid in the first offering.

We also began to sell, as strategically as we could, a number of the estate's other real estate interests, analyzing each interest, and each interest's connections to other interests, in order to maximize return. Harry Helmsley had struck different partnership arrangements with real estate investors covering different properties at different times, the partners having different financial interests and different rights under each agreement for each property—a maze of entities and partnerships.

The chips we were playing with were immense. We ultimately sold the estate's interests in all the properties; in hindsight, we got good to terrific prices on all. The deals involved intricacies that weren't surprising since the stakes were so high; you'd nod off at the details of most. But:

The most fascinating for me was the sale of the estate's interest in the Empire State Building. You doubtlessly know: The Empire State Building is the world famous 102-story skyscraper located at Fifth Avenue and 34th Street in Manhattan. It was built in thirteen and a half months (about as long as it took a contractor to renovate my kitchen a few years ago) during the Great Depression; has nearly three million square feet of office and retail space; a world famous multi-floor observatory visited by four million people every year; and antenna facilities leased to broadcasting companies. The observatory generated over 42 percent of the building's revenues, and the broadcasting licenses over 8 percent—half the revenue came from the top of the building.

I've spared you the details of the ownership and management structures of Helmsley's interests in most of the properties. But let me feed you a bit of financial spinach involving the Empire State Building. It's interesting; stick with me; you'll get it.

In 1961, Harry Helmsley and a lawyer named Larry Wein bought control of the Empire State Building ("ESB"). They didn't actually buy the building or the land, but bought the right to manage ESB, operate it, rent it, and reap the profits for the next 114 years—effectively owning it during that time period. The price was $65 million.

(Wein was a highly skilled lawyer who invented the concept of real estate syndication. His name was familiar to me: He was the lawyer my father had introduced me to decades earlier, to convince me that going to Harvard Law School would be a better choice than postgraduate work in English.)

Much of the price for ESB was paid with other people's money. Here's a stick-figure outline of the financial structure.

Wein and Harry Helmsley—Larry and Harry—set up a partnership named ESB Associates and sold 3,300 participation units in that partnership for $10,000 apiece to members of the public, generating a total of $33 million. That's "syndication." Each of the unit-holders held only one or a few participation units.

ESB Associates would be simply a passive partnership—it wouldn't actually manage the building. Simultaneously with acquiring the long-term lease of the building, ESB Associates sub-leased the entire building to another partnership Larry and Harry set up named ESB *Company*—this one having just three partners. "Company" was established to operate the building—leasing office and retail space, collecting rent, operating the observatory, and generally managing the entire property.

The two tiers of ownership—Associates and Company—would share the profits on roughly a fifty-fifty basis. Associates' half would be split proportionately among the holders of its 3,300 units; and Company's half would be split among Company's owners. Harry Helmsley—and now the estate of Leona Helmsley—owned 63.75 percent of Company (fractions of a percent mean big money); Wein and others he represented owned 23.75 percent; and another investor owned the remaining 12.5 percent. So: Harry Helmsley owned 63.75 percent of 50 percent of a 114-year lease in the Empire State Building. That was essentially ownership of 31.875 percent of the building for 114 years—until 2076. Nobody else owned close to that. The estate of Leona Helmsley now owned Harry's 31.875 percent. Got it?

Larry and Harry had other substantial sources of revenue from ESB besides their ownership interests in ESB Company and right to share in the building's profits. Larry was the senior partner in a law firm, and that firm earned hefty legal fees incurred in running the building. Harry owned a major real estate management firm, Helmsley-Spear, which also made bundles of money managing, leasing, operating, and providing other services to the building.

Larry and Harry were old friends who made deals on a hand-shake and memorialized them in short, bare-bones agreements. Their partnership agreement for ESB Company—the contract that set forth the financial, management, and other rights for controlling the Empire State Building for 114 years—was eleven pages. Today, an agreement like that would run hundreds of thrilling pages, plus exhibits galore.

Larry and Harry had also acquired ownership or control of eight other major midtown Manhattan office buildings—some mammoth, some only extremely large. All told, those eight other buildings had an additional five-million square feet of office space. The nine buildings were marketed as the "W&H" properties. Three of them—ESB and two others—were subject to regulation by the Securities and Exchange Commission because they were publicly owned: syndicated to large numbers of investors who owned passive participation units. Harry and Larry controlled their other joint properties through private partnerships.

Wein died in 1988. After he died, his interests in the W&H properties were run by his son-in-law, Peter Malkin, who had worked with Wein for many years, and then by Peter and his son Tony Malkin, both indefatigable workers with sharp minds and total knowledge of the business.

When Harry Helmsley became incapacitated shortly after Wein died, Mrs. Helmsley took practical control of Harry's interests in the W&H properties. When Harry died, she inherited all of his interests in those properties, along with the rest of his estate.

The "Larry and Harry" relationship did not pass seamlessly to their successors. The skeletal contracts, adequate for two friends, were grossly inadequate to govern the frosty relationship between Mrs. Helmsley and the Malkins. Issues of management, control, and financial entitlement, which Larry and Harry had sorted out amicably for decades, resulted in seven major litigations pitting Mrs. Helmsley against the Malkins. I'd represented Mrs. Helmsley in a few. When she died, the Helmsley-Malkin relationship was, at best, very contentious.

Contractual provisions governing management and control of the W&H partnerships varied from building to building. Each building had its own ownership structure. The Malkins supervised all of the properties though we believed various of the contracts provided otherwise; and the Malkins controlled all the properties' books and records.

Selling the Empire State Building and the other W&H buildings, and splitting the proceeds in line with each partners' percentage interest in each property, would be ideal for the estate. But we had no right to force the Malkins to sell anything. Moreover, the Malkins had a contractual "right of first refusal" for the estate's interest in ESB: We couldn't sell the estate's interest without first offering the Malkins the opportunity to buy it at any price we were offered by anyone else. That provision would put a severe damper on any possible purchaser's interest in buying our rights, since any offer would be preceded by extensive due diligence, a time-consuming and expensive exercise that would be for naught if the Malkins simply chose to match the buyer's offer. Add to that the fact that the real estate and economic environment had plunged to disastrous depths, and you could see that we were in a bit of a pickle.

The Malkins knew we had to sell; they knew their right of first refusal would depress the price any prospective purchaser of our interest would be willing to pay; they knew a dispute over management rights would further depress the price; and they had a strong financial motive for exercising all of their leverage, since the best result for them would be to purchase our interests at bargain-basement prices. The Malkins were not shy and retiring, and when it came to Helmsley money neither was I, so we did some headbutting at the beginning.

With all the battles the Malkins and Mrs. Helmsley had fought after the end of the Larry-and-Harry duo, I had learned that the world of New York real estate operators was rife with people you or the Malkins wouldn't want to do business with. The devil you know is better than the devil you don't know. We knew who the Malkins would regard as ogres they'd never want to be partners with—including Donald Trump, who'd previously unsuccessfully attempted a takeover of the building years earlier, and his ilk—and they knew we knew. Each side had the capacity to inflict harm on the other—sort of the real estate equivalent of superpowers with the ability to inflict unacceptable damage on each other.

We knew what they knew we knew they knew, etc. and vice versa. Both sides began the dance by discussing a possible sale of the Empire State Building. Analysis required my immersion into the entire financial structure and operations of the building, a formidable job for someone taking a crash course in Real Estate 101. The estate owned the major interest in the longterm operating sublease; the Malkins controlled the direct lease and, through a purchase they had made as agents for the public participants during Mrs. Helmsley's lifetime, the land and the building.

Both sides considered selling the building, and that would involve allocating the purchase price among the different tiers of ownership and control. In assessing which tier of ownership was more valuable—the sublease and management tier, in which the Helmsley estate owned a 63.75 percent interest, or the master lease and ownership tier, in which the estate's interest was minuscule—shifting a single percentage point of value in either direction would involve reallocating tens of millions of dollars. In considering options, each side hired its own appraisal expert and—surprise, surprise—each expert's opinion favored the side that paid for its services. Eventually, real life took over: the real estate market and economy crashed, and sale of the building became economically unwise.

Both sides were now left to joust over control of the buildings.

We argued that the partnership agreement for ESB, sparse as it was, gave Helmsley shared rights with the Malkins over management and leasing decisions. They said no, that they had sole control, and pointed to years of inactivity by Mrs. Helmsley in the building's operations. We said that didn't matter: the contract says what it says, and it says we've got shared control. The issue involved potentially hundreds of millions of dollars: The value of the estate's interest would be worth far less if it simply was a passive income stream rather than including management, leasing, and other control rights.

Litigating against the Malkins over that issue would be expensive, time-consuming, and filled with headaches and uncertainties. But the issue was worth enormous sums of money. I'd learned long ago that asserting a legal position forcefully often results in not having to litigate it at all; you can achieve a good resolution without the need to actually wrestle in court by simply showing seriousness of purpose coupled with a legitimate legal position and the ability to fight ably and for as long as necessary.

I knew how to assert our position forcefully and to draft a compelling set of legal papers. But I was now wearing several hats: practicing lawyer, co-executor, and a co-trustee of the charitable trust which would eventually receive whatever money the estate received. Litigating over control of the Empire State Building and other valuable properties would be a full-time job requiring a large legal team, and it was important for our potential adversaries to recognize that we had the manpower to attack full bore. So we retained a superb lawyer from a highly regarded large firm with whom I'd worked over the years and would continue to work with on the Empire State Building matter —there would be no question that the estate had the wherewithal to go to war if necessary. The Malkins also hired first-rate lawyers.

We'd have regular meetings at the Malkins' large conference

room on the 48th floor of One Grand Central Plaza: Business people and real estate lawyers discussing, litigation lawyers arguing, each side knowing the other's arguments, concerns, vulnerabilities, constraints. We reached agreement on some issues of control of ESB, but the big questions—would the Malkins be able to buy the estate's interests cheaply, would the estate sell its interests to someone the Malkins wanted no part of—still loomed. So we'd sit and discuss, continually, until:

A solution emerged. Essentially, ESB and the other W&H properties would be bundled together, along with twelve unrelated Malkin-controlled properties in the New York City metropolitan area, into a single entity: A "REIT" (or Real Estate Investment Trust). Shares in the REIT would be offered to the public in an "IPO" (Initial Public Offering) and would be sold on the New York Stock Exchange. The Malkins would operate the REIT, and the Helmsley estate would be able to cash out at full market value by selling its shares to the public in the IPO.

Sounds simple, right? The cost for lawyers, accountants, appraisers, investment bankers, registration and filing fees to government agencies, printing, and other expenses: Pick any large number and then triple it. We had no end of meetings with the Malkins; negotiated veto rights over the entire transaction if the final result didn't suit us; worked with expert after expert; resolved knotty issues with accountants and lawyers; addressed tax issues; and fought over property valuations in order to maximize the amount the estate, and ultimately the charitable trust, would receive. We had to agree on relative values of twenty-one properties, and of different ownership tiers within many of those properties; had weekly conference calls with the Malkins and their battery of advisors; and dealt with voluminous issues.

Added to this mix was the fact that three of the properties, including ESB, were partly owned by publicly registered entities involving thousands of participants, and the Malkins were therefore required to submit numerous filings, amendments, and assorted other documents to the SEC, all of which required discussion and review with us. It was over three and a half years of heavy lifting, not for the faint of heart.

Periodically, Tony Malkin would call to meet with me and we'd resolve some problem that had come up; just two businessmen sitting together, quietly solving some conundrum, without playing to any audience. Tony and I had occasionally been at loggerheads, punctuated with heated words, until we began working toward a common objective. After the transaction had been brewing for over a year and we were shooting at the same goal, he needed to discuss an issue and tracked me down in the middle of the Negev, Israel's desert. A year ago you wouldn't take my calls, he began; now I can reach you in the middle of the desert—really good progress.

World events were viewed through the prism of their possible effect on the IPO. Would Middle East turmoil affect ESB, frightening people away; or how successfully would the new observatory planned for the top of the nearly completed new World Trade Center compete with the ESB observatory; or would the wild gyrations of the stock market affect the IPO itself?

The transaction moved forward at a glacier-like pace. Every move had complications, and the complications had complications. As we approached the finish line, a new set of obstacles arose: A battery of lawyers brought six lawsuits, including class actions on behalf of public participants in the properties subject to SEC regulation, claiming they were being shortchanged by the transaction and seeking to block it. They alleged that the protracted, expensive, and hard-fought pulling and tugging that had resulted in the valuations of each of the properties, and tiers within properties, had been rigged. They tried to enjoin completion of the transaction, asked for recovery of enormous damages against the Malkins, and for good measure threw in the Helmsley estate as a defendant. The lawsuits demanded substantial reallocations of relative values ascribed to many of the properties, and particularly the value attributed to the tier of ownership in ESB in which Helmsley held its interest. If successful, the cost to the estate would be astronomical.

The greatest beneficiaries of class action lawsuits such as these are often the lawyers. We knew that, and danced the necessary minuet with them. We gave voluminous voluntary disclosure to the teams of plaintiffs' lawyers—an endless stream of documents. This permitted the plaintiffs' lawyers to determine that the process we'd been pursuing had indeed been fair, while at the same time allowing them to spend countless hours—but they counted them— in order to justify a tremendous fee they'd ask the court to set when the cases would finally settle.

From everybody's vantage point the cases had to settle—in reality, everyone was rowing toward the same objective but with different interests. If the suing participants blocked the transaction, they would be depriving themselves of the ability to sell their own investments, and those investments would therefore remain illiquid. Most important, the plaintiffs' lawyers, who were handling the cases on a contingency fee basis, would not receive a large fee unless the transaction went ahead; if they were to actually block the transaction, there'd be no big money trough. From the Helmsley and Malkin perspectives, if the transaction tanked, tremendous costs that had already been incurred would be lost. Moreover, if the litigations continued for more than a few months, market conditions and other economic circumstances might have scuttled the entire transaction, and the estate would have been back to square one, arguing with the Malkins over who had what rights, and saddled with disposing of real estate interests that were highly illiquid and of indeterminate worth. If the transaction went through, the estate would get a staggering amount. Settling was imperative.

My grandmother, Enny, who used to throw down sandwiches to me when I played in the lot behind 690 Gerard Avenue in the Bronx, had an expression: Sometimes a dollar is a penny, and a penny a dollar. We—the combined Malkin and Helmsley interests—settled the class actions for a total of $55 million—chicken feed, if you'll pardon the phrase in this context, compared to the estate's loss if forced back to selling its illiquid interests and uncertain contractual positions. The transaction proceeded. The plaintiffs' class actions lawyers got $11.6 million of the settlement money. They were big winners—not an unusual outcome in such matters.

The culmination was a bell-ringing ceremony on the trading floor of the New York Stock Exchange, with Empire State Realty Trust as a publicly traded REIT and $879 million going to the Helmsley Charitable Trust. We'd come a long way from warring antagonists to everybody-wins capitalists. And that's how come, as I'm writing, you can own a piece of the Empire State Building and its sibling buildings for $11.76 a share.

There's only one Empire State Building; everything else is relatively small potatoes. But many of the small potatoes were huge—huge—buildings.

Harry Helmsley had won big at Monopoly and had a building in every space. Our job was now to dismantle the entire empire—every brick. We took our time, waited for the economy and the real estate market to emerge from recession, disregarded the admonition that we couldn't be criticized if we'd just unload all the properties right away, and made some big sales. Here's a tasting:

- The New York Helmsley was a 773-room hotel which the estate owned through a web of legal entities. It had outdated heating, air-conditioning, and electrical systems, and union problems. We sold it for $313.5 million.

- The Carlton House is a 161-room hotel on Madison Avenue and 61st Street in Manhattan. The estate didn't own the building, but owned the operating leasehold—the right to occupy and lease the building to others—until the year 2169. Because of contractual issues in the lease with the owner, the appraised value of the estate's interest when Mrs. Helmsley died was $44 million. We negotiated out those deficiencies with the owner, and sold our interest for $166 million.

- The estate was a major owner of the 193-room Middletowne Hotel and an adjacent apartment building in midtown Manhattan. The hotel was losing money. The co-owners were sophisticated real estate operators who knew of our legal obligation to sell our interest and raised every conceivable impediment, to force us to sell to them at a deep discount. We sent them a draft of a lawsuit we threatened to file, and induced them to pay the estate $41.6 million.

- The estate owned a 50 percent interest in partnerships owning two large apartment houses on the upper east side of Manhattan. The partnerships sold both buildings, and our take was over $220 million.

- The estate owned a one-third interest in a large office building at 1001 Sixth Avenue in Manhattan. We outwaited a series of operating problems that time and an improving economy cured, and sold our interest for more than $41 million.

- The estate owned an interest in an apartment building at 575 Park Avenue. We sold our interest for $36 million.

- We sold Mrs. Helmsley's Dunnellen Hall mansion for $35 million.

The list goes on: $10 million for the estate's interest in a 185-unit apartment building in midtown Manhattan; over $7 million for the estate's interest in a retail condominium of stores and a garage in midtown; $9.5 million for the estate's interest in a commercial building in the Bronx a few blocks from where I'd grown up; over $11 million for the estate's interest in garden apartment buildings in Houston, Texas; $24 million for the estate's interests in six properties leased to Walmart scattered throughout the United States; $2.3 million for the estate's 12 percent interest in another Manhattan office building; $10 million for the estate's interest in a multibuilding warehouse and office complex in Passaic, New Jersey; $7.5 million for the estate's interest in two apartment buildings in Florida; other buildings in Manhattan and Florida for millions; and many more. Issues were resolved, problems navigated, partners dealt with, sales negotiated, and the money kept pouring in—none without considerable work, effort, and angst.

One of the last properties we sold was the Sandcastle Hotel in Sarasota, Florida where Mrs. Helmsley had first asked me to draft a will for her. The Florida real estate market recovered very slowly from the Great Recession. We held off selling for years, and finally decided to test the waters in early 2011, more than three years after Mrs. Helmsley's death. Experts advised that we'd get $14 million at best, even at that late stage. So we continued to delay a sale, instead keeping the hotel's operations going. We finally sold it three more years later for $45 million.

My crash course in real estate was coming to an end. The money from these sales was given to The Leona M. and Harry B. Helmsley Charitable Trust. Harry Helmsley had devoted his life to building a real estate empire, Mrs. Helmsley had helped nurture it, and we had dismantled it—over $5 billion-worth—all for the public good. Now, let me tell you about that.

building a real estate empire, Mrs. Helmsley had helped nurture it, and we had dismantled it—over $5 billion worth—all for the public good. Now, let me tell you about that

Chapter 11

Giving Billions Away

So you think giving away billions of dollars, while juggling other billions, is easy?

Trying a major case is far more stressful, for sure. Construction, bricklaying, coal mining, fire fighting—all heavy lifting, and far harder. Giving away money is mostly indoor work. But you don't give away billions of dollars by just writing out some checks.

I had no background in philanthropy, and was starting from scratch. Early on, I wrote to Bill Gates. I'd never met him, and I sent him a cold-call four-sentence letter saying I'd just become a trustee of a multi-billion dollar charitable trust and would like to meet with him, any time and any place, for guidance on what I should and shouldn't do, and how to avoid blunders. I FedEx'd the letter so whoever sorted his mail might notice it.

A few days later, I received a call from Patty Stonesifer. She had headed the Gates Foundation since its inception a decade earlier when it operated out of a small office over a pizza parlor in

Redmond, Washington. For many years before, she'd held high-level technology and executive positions at Microsoft.

Patty met with me for lunch in New York. She shared her experiences in helping establish, build, and operate by far the largest private philanthropy in the world. I asked her to meet with my co-trustees, and she immediately agreed to. In exchange, she and Gates asked for nothing. No charge, nothing expected in return.

In my world of litigation, that simply didn't happen. You fight an adversary to the end, or until you beat him into a weak negotiating position. There's a give-and-take, but rarely—I'm tempted to say never—does one simply give something for nothing. There's always a quid pro quo—no quid, no quo. My first lesson in philanthropy was the opposite: Philanthropy involves giving, with no expectation of anything in return other than the wise and productive use of what's given. There's a world of difference between lawyering and philanthropy.

I had no experience in philanthropy, and neither did my co-trustees. Fate and Mrs. Helmsley's anointment had put us in this lovely spot. Each of us had to decide where the Trust's enormous pot of money could do the world good; Mrs. Helmsley had left it all in our hands, without directing any money to any specific charity. We were painting on a vast empty canvas, with a palette of infinite colors.

We weren't a group of friends or colleagues with common interests, backgrounds, values, or passions, but very different people whom Mrs. Helmsley had thrust together to do the best we could to—if you'll pardon the hyperbole—help the human race. And we had to act together as a unit; we were not separate trusts.

We were in charge of the whole shebang. We had to create, from inception, an organization that would responsibly dole out a vast fortune, beginning with nothing but money—no staff, no knowledge, no expertise, no philanthropic experience. Out of the blue, we were suddenly responsible for more money than I could imagine. We had to set up program areas, hire staff, establish policies, procedures, and strategies, ensure effective grant-making, develop by-laws, create a financial structure for the prudent investment of billions of dollars, establish budgets, set up internal controls, set compensation levels for staff, ensure the honest and ethical handling of these extraordinary sums, comply with a sea of legal and regulatory requirements, and . . . and. . . . This wasn't just a new legal case coming in the door; we were setting up a multi-billion dollar charitable business. My life's experience was my only operating manual for the new responsibilities and opportunities given to me by an angry, resentful, lost, lonely woman of unimaginable wealth.

I was also determined to continue practicing law. I'd trained too long, had developed some ability in the profession, and saw no reason to give it up. And I haven't.

Here I was, after decades practicing law, in a position to help determine where billions of dollars should be spent, and with no guidepost other than to have a real impact on helping people. That sounds general.

It was. I'd grown used to fighting legal battles mano a mano, and now there'd be a seismic shift in my frame of reference: no longer trying to win or to subdue an adversary, but simply to do good. And how does one "do good" when the choices encompass all the opportunities in the world? What would *you* do?

There are no training camps for inexperienced newly-appointed trustees of newly-operative multi-billion-dollar philanthropies. But I was surprised to learn that there are organizations that teach charitable organizations how to do their job and help them begin doing it. Although other philanthropies have used their services, we were unique. Philanthropies our size don't suddenly materialize every Monday and Thursday. Yesterday we had nothing, and virtually overnight we had billions. We would soon be one of the largest private philanthropies in the world, and the organizations we interviewed to guide us were all eager for the catch.

We settled on Rockefeller Philanthropy Advisors, a New York City non-profit organization. Rockefeller's roots extended back over a century to John D. Rockefeller Sr., who decided to run his philanthropy as if it were a business.

Each trustee brought his own interests and background to the common table. I thought long and hard about program areas I might create, and what I'd like to accomplish. It wasn't easy to decide: Try it yourself. The goal isn't just to write out checks in large amounts, but where you can do real good. We're not talking about thousands of dollars here, or hundreds of thousands, or millions, or tens of millions. We're talking, over time, about amounts of money difficult to fathom.

I thought of the charitable contributions that I personally made. Probably like you, every year I receive dozens of envelopes with form solicitations from charities. My assistant files them away until the end of the year, then sorts them and gives them to me rubber-banded in stacks, categorized: cancer, blindness, general medical, poverty, Jewish causes, veterans organizations, others.

I mentally sorted through those stacks. All were plainly worthy, or I wouldn't accumulate their envelopes each year. Which were the most important to me? Where could the Trust make the greatest impact?

As my thoughts began to crystallize, I talked them through with Ruthie, and then met with the president of Rockefeller. I told her there were two programs I'd like to set up and lead for the Trust, and wanted her views on my choices.

First, I said, was a health-related program. My thickest set of year-end rubber-banded envelopes were cancer and blindness. I supposed that those causes were already the subject of tremendous amounts of charitable giving, and a Helmsley Trust program in either area probably wouldn't make much of a dent. She agreed.

I told her that someone extremely dear to me had Crohn's disease, a chronic inflammatory condition of the gastrointestinal tract. Crohn's seemed like a discrete disease where substantial funding could in fact make a difference. Millions of people suffer from the disease. In the metaphor du jour, we might be able to move the needle in Crohn's research, helping to find the cause of the disease, funding the development of new diagnostics and therapeutics, and eventually helping discover a cure.

A second program I wanted to establish was support of Israel, a country to which I had deep and abiding ties, and without which Judaism would be in peril and the Holocaust could recur. What a privilege it would be to help contribute to the continued development and security of the country—for that country's benefit, for the United States, and for humanity in general. Thus was born the Trust's Israel program.

I would be the lead trustee of both the Crohn's and Israel programs, and two were enough. The goal was to have real impact, and aiming in too many directions would dilute our impact on any of them. We were in a position to achieve significant results by concentrated effort in highly focused areas, and I'd shoot for that.

The other trustees established their own priorities. One co-trustee, David Panzirer, a grandson of Mrs. Helmsley, has a young daughter who'd recently been diagnosed with type 1 diabetes; he wanted to devote his life to trying to find therapies, and ways to make life better for those suffering from the disease. His half brother Walter, whom Mrs. Helmsley had also appointed a trustee, lived in South Dakota and had seen the shortcomings of rural healthcare; he wanted to build a program to remedy that situation in rural communities throughout the United States, and then extend it elsewhere in the world. Codey's professed interests were healthcare and conservation. Alvin was less focused.

With Rockefeller's help, we each presented strategic plans—written frameworks of our objectives and how we proposed to achieve them. None of us would have unilateral power to give away money. Every program would have a staff; all proposed grants would be thoroughly vetted by that staff; those that passed muster would be fully described in a written recommendation submitted to the other trustees for consideration; and all trustees would vote on all proposed grants at formal meetings. No grant could be given by any single trustee—a majority vote is required, with the recommending trustee or his staff answering any questions the others might have. Each of us would be lead trustee, with primary oversight and responsibility, for the programs each brought to the table.

I decided, as did several of the others, to serve in more than a trustee's traditional role. The usual practice, I learned, is for trustees to meet every few months, review recommendations of the staff, say yes or no, give instructions to the staff, and generally oversee the Trust. That is not what I chose to do. The opportunity was too awesome, and my background and training too controlling, to passively take a backseat. I decided to actively involve myself in the Crohn's and Israel programs, and help run the foundation, on a daily basis. I'd split my time between my law practice, the estate, and the Trust, figuring time would expand for whatever became necessary. The opportunity to achieve important results was once-in-a-lifetime, and I couldn't pass it up.

The dollars would be staggering.

The Dollars

By the end of our first full year of operations, the Trust had received more than $2.2 billion from Mrs. Helmsley's estate. The precise figure was $2,267,531,657. Rounding the number down ignores $67,531,657. It's hard to get used to ignoring over $67 million in a round-off.

Rounded or not, we had to dole out a lot of money, quickly and responsibly. The law required both.

Charitable foundations don't just give grants when they feel like it. The Helmsley Charitable Trust is a "private foundation"—a non-profit, nongovernmental organization set up for charitable purposes and receiving all of its support from one "person," the estate of Leona Helmsley. Basically (there are of course complexities, since the IRS is involved), a private foundation is legally required to make annual charitable distributions equal to 5 percent of its previous year's assets (some expenses count toward the 5 percent), with latitude for the first year of operations. So a charitable trust with $8 billion in assets—the amount in the Trust as I write—is required to pay out $400 million annually. The best way to fathom that number is in small pieces: that's over $1 million per day if we were to pay equal amounts every day during the year, Monday through Sunday, no time off for holidays or weekends. Or look at it another way:

Pick a random number that seems generous by normal standard—say, $20,000. If we gave our required annual minimum in grants of $20,000 each, we'd have to give 20,000 grants per year— or an average of about seventy-five $20,000 grants *every workday*. Here's another way to look at it: Suppose we converted the money to cash—greenbacks—and kept it all under a pillow, without investing a penny—no interest, no dividends, no capital gains, nothing but principal. If we simply gave out $20,000 every workday, it would take over 1,500 years for the money to be gone. You can get the exact figure with a calculator and a lot of calendars.

Our aim would be for large impact with large grants, not scattershots. And we had the opportunity to take risks—measured and thought-out—where the opportunity for significant impact was worth the risk.

For decades as a lawyer, I'd been fighting to get money for clients, or prevent others from getting my clients' money. Now, I had an obligation to give money to others, in hard-to-imagine amounts, thoughtfully and responsibly. Lawyering one minute and philanthropizing the next required a radical change in attitude.

Plenty of people came asking for money. Rather than trying to please and persuade judges, hoping to avoid their displeasure and chuckling appreciatively at their humor, I was no longer the supplicant. Strange what money can do. One cynic put it best: A foundation is a large body of money completely surrounded by people who want some.

We give it out carefully. All of our grants are supported by detailed budgets provided by the applying institution: how much for whom to do what; how much for construction, what are the elements, what does each piece of scientific or medical equipment cost, how many assistants will we be paying for and what will each be doing, how much will each person receive, who'll be travelling where and for what, and the like. Even if it's not down to the last pencil, we always know what we are paying for, in detail. And we have a Trust-wide policy designed to make sure we pay for results and not to help other charitable institutions sustain themselves; not more than 10 percent of any grant can be used for administrative expenses of the receiving organization.

We don't just dole out money, accept a "thank you," and walk away. We become our grantees' partner. They account to us not only financially (which assuredly they do), but also in terms of the particular project's progress. We interact with them after the money leaves our coffers, follow what they're doing, understand

and help with problems they may be having. We've got the luxury of being able to focus on how our money is being spent, without our time and attention being diverted by a need to fund-raise. We're a private philanthropy with enough money, thank you, and can concentrate on each program's goals, and the role of each grant in helping satisfy the goals.

Many of the applicants for money are highly respected institutions, ideal candidates for grants in our program areas, but a constant flow of people are decidedly not. Some people approach me about a favorite charity; could the Trust contribute? A friend's father was an on-staff doctor at a hospital; could the hospital get some money? Someone taught at a college; would the Trust give some money there? A lawyer had a client involved in rescuing horses; would we consider grants for horses? A charity wants to buy a building instead of renting; could we help? A client wanted funding for a business venture; could it qualify as a charity? Someone wants us to invest in a new brand of gluten-free kosher vodka sold in a uniquely designed bottle; or a college scholarship or some help through financial difficulties; or money to help find a job, or to travel for research, or to pay the mortgage and taxes on a home. A friend has a friend. . . . An accountant has a client. . . . You've got billions; why can't you just give a little to my favorite place?. . . . Just passing through New York, would love to stop by and say hello. . . . I'm having lunch with a friend, and he casually reaches into a breast pocket and says "Oh, by the way"—as if he's just thought of it—and out comes a proposal. Or a stranger writes to say he's contacting me "at the suggestion of the Prime Minister's Office," and when I respond by asking "Who in particular?" the writer vanishes.

In Rockefeller's offices, I saw a photo of John D. Rockefeller standing next to an oil gusher. The thought struck me: I'd become an oil gusher.

There's a price to pay for such perceived control of so much money: People no longer see you for who you are, but for what they think you can give them.

In the courtroom, lawyers are always "Your Honor"ing, trying to ingratiate themselves with a judge to get an edge. My role changed from genuflector to genuflectee. My personal lodestar for avoiding the disease of genuflectitis is to remember, always: It's not me, it's the money; remember who you are.

Some charitable foundations have limited life spans. The founder may want to see all the money spent in his or her lifetime, or within a few years following the founder's death. Others, including Mrs. Helmsley, direct that the foundation live in perpetuity. She said so in the document she signed which set up the Trust.

"Perpetuity" is a long time. It was too long for Codey.

When Mrs. Helmsley died, Codey was sixty-nine years old. I was sixty-four, David thirty-eight, and Walter thirty-one. Under the document establishing the Trust, there will be no other trustee until only one of us is still alive. The last man standing must then appoint a corporation—since corporations theoretically live forever—which will be the sole trustee after all of the original trustees have gone on to their next adventure. The Trust's designated life span is forever.

The actuarial odds of David or Walter being the survivor are very high. Codey was not satisfied with us giving 5 percent per year of the Trust's money. At the time, each of us was responsible as lead trustee for grants totaling over $50 million per year in our fields of interest, along with oversight responsibility for grants of another $200 million or so (the numbers have grown considerably since then). But if the Trust were not required to last in perpetuity but were to be spent down in a fixed number of years—say, the lifetimes of the four remaining trustees appointed by Mrs. Helmsley—then we'd be giving away billions of dollars in a few quick, gigantic chunks, comfortably over $1.3 billion per man. That could convert a suddenly very popular and powerful person into an even more suddenly popular and powerful person. It would also minimize the likely fact that Codey would have nothing to do with the eventual appointment of a permanent trustee, since by then the money would be largely gone.

Codey asked me several times to join him in claiming that Mrs. Helmsley did not intend for the Trust to last in perpetuity, but I'd refer him to the language of the document establishing the Trust. You'd think that each of us already having responsibility for so much money would be enough, right? Especially for folks whose experience with philanthropy, until a few years ago, had been arranging solicitation envelopes into piles to make year-end contributions. When is enough enough?

Codey buttonholed me one day and made his final pitch; I paraphrase, but it's real close:

"We both knew Leona closely," he said to me. "You were alone with her when she signed her will and the document establishing the Trust. I can just imagine her saying to you: I know the five people I've named as executors and trustees, and I want them to be the only ones to give away my money; I don't trust anyone else, and I certainly don't want some stranger I've never met having anything to do with it. Sandy," Codey concluded, "can't you just hear her saying that to you?"

"Yes," I answered. "I can certainly imagine it. The problem is that it didn't happen."

That was the last time Codey broached the subject. Perpetuity outlasted him a few years later. Just the two grandsons and I now run the Trust.

Here's how we deal with all that money.

To achieve the goal of lasting into perpetuity, the Trust's money has to be carefully and successfully invested. Experts we consulted projected an annual rate of 2.4 percent inflation over the near future. Adding that to the 5 percent legally required annual minimum payouts in grants, the Trust's money had to achieve roughly a 7.4 percent return to retain its purchasing power into the near future. As inflation would vary over time, our financial resources and requirements would change—the ultimate goal being to achieve a rate of return necessary to maintain the Trust's beginning real value into perpetuity after giving away 5 percent each year.

Investing billions of dollars requires financial expertise, and handling that amount imprudently can have really bad ramifications—including the trustees being held financially liable for miscues. Over the years, I'd met folks in the financial industries, and several called to offer their services when they learned of my new position. In fact, several I'd never met offered their services—I'd instantaneously developed a broad and brand-new circle of financial friends.

Responsible investment of this fortune required the best and the brightest, and we undertook the search for those. Because of the vast initial transfer of money from the estate to the Trust, we couldn't dilly-dally. We interviewed several large institutions. Their top executives came to see us, as we would be a catch for any. I wasn't particularly used to being courted by big banks, but it's something that a person can get used to. Ultimately we concluded that JPMorgan was best in class, and retained them for financial guidance during our start-up phase.

We could not, of course, be gamblers. Our financial needs would be substantial and continual. We needed to maintain sufficient liquidity—available cash—not only to pay for the operations of the Trust itself, but to pay out the grants. Making a grant is a formal process: After it is awarded, we present the grantee with a written contract, obligating the grantee to spend the money as agreed and account to us periodically, but also obligating us to pay the money, usually over a period of years. We set up a three-year limit for ourselves on the life of any grant.

When the time would come for us to pay out the money in years two and three, we had to make sure we had enough ready cash available; making a grant is voluntary, but making the payments after signing the grant agreement is a legal obligation. For a trust that would be paying out grants totaling over a quarter of a billion dollars every year, making sure we retained sufficient liquidity wasn't a back-of-the-envelope calculation. If we didn't have the money to pay our obligations, legal havoc would ensue—it didn't matter that we were a philanthropy, or that we were giving the money away for nothing.

With so much money at stake, we plainly needed immediate full-time in-house investment guidance, and were lucky enough to find an expert who was about to retire as Chief Investment Officer of the Ford Foundation, where she'd served in various investment capacities for nearly thirty years. We established a seven-person investment committee to independently review JPM's recommendations regularly and hold formal meetings quarterly at which JPM would report in detail regarding proposed investment decisions. With the professionals' recommendations, my co-trustees and I determined asset allocations: the range, in percentage terms, of what could be invested in cash or fixed income, equities (large-, mid-, small-cap, international, sector, cyclical, defensive, value, growth, blend, emerging markets, you-name-it), and alternative investments (hedge funds, hard assets, private equity—we had no need for outside real estate investments, in view of our large real estate holdings). Five of the investment committee members were pros—people with real financial background and experience, capable of meaningfully reviewing JPM's performance and recommendations. They served without fee. As a substitute for compensation, we allowed each to recommend to us grants of $50,000 per year for the Trust to give to their designated charities.

The other two members of the committee were my co-trustee David and me. Neither of us had a background in finance or investing that would permit us to meaningfully contribute to the investment committee's meetings or decisions. But the smooth and effective functioning of the investment process was essential to the Trust, and I wanted to be in the mix even if my contribution wasn't much. I read the materials, attended the meetings, and did the best I could. This was a whole new world for me: valuations, inflation sensitivity, frontier markets, macroeconomic factors, liquidity risk mitigation, private versus public markets, risk, volatility, credit spreads, deleveraging, mean variance optimization, hedge fund strategies, structured investments, projected payouts, liquidity tiers, detailed analyses of fund investments, alpha, beta, everything but gimmel, investing hundreds of millions of dollars at a clip—it was big-money stuff.

We grew from zero dollars to several billion in a flash, and added tens and hundreds of millions of dollars at a pop. We weren't just building an airplane while it was flying, but juggling fine china at the same time.

Eventually, we built a full-time investment staff in-house. We hired a chief investment officer and experts in alternative investments, public markets, risk, and associated areas—a twelve-person full-time investment department with expertise, able to dig deeply and knowledgeably into prospective investments. The large amounts of money flowing in—well over half-a-billion dollars at a time when we sold the Park Lane and our interest in the Empire State Building—had to be invested wisely and prudently; but if it wasn't invested reasonably quickly, large potential earnings would evaporate; but if it wasn't invested smartly, we could lose principal; but if. . . .

Because of the size of the Trust and its investment portfolio, we have access to deal opportunities—among the best of the best—unavailable to ordinary folks. When the investment staff recommends an investment, they write a detailed defense of the recommendation: the reasons for the Trust to invest in it, the terms, risks, return expectations, the people behind the investment, how the investment fits within our overall investment strategy, regulatory and other legal issues, analysis of co-investors, and many other factors. When an opportunity requires speedier decision than our quarterly meetings permit, we convene on short notice via conference call. The investment committee reviews the staff's recommendations, questions the staff, and votes on the staff's proposals. The vast majority are approved because of the staff's thorough investigation before submitting a recommendation. When you're investing tens or hundreds of millions of dollars at a clip, analysis is not done loosey-goosey.

Getting a grip on the Trust's finances wasn't simply a matter of learning to say "millions" instead of "hundreds" or "thousands." We established written policies and procedures. We also had to plan for worst-case scenarios. How do we prevent our computer systems—for investments, grants, management, and more—from being hacked? What if the financial markets collapse—the investment staff subjected our finances to various "stress tests." We obtained a multi-hundred-million dollar line of credit—in case a market collapse were to strip us of our ability to honor our grant commitments, or would otherwise force us to sell into a plummeting market. And what if, in a worst-case scenario, the banks wouldn't honor the line of credit and lend us the money, even if we'd paid the premiums? How does one plan for uncharted potential economic catastrophe?

Carefully. The severe financial impact of the coronavirus crashed harshly on many foundations, severely impacting their ability to honor their grant commitments and make new grants, and hurting philanthropies that depended on donors who stopped donating when the economy swooned. But our investment team hadn't swung for the fences, instead managing our billions prudently so that we had safe and liquid assets available to continue grant-making without interruption even if the plague were to last for several years. Without shooting for the stars, we had assumed the right amount of risk to generate returns adequate to pay our grant obligations and make new ones, without having to do any cutting back or jeopardizing our mandate to last until perpetuity.

Over the years, I'd taught myself some basic principles of value investing and had learned that the four most dangerous words in the world of investing are "This time is different." Now I learned a new dangerous phrase: "We're not expecting any surprises." When you're responsible for managing billions of dollars, surprises are the last item you want on the menu.

Finding and hiring a talented investment team, and then overseeing but not interfering with them doing their job, has resulted in some fortunate financial alchemy. Sales of all of Leona Helmsley's assets generated roughly $5.4 billion; we've given away (as I write) $3 billion (hard to believe); and our remaining assets total $8 billion. How's that for arithmetic?

The Trust also grew quickly in other areas. We established departments of finance and operations, hired a CEO, an in-house legal counsel, and outside auditors, and set up a grants management team and a communications department. We needed to have cyber experts to protect our computer systems—hackers would love to figure out how we direct large amounts of money so they can misdirect some in their direction. We had become a large operation, with one hundred people in-house plus a raft of outside consultants, far from the modest law firm I was used to running.

Because we are essentially a tax-free organization (except for a

1 percent or 2 percent (depending on boring stuff) excise tax), we are heavily regulated by the government, and I do mean "heavily." Regulations stick out of so many of our organizational orifices you can't imagine. We filed 240 (yes, *240*) tax forms last year. And you think you have a knotty financial life? We've got inside accountants, outside auditors, and people in the middle. We are under a continual microscope.

But, you ask, eyebrows raised: With all that money floating around, some of it must slip into pockets it doesn't belong in, no?

No—and if I find out it has, I will be very unforgiving. We established a ground rule mandating that any expense of over $5,000 requires at least one trustee's written approval. As my law office is near the Trust's office, a bottomless sea of papers crosses my desk for signature—contracts, approvals, bills, checks, transfers. I've signed payments and transfers totaling hundreds of millions of dollars flowing from one place to another, in checks and other authorizations for investments, grants, purchases, and what-not. We've got a carefully crafted system of protections in place, including layers of required approvals and multiple sign-offs, but I've got to know why I'm signing everything I sign. If I make any mistakes, it—or they—could range from minuscule to supersized. I try to be very careful, and sure hope it hasn't happened.

W hen you control so much money, people try to play you.

I met with the president of a prominent institution that had received a large grant from us. He was making a follow-up thank-you visit, paving the way for what would doubtlessly be a later request for another grant, and was friendly to the point of letting down his guard.

I told him that much of his time seemed to be spent on fund-raising, and asked whether he found that tiresome.

He answered No, I find it psychologically fascinating to see what makes donors tick and finding the on-off switch that leads them to say yes.

And what's my on-off switch, I asked.

He answered with some vague flattery that, to me, translated into "Whoops."

That just illustrated this occasional unexpressed viewpoint: How bright can these charitable organization people be, just giving away money to others without getting anything in return? Who gives away money for nothing? So since we're not so smart, they'll sometimes not answer a question, or give an indirect or diversionary response. Eventually, they come around to understanding that when we ask a question or request information, it's because we want that particular question answered, or that piece of information given, directly. They get the point, though it sometimes takes more time than it should.

I've only had one incident where the "in return" mentality seemed to click in ugly. Someone who ran a supposedly charitable enterprise sent me a request for a grant, and when I didn't answer quickly enough for him, followed up with a call. I told him, nicely, that what he'd proposed wasn't really in our wheelhouse. He asked me again, and I answered that as worthy as his enterprise was, it was simply outside our spheres of involvement. He asked me again, and I just said no. Am I being rude, I asked myself? Too big for my britches? Until he asked one more time and added, delphically, there'd be enough for both of us. I hung up and never heard from him again.

The Trust's policy is not to accept unsolicited grant requests: Don't call us, we'll call you. But that's not what happens in real life. We get a steady flow of unsolicited requests, read them, and decline further inquiry as to most.

The avenues for productive use of charitable dollars is virtually boundless. As the Helmsley philanthropic name became known, unsolicited requests from organizations grew significantly. I tried to respond to everyone, imagining myself on the other end of the process wondering whether my request had been received and would get a response. Who do these Helmsley folks think they are, I'd ask myself, and will they even acknowledge my request?

I was brought up to be polite—even decades of battle in litigation trenches couldn't knock it out of me—and simply ignoring people is not in my DNA. So I respond with polite turndowns to a plethora of unsolicited requests—sometimes to worthy causes, but sometimes to requests for financial support for a proposed book, or a sports project, or a cultural event, or a private venture, or a project not permitted by legal requirements, or a project which, though promising in the abstract, doesn't sound like a real deliverable by the organization presenting it.

I've turned down requests because they don't fit within our goal of funding where we can have a significant result, or they don't fit within our program areas or objectives. Other requests come from the kinds of institutions we do assist—educational or health-related, for example—but without any real thought or planning apparent in the request: They feel like "Helmsley has a pot of money, let's just ask for some and see if we get lucky." Or innumerable other worthy causes we haven't been able to fund because, though we are one of the largest charitable foundations in the country, our resources are finite. Others I turn down because we've already spent enough in a particular area. I generally don't give reasons, to avoid being drawn into argument about why my reasons are wrong. I spend enough time arguing in my law practice.

Some out-of-the-blue applicants are indefatigable. They figure "No" doesn't mean No as long as they keep getting a response.

Reminds me of a legendary Harvard Law School story. At the beginning of the first year, a professor announced that class starts promptly at 9:00 a.m. and he'd lock the door at exactly that time. Sure enough, a few days later, a latecomer rattles the door at 9:02 and the professor won't unlock it. The student keeps pounding, uselessly. Finally, a window opens, and the student climbs in and takes his seat. "I paid tuition," he tells the startled professor, "and no locked door is going to keep me out." "Welcome," the professor replies. "You'll make a fine lawyer." But that doesn't work in soliciting Helmsley money.

I've learned that, as in so many aspects of life, being direct and honest in responding to grant requests is the best policy; leaving people with a false sense of optimism does a disservice by disincentivising them from looking elsewhere. Learning how to say "No," clearly, is important.

Some applicants are creative. I met with someone involved in a small charitable organization active in Israel and interested in applying for a grant. After hearing about his organization, I told him that although its work sounded very important, the organization simply wasn't the type that the Trust supports. He thanked me for my time and candor, and as we walked to the door, told me how he'd overcome a previous rejection.

He'd been hoping to arrange a meeting with another major foundation, but they wouldn't see him. At the time, the actor Paul Newman was active in the applicant's organization, so he called the foundation and said that he and Paul Newman were wondering if they could both make an appointment to see someone about a possible grant. The immediate response was: Yes. When he and Newman arrived, the halls were lined with women, gawking. By the end of the meeting, the foundation had committed over $1 million to the organization. On the elevator ride down, Newman peered over his glasses and said, "Still sexy at seventy."

Most of the applicants we reject accept the decision without protest, often with a "thank you for your consideration." Others challenge the decision, and I try to be responsive to their protestation, within limits. Others try a different tack: Someone I meet at an event approaches and asks whether I'd be willing to read some materials. I let him know his project isn't really up our alley, but when he extols its potential glories and won't let go, I finally say I'll read what you send me. Materials then arrive in the mail, with a cover letter beginning: "As you requested, I am enclosing. . . ."

Ultimately, there is no algorithm or scientific formula: It's a question of judgment. I do the best I can, and assure unsuccessful applicants that the turndown simply reflects the limits of our funding capacity and not the merits of their work. It's not you, it's me.

But wait, you say: Didn't Leona Helmsley leave her money to her dog? Or to dogs in general?

Here's the scoop.

Mrs. Helmsley's dog, Trouble, was surely one of the richest and most notorious dogs in the world. She often said that she could trust nobody but Trouble.

For one of Mrs. Helmsley's birthday parties, Ruthie and I bought a sterling silver picture frame. She sent us a letter thanking us for attending the party and for the frame, writing "I have the perfect photo for it . . . one of Trouble, naturally."

She ran full-page *New York Times* ads for the Park Lane Hotel featuring a photo of Trouble seated in a chairman-like chair behind a chairman-like desk, the dog's mouth open and the caption reading: "Let's get down to business."

In truth, Trouble was a vicious nondiscriminatory people-biter, attacking without regard to the victim's status in life. One of her alleged victims was a housekeeper in Mrs. Helmsley's Park Lane apartment. The housekeeper sued Mrs. Helmsley, claiming that Trouble had ferociously attacked her, causing severe injuries, and that Mrs. Helmsley had acted maliciously because she knew the dog was fierce and dangerous. The claim was covered by Mrs. Helmsley's insurance policy, with the insurance carrier having the right to select as a lawyer someone on the carrier's roster of outside lawyers. I told the lawyer selected by the carrier that I'd like to draft legal papers seeking immediate dismissal of the case, for him to sign and file. He agreed.

The case was problematical. It was credible that the dog had bitten the housekeeper, and my concern was the housekeeper's right to demand a "Bill of Particulars" requiring Mrs. Helmsley to identify everyone the dog had ever bitten. The list would include numerous other employees, corporate officers, outside professional advisors—and even Ruthie and me, as we too had felt the nip of Trouble's fangs. That compulsory disclosure could result in additional liability for Mrs. Helmsley, and New York's tabloids would have a field day splashing the litany of victims' names, including ours, across its front pages.

Fortunately, we found a very helpful legal chestnut. Before suing, the housekeeper had filed a claim under the Workers' Compensation Law, and that claim barred her from suing in court, a little-known hitch in the law that the housekeeper's lawyer hadn't known. The case was dismissed.

Trouble provided the one occasion of my not being completely candid with her owner.

Mrs. Helmsley's apartment had a spacious dressing room, decorated completely in white—the flooring, the wallpaper, the credenzas, everything. One afternoon, I arrived at the apartment to report on a legal matter. A housekeeper led me into the dressing room, where Mrs. Helmsley was sitting under the large hood of a hair dryer. The dog lay at her feet, white fur blending seamlessly into the white carpet. Mrs. Helmsley set the dryer on "low" so she could hear me.

In the midst of our conversation, the phone on one of the credenzas rang. After a few rings, I realized Mrs. Helmsley couldn't hear it because of the dryer enveloping her head, so I hurriedly got up and raced the few steps to answer the phone. But I'd forgotten Trouble was there, and didn't notice her, white on white. As I bolted toward the phone, the front of my right shoe struck Trouble square-on, and she flew through the air like a punted football. The phone stopped ringing before I could reach it, and Trouble, after what seemed like hours of floating end-over-end in the air, finally landed back on earth on the other side of the room. She began screeching, and lunged at me. Mrs. Helmsley, who hadn't noticed the kick, grabbed her.

What's wrong, she purred to Trouble.

Trouble growled at me.

What got into her? Mrs. Helmsley asked me.

Must have been startled by the phone, I answered.

Mrs. Helmsley held onto the dog until our meeting was over, which I made sure was soon.

Mrs. Helmsley's will left Trouble to her brother Alvin, but he declined to accept her. The declination became publicized, and strangers wrote to me offering a warm and loving house to the dog and a repository for the dog's $12 million trust. A longtime Helmsley employee in Florida volunteered to care for the dog, and we accepted. Even Trouble's moving to Florida was considered sufficiently newsworthy that the New York Post ran an old picture of Mrs. Helmsley holding the dog—full page, front page—with a screaming headline: "Rich Bitch Flees—Death threats chase Leona's 12 million pooch."

The income generated by a $12 million trust would clearly exceed even the lifestyle that Trouble had grown accustomed to. Trusts for pets are legally valid, but the Surrogate's Court is empowered to reduce any trust for a pet if the amount substantially exceeds its intended use. Here, it did. We submitted an affidavit from Trouble's new caretaker itemizing the costs of all of Trouble's queen-sized annual needs—fulltime private security, grooming, veterinarian costs because of Trouble's kidney condition and age, and other expenses, all totaling $190,200 per year. Hard to believe, but that's the total for a super-rich dog's life, Rolls Royce style.

We told the judge that reducing Trouble's trust to $2 million would leave more than enough money to provide for Trouble's care at the highest standards for the rest of her life. The judge agreed, and reduced Trouble's trust from $12 million to $2 million, with the $10 million reduction immediately transferred to the charitable trust. The remaining $2 million trust (plus earnings on that amount) would be quite sufficient over the course of Trouble's lifetime, with whatever remained being transferred to the charitable trust when the dog died.

When the judge reduced Trouble's trust, newspapers and other media worldwide again carried the story. The *New York Post* thought the reduction sufficiently important that it ran yet another full-page story under the headline "Screw the Pooch," with the obligatory picture of Trouble in Mrs. Helmsley's arms.

The $10 million reduction of Trouble's trust paled by comparison to the next legal brouhaha involving Mrs. Helmsley and dogs.

Ten months after Mrs. Helmsley's death, the *New York Times* ran a front-page story headlined "Helmsley, Dogs' Best Friend, Left Them Up to $8 Billion." Based on anonymous sources, the article reported that Mrs. Helmsley had directed that her entire (and exaggerated) multi-billion dollar estate be used for the care and welfare of dogs. This sensational disclosure was repeated in media worldwide.

Nobody seemed to care that the story was simply wrong. In fact, in the documents establishing the Trust, Mrs. Helmsley had given the trustees complete discretion to determine which charitable purposes to support and the amounts to give each grantee we chose. The documents relied on by the *Times* had been superseded by later trust documents, and were inoperative for a host of other reasons. Dogs had no entitlement at all.

In view of the billions of dollars at stake, however, and the irreversibility, in case we were wrong, of the large grants we would be making to charities having nothing to do with dogs, we decided that prudence dictated our presenting the issue to the Surrogate's Court to determine whether our reading of the operative documents was correct—though we were sure it was. After Mrs. Helmsley's death, I had asked all lawyers who had been involved in any way with her wills and the Trust to send me all of their records, and received a mass of papers.

We made full disclosure to the court, filing all conceivably relevant legal documents, including those cited by the *Times*, and asked the judge to rule that we had complete discretion to disburse these billions of dollars of charitable funds as we saw fit, with no obligation to give grants to dog-related charities. New York State's Attorney General, who by law represents all unnamed potential charitable beneficiaries, agreed with us. So did the court, ruling: "The trustees may apply trust funds for such charitable purposes and in such amounts as they, in their sole discretion, determine."

But that did not end the matter. A few weeks after the court's decision, I received a phone call from a former law school classmate of mine. We had also served together in the U.S. Attorney's Office, and in the intervening decades had occasionally socialized. Over the years, he had built a large law firm based in Washington, D.C. A few years earlier, he had asked me to join his firm and head its New York office, and when I thanked him for the flattery but declined, he had asked, to my astonishment, whether he could ask my partner to join instead. I gave him permission, knowing that my partner was perfectly content with our small firm, but dumbfounded by being asked to allow him to try to lure my partner away from me.

The purpose of the call, my former classmate said, was that "as a friend" he wanted to "give a heads up" to me. I would shortly be contacted, he said, by a partner in a nationally prominent law firm, with whom my former classmate was working, representing one of the country's leading charitable organizations devoted to the care and welfare of dogs. "Don't worry," he said, the caller is "a good guy" and would be calling "to work things out" concerning the Trust's obligation to dogs. I asked what that meant. The answer: an agreement as to how much of the Trust's money should be given to dog-related organizations.

I responded that the question had already been determined by the court: Dog-related charities had no claim on the Trust's giving. I thanked him for giving me a "heads up" that he and his colleague were about to sue me, and ended the call.

Shortly afterwards, the promised lawyer called, purportedly on behalf of all dog-related charities, seeking a negotiated portion of all grants to be made by the Trust. We declined to negotiate. The documentation establishing the Trust and giving us complete discretion was clear, and the court had already ruled in our favor on the issue.

Then came a barrage of legal papers, filed by three major law firms representing the ASPCA and several other dog-related charities. Through a legal procedure called "intervention," they sought to convince a newly elected Surrogate, who had replaced the Surrogate who had already determined we had full discretion, that the prior Surrogate was wrong. We filed papers opposing their request on numerous grounds, saying that the dog charities lacked standing to "intervene" in the case, which was now over, and that in any event the decision of the first Surrogate was correct.

The new Surrogate denied the dog charities' request to intervene. The dog charities and their lawyers were not deterred. They filed an appeal, which would ultimately determine whether the Trust would be improving the lives of people instead of dogs. I admit to hubris: The stakes were so high I wanted to draft the Trust's legal papers in opposition to the appeal. I did, with my associate Breeze McMennamin, and the appellate court (called the Appellate Division), which hears cases in five-judge panels, voted 5–0 to affirm the Surrogate's decision denying the dog charities' application to intervene.

But the dog charities and their lawyers were indefatigable. In New York, there are two primary layers of appellate courts. The Appellate Division is available as of right to any litigant that loses a case. There is a higher appellate court—the New York State Court of Appeals—but litigants dissatisfied with the Appellate Division's ruling do not have an automatic right to further review by the Court of Appeals; they only have the right to ask that court to accept the case for further review. So the dog charities filed more legal papers, asking the Court of Appeals to hear the case, claiming it raised issues of extreme importance. We claimed it didn't, and urged the court to turn down the request. The Court of Appeals unanimously turned it down.

The dog case was now over. All told, thirteen judges had considered the case, and none voiced any disagreement with our conclusion that Mrs. Helmsley had granted the trustees full discretion to determine what charitable uses the money should go to, and in what amounts. Media worldwide had gotten it wrong. Finally, case closed.

Postscript: When Trouble died, the remaining money in the Trouble trust was all transferred to the charitable trust.

And by the way: If you've got a dog joke, I've heard it.

Chapter 12
Trying to Cure a Disease

How do you create and oversee multi-multi-million dollar funding aimed at improving lives of people with a serious disease, and ultimately finding a cure, when the disease's cause (or causes) is (or are) unknown, when you are untrained in science or medicine, and indeed all your scientific and medical knowledge could be poured into a thimble and still leave room for your thumb? And why would I try to?

The second question is an easy one, though I've got to be a little coy with you here. The somebody close to me who has Crohn's is a very private person. He or she would be very angry if I were to publicly disclose anything personal about him/her. So I'll have to ask your indulgence and not tell you who it is. Suffice to say that I love him, or her, very much, and saw my new trustee position as a godsend to try to help. I'll refer to him or her as "him," because I've go to pick a pronoun, and "it" doesn't feel right and "they" isn't grammatically correct.

But is it legal to start a philanthropic program that would

benefit him, and pour unheard-of amounts of money to try to help cure, and in the interim develop diagnostics and therapeutics to help, someone dear to me? I've always been straightlaced as a lawyer, and wasn't about to relax my scruples now that I controlled zillions of philanthropic dollars. Could I legally, properly, ethically pour vast amounts of money toward a disease for personal, selfish reasons?

I expressed concern to our Rockefeller expert and my lawyer about whether establishing a program that would result in prodigious funding, where the impetus of the program and a possible ultimate beneficiary was someone dear to me, would be problematical—could I or the Trust be subject to criticism, or even worse? No, they assured me, philanthropic giving is often directed toward health issues in which philanthropists have vested and highly personal interests. Far from being improper, personal interest spurs devotion to a cause and is common. Since Crohn's is a serious disease that afflicts a vast number of people, selecting it as a program area would not be at all questionable. David's establishing and leadership of the type 1 diabetes program, which could help his daughter, fell into the same category.

And so was born the Trust's Crohn's disease program, which has become the largest private philanthropic Crohn's disease program in the world. Our goal is to help people throughout the world, but the true impetus was one person, him. I remember when a doctor first explained his disease and I tried to fathom what it meant, to absorb the biological mechanisms and contemplate the lifestyle implications; walking in the streets around the hospital the first time he was admitted, hoping he'd soon be able to return to a normal routine; and crying from relief after learning the surgery had been successful—everything else was secondary and unimportant. Now, I could try to help end the disease, or at least help soften its impact, despite being a layman about it.

Crohn's disease is a chronic, relentless condition—it never goes away—affecting the intestinal tract. It can appear in any part of the tract, and causes severe abdominal pain, rectal bleeding, persistent diarrhea, fever, malnutrition, weight loss, fatigue, and other debilitating symptoms. Its causes are unknown, involving the interplay of genetics, the immune system, the microbiome (trillions of bacteria and other microorganisms that reside in the human body), and environmental, nutritional, psychological, and other factors. Researchers now believe Crohn's is really different diseases —variants in different genes (many by now identified) predisposing an individual to "triggers" activating the disease. The triggers may be in the individual's microbiome, or in immunological responses, environmental exposures, nutrition, stress, or elsewhere—or in some combination. Certain genetic variants make an individual more susceptible to certain triggers, while other genetic variants are protective. Discovering the predisposing or protective variants within identified genes is an essential step to fully understanding the disease and devising therapeutic compounds to prevent, treat, or cure it.

Crohn's is a disease of relapse and remission, with flare-ups causing pain and discomfort and impacting the quality of life. The goal of treatment is to reduce the severity of symptoms or, better yet, keep the disease in remission, meaning that the patient is symptom-free. Most patients require surgery, or multiple surgeries, to remove diseased portions of their intestines. Though estimates are imprecise, about 2 million people worldwide suffer from Crohn's, including nearly a million in the United States, and the numbers are increasing.

"He" is one of them.

Low do I help scientists, doctors, and other experts find improved diagnostics for the disease, and devise better therapeutics and ways to prevent, manage, and, eventually, cure it? And who am I to undertake this journey? Where can I, should I, do I, begin?

I had to start somewhere, and the top seemed like the right place. I knew of Dr. David Sachar at Mount Sinai Hospital. That hospital is generally recognized as a world leader in research and treatment of Crohn's. Dr. Burrill Crohn had first described the disease while a gastroenterologist there, and thousands of Crohn's patients come there annually from all over the world for treatment.

Dr. Sachar is a preeminent Crohn's expert at Mount Sinai. He has devoted his professional life to the disease and those suffering from it, as a caring clinician, researcher, teacher, and author of innumerable publications in the field.

I called Dr. Sachar, introduced myself, said the Trust was considering establishing a Crohn's program, and asked if I could meet him at the hospital. No, he said, he'd come to see me as soon as I was available. We met the next day.

The Trust was still working with Rockefeller, and they had assigned an experienced philanthropic adviser to work with me. I had him join me at the meeting with Dr. Sachar. Later, I'd build an expert staff at the Trust to work on the Crohn's program. But in the beginning, it was only me and one non-scientist advisor from Rockefeller.

I explained to Dr. Sachar that the Trust was a start-up and establishing its fields of concentration, and Crohn's would be one. I said I was a scientific greenhorn, and asked how, where, and with whom to begin. I told him I had no interest in tinkering around the edges, but wanted the Trust to make meaningful investments—big bets on potentially transformative science—to help people with the disease and, ultimately, find improved therapeutics and a cure. I wanted us to be game-changers, even though we weren't playing a game and in any event I didn't know the rules.

I told him the possible range of available dollars if they could be productively spent on the disease. He was flabbergasted at the once-in-a-lifetime opportunity, and suggested we also meet with Dr. Lloyd Mayer, the director of Mount Sinai's division of gastro-enterology and a brilliant doctor and researcher in the field. I asked Dr. Sachar if he could arrange a meeting for us, though I was leaving town that day and wouldn't be back until next week.

I've waited forty years for this moment, Dr. Sachar said, and another week won't hurt.

The following week, I met with the two doctors. In the intervening days, they had discussed the opportunities for large, concentrated, high-risk high-reward funding in Crohn's.

They explained that much of scientific research is done in "silos"—individual researchers working separately, without cross-pollination of ideas, data, and findings. They suggested the Trust fund a consortium of the best Crohn's research centers in the country—they knew all of them—to share resources and knowledge, conduct joint projects, and deal collaboratively in order to better understand, treat, and ultimately—maybe—cure the disease. Mt. Sinai would be the coordinating hospital for the first year, and that position would rotate annually; they weren't interested in being captains or getting any glory, but only in helping people with the disease and preventing others from getting it. The project would be called SHARE—Sinai-Helmsley Alliance for Research Excellence. This multi-centered program would allow the best and most creative minds in the field to feed off each other's work and ideas, rather than work in isolation.

That sounded like a fine idea. Even without a scientific

background, it seemed self-evident that if you bring smart, talented, dedicated, and knowledgeable experts together, something good can come of it. And the doctors recommending it were tops in the field. So I brought the idea to others whose views I respected, examined it further, and thus was born the Trust's SHARE program, which ultimately grew to seven institutions with over $25 million in Helmsley funding and was a precursor to many later multi-institution grants we gave to support collaborative world-class scientific research.

But little did I understand the difficulties of scientific sharing. You don't blindly invite a bunch of geniuses into the same room and hope something good will happen. You've got to know what's to be shared, by whom, how, when patients consent, and a host of other scientific, legal, and ethical issues. How to take tiny samples of the human body, analyze and make them accessible to others, share findings and insights, share credit and ownership, and ultimately fully understand their significance and translate everything into helping patients is a very sophisticated process. It is not a task for your run-of-the-mill lawyer, not a casual scientific detour from a lifetime litigating.

I began gradually assembling an in-house staff, and did it in exactly the wrong way. The people I chose were experienced in philanthropy but not trained in science. So when scientists submitted requests for funding and reported on the results of their research, their submissions were evaluated through a philanthropic lens—making sure all the money was being spent properly, and all the regulatory i's dotted and t's crossed—but not through the perspective of whether the work being done was scientifically significant or potentially transformative.

I was the leader, but not qualified to lead scientific research by major medical institutions and the world's preeminent scientists and doctors in the field—like my giving antitrust advice to Exxon.

A generous dollop of humility is helpful in spending hefty doses of money to search for new ways to help people suffering from disease. I brought considerable humility to the table, all of it justified. Beyond a superficial threshold, much of the experts' medical-speak could have been Aramaic to me, and indeed may have been; often the threshold was "hello." From having been a control freak able to survey the landscape of legal problems and devise and implement (sometimes) solutions, to being in a foreign professional country with no ability to understand the language or evaluate the science—watching a foreign language film without subtitles—was tumbling into a vastly different intellectual world.

After flailing around and ultimately realizing I was far out of my depths, I began relying on an informal group of advisors, experts in the field who gave direction, advice, and criticisms. This developed into a formal advisory board—distinguished and accomplished doctors and scientists who evaluated our approach to Crohn's funding, suggested avenues we might otherwise have missed, and advised us on prospective grants. I wasn't shy about asking them to speak in plain English so I had a shot at understanding, and they were sufficiently expert to be able to express themselves in terms basic enough for me to understand.

With all that help, though, I still had difficulty reading about such things as a "gene-targeted approach for 454 pyrotag sequencing and quantitative polymerase chain reaction for the final genes in the two primary bacterial butyrate synthesis pathways, butyryl-CoA: acetate CoA-transferase and butyrate kinase." Easy, right? But I evaluated scientists and others the best I could: Were they highly regarded by their peers? Did they have proven track records? What did our scientific advisors and other experts think of them and their work? Could they execute what they proposed? Were they associated with world-class institutions? Were they able to explain concepts with sufficient clarity that even I could understand? Did they appear to be smart? Honest? Did they appear to be scientists to the core and not salesmen? Were they stroking me to get at the Trust's money?

I finally got smarter: I realized that philanthropy was fairly straightforward—the governing rules and processes are simple even if occasionally technical, and we had built a sufficiently competent administrative staff to provide guide rails for the do's and don'ts of philanthropy. What I needed was a staff of scientists and public health experts, not philanthropists, to achieve meaningful results. I had built my law practice by hard work, treating each client's problem as if it were mine, and surrounding myself with colleagues who themselves settled for nothing short of excellence; now I needed a new Crohn's staff with comparable talent and devotion to the cause. Warren Buffett, explaining why he lets expert managers run Berkshire Hathaway's businesses without telling them what to do, counsels that you don't teach a .400 hitter how to swing a bat. The same with me: I'd leave the science to the scientists. But finding .400 hitters is difficult, and so is recognizing when you've found them. You can't find scientists with those qualities by standing on a street corner and wearing a "help wanted" sign.

I eventually found skilled, motivated scientists and public health experts eager to join the program and dedicated to its mission. But in the interim before that happened, times were tough: I had to be the ultimate judge and jury for many millions of dollars in scientific grant applications and oversight—and who knows whether I did it well. I usually know when my lawyering is up to snuff, but science, not so much. Toggling back and forth between practicing law and overseeing a sophisticated scientific medical program—along with running, with two co-trustees, a multi-billion-dollar charitable trust—requires mental gymnastics. Properly handling a case requires total control—of facts, of law, and, when possible, of your adversary—and there's always an adversary. In overseeing the

Crohn's program, I brought none of that expertise, training, or experience to the table, and there was no adversary. And running a several-lawyer boutique law firm was far less bureaucratic than running a one-hundred-person charitable organization.

One day, or one morning, or for a few hours, I'd be working on a case—questioning a witness, arguing before a judge, grinding out legal papers, fighting, and certain about what I was doing. Then, I'd be meeting with a brilliant doctor or scientist, asking him to re-translate, in words of one syllable or less, what to him (or, often as not, her) seemed perfectly clear. I'd be in control one moment and befuddled in another, depending on the professional hat I was wearing and what office I was working out of. The Crohn's hat was particularly frustrating because the stakes were so high and personal.

I'd sometimes be thinking of one role while in the other. In my legal practice, a million-dollar case, or a few-million-dollar case, was a big one. But now, after fighting in my law office tooth-and-nail over every client's dollar, I'd go to my Trust office and decide how many millions to dole out to whom. In my law practice, I'd want something for something from my adversary; in philanthropy, I'd want nothing but excellence and devotion, for millions. My mental on-off buttons required constant adjustment.

We've spent over $415 million so far on Crohn's research—our annual budget for the Crohn's program is over $38 million. That buys a lot of learning, but so far we haven't cured the disease. Medical research of this sort is slow, plodding, and frustrating to someone personally vested in reaching significant results, even with the best of minds and devoted scientists doing their level best. "Cure," I've learned, has linguistic gradations in the worlds of medicine and science. On one end of the spectrum is things remaining as they've been—no improvement; on the other end is a magic potion that would completely eradicate the disease, or at least induce permanent or long-term remission without significant side effects. There's a whole range of spots along that continuum—we've moved past "a," but remain far from "z." I'm still shooting for the moon.

Our program is patient-centered, with four basic, often overlapping pillars: preventing Crohn's in people genetically predisposed to the disease, or delaying its progression; early diagnosis of the disease to permit personalized targeting of the best treatment for each particular patient; developing safe and effective drugs and getting them to market; and optimizing patients' quality of care. The key is to find the right course of action for each particular patient at the right time, as one size doesn't fit all.

We fund Crohn's-specific scientific investigations worldwide—throughout the United States, in Canada, Israel, Europe, Australia, Hong Kong, China, and still growing. We've eliminated barriers that have traditionally isolated scientists from each other, funding many large-scale collaborative networks bringing the greatest minds in Crohn's-related research and other relevant scientific fields into the same metaphorical and often literal room, working together toward developing knowledge, drugs, diagnostics, technology, and other mechanisms that will eventually help, we hope, people all over the world. We have mobilized a global community of scientists and doctors committed to finding effective solutions to improve Crohn's patients' lives while seeking a cure, and we function as their partner—speaking, meeting, and sharing ideas with them in a continual collaboration.

Even as a layman, I have witnessed the benefits of collaborative scientific research. Our funding of joint projects became known in the IBD community ("IBD," or inflammatory bowel disease, includes Crohn's and ulcerative colitis). A group of a dozen doctors and scientists from the U.S., several European countries, and Israel studying very early onset IBD—striking children younger than six years old (many under two)—asked for a small grant to meet for a few days in Amsterdam, to discuss establishing a consortium studying the disease. Scientists from ten institutions convened there for a weekend of meetings. Some knew each other; some knew only each other's works; and some were strangers.

By the end of the second day, having met, eaten, and informally interacted among themselves, they began to feel comfortable around each other, and the human element kicked in. One of the scientists mentioned having found that a variant of a certain gene causes a particular reaction in Crohn's patients. Genes have names, but he didn't name the gene.

A second scientist said he'd also found—independently—the same phenomenon. Each of the two plainly regarded the finding as potentially significant, but proprietary. They'd been with each other for two days, though, the spirit of the meeting was interactive and interpersonal, and after some hemming and hawing, each identified the gene he'd been talking about—and it was the same gene. Each scientist now had the corroboration he needed, and the rest of the group shared the benefit of this insight.

Detailing everything we've done would numb your mind, but let's sample a plain vanilla version of a little of the science, medicine, and technology we've paid for, seeking the magical potion that will meaningfully improve patients' lives. Here's a short and sweet overview of a few Crohn's projects we've funded, but I promise—promise—each is far more intricate than it sounds. The reason for the simplification is because this ain't a science textbook and, anyway, I'm not sure I could do all of them full scientific justice. Needless to say, most of these projects are very expensive, and some cost many millions. A handful of over 200 Crohn's grants:

- Developing a tethered high-tech capsule that the patient swallows and which transmits detailed video of the inside of the intestines, allowing a close-up view without invasive surgery or the unpleasantness of bowel preparation and sedation used in typical colonoscopies. The pill is so small it can pass through strictures—narrowings—that develop in the intestines of many Crohn's patients, and allows views of parts of the intestines which can't be reached with standard procedures.

- Recruiting five thousand siblings or offspring of people with Crohn's, who are at risk for developing the disease, and following them over years to try to uncover information about the triggers of the disease and clues toward how to prevent it from developing.

- Investigating whether different diets will reduce the severity of the disease, and help maintain remission.

- Studying the increased occurrence of Crohn's in China as a window into learning the impact of increased westernization of diet and lifestyle on a genetically similar population.

- Evaluating, as a possible therapy, transferring fecal matter from a healthy donor to a patient to change the composition of the patient's gut—or putting stored fecal matter obtained from a patient in remission back into the same patient during relapse. As unappetizing as that sounds, it's a procedure that has been helpful in treating another intestinal disease called C. difficile—but now I'm showing off.

- Development of drugs to treat fibrosis (excessive scar tissue formation) which narrows many Crohn's patients' intestinal tracts and hinders intake of food and proper digestion.

- The Human Cell Atlas is a vast global scientific collaboration to map the trillions of cells in the human body. One of its principal scientific and financial supporters is the Chan-Zuckerberg Initiative—that's Zuckerberg as in Facebook, and Chan as in his wife. We are partnering with them by funding development of a Gut Cell Atlas, mapping the cells in the human gut to increase understanding of individual cell functions and their impact on Crohn's.

- Exploring how smartphones and wearable devices can track biomarkers and help predict flares, permitting early intervention.

- Developing passive, non-wearable, at-home wireless monitoring technology to collect patient data and help predict flares.

- Developing an ingestible device capable of sensing Crohn's-related biomarkers in the intestines and creating a signal transmitted to an external recording device outside the body.

- Identifying biomarkers to predict patients' responsiveness to particular drugs, allowing individualized therapies.

- Using saliva as a diagnostic tool to identify the presence, location, and severity of Crohn's disease, without subjecting patients to invasive examinations.

- Developing alternatives for bowel preparation before colonoscopies, to replace having to drink the repulsive goop that is today's standard.

- Creating a three-dimensional imaging tool allowing surgeons to perform safe, minimally invasive procedures.

Exposure to the brainpower behind projects like these is a humbling experience. But if you want real humbling:

The Broad Institute of MIT and Harvard is a beyond-top-tier biomedical research institute that seeks to understand and treat human disease by applying genetic discoveries to design therapeutics—developing drugs that hit genetic targets. We have given them over $40 million to focus on Crohn's. I was invited to an informal dinner meeting of the Broad's board of directors at the home of one its members, Eric Schmidt, the retired chairman of Google. In a free-ranging discussion, Eric asked a question about data-sharing to accelerate scientific research. Wanna feel like you're in the big leagues, or out of your element? Try adding value to a conversation with the former head of Google about data-sharing.

Covid-19 deeply affected our program. Research stalled: Many researchers switched from Crohn's to Covid; labs shut down or converted to emergency work; patient recruitment for research was hit as patients avoided medical centers and new patients couldn't be recruited; travel restrictions impacted research and collaborations; workers were furloughed; and a bevy of other problems arose.

Grantees entitled to receive additional money couldn't spend what we'd already given them—our payments for each grant are staggered, recipients must satisfy periodic milestones to receive the next tranche of money, and many couldn't. Fortunately, we'd developed a bullpen of promising projects we could accelerate to satisfy our required minimum distribution—the object never is simply to spend money, but to spend it productively.

I'm constantly asking the scientists: Why does it take so long, why aren't we there yet? Medical research of this type is a slow process, they say. Well, I know that. It can't be their fault—they're dedicated and best in class. Is it my fault—am I missing something, or someone, somewhere? Or does this kind of scientific journey, by it nature, require tediously navigating multiple scientific pathways, inch by inch, in-the-trenches warfare against an indefatigable enemy that can only be slowly wrestled to the ground?

I've been in many courtrooms watching other lawyers present their cases, cross-examine witnesses, and argue to judges and juries, often saying to myself they're not doing it well and knowing what they should be doing. But in scientific research, lacking that knowledge and experience, I'm relegated to hiring a talented and dedicated program staff and relying on the best scientists we can find doing the most cutting-edge research they can do.

The goal isn't simply to throw money at the disease, but to spend wisely on projects that can improve lives. We look for potentially transformative scientific ventures. Our bets seek to harness the efforts of the most brilliant minds in science. Being unschooled in the science, genetics, biology, and chemistry of Crohn's is certainly not a plus, but leaves me untethered by the constraints of scientific reality. My objective, and the Trust's—and the scientists'—is not simply to learn more about the disease, but to alleviate the suffering of those with the disease and improve their lives, to develop new drugs, and ultimately to cure the disease—nothing less will do.

Our grants are not given lightly. The application process is rigorous, and follows intensive pre-application meetings and analyses. After a grant is given, we remain heavily engaged with grantee scientists, tracking their progress and offering help—we're their partners, not their bankers.

But though our grants are enormous, they are insufficient to bring to market drugs and a cure. The really big money needed to vanquish disease—amounts that dwarf even the Trust's—comes from pharmaceutical companies when they perceive a profit-making opportunity by developing drugs for a potentially large target population. Money and profits talk. Analyses of relevant genetic variants, discovering the non-genetic "triggers" that activate the inflammatory process, and developing productive therapeutics is a long, hard, expensive, frustrating, and potentially lifesaving process. Efforts we've financed have led major drug companies to begin developing more, and hopefully more effective, medications for Crohn's.

The causes of Crohn's are still unknown, really effective treatments and the cure still elusive. But scientists now know far more about the disease than they did when we first established our program. Philanthropists often speak of "metrics"—a small word with a big meaning: How to measure success. To me, it's very simple. My metric is: Does he feel better today than yesterday? When you've got a canary in the mine, hyper-sophisticated scientific gobbledygook doesn't cut it.

The experts tell me that Helmsley funding is responsible for tremendous strides in understanding and treating the disease, but I'll believe it when he tells me he feels really good. For decades, I've kept a Chinese fortune cookie proverb in my desk: A handful of patience is worth more than a bushel of brains. I'll keep pushing the wall.

Because of him.

You probably suppose that he's surely getting the world's best treatment because I can pull strings to make certain someone dear to me is taken care of by the tops. Nope. Like I said earlier, he's a very private person. He tells me nothing about how he's handling the disease—whether today was a good day, is the medicine working, how he's feeling in general. And though I think about him constantly, I don't push. If I did, he'd push away.

I recall a story Leona Helmsley told me. Her son died young, from a heart condition. Mrs. Helmsley believed she was indirectly responsible for his death: Had the doctors treated him as they'd treat anyone, he still would be alive, she thought; only because they wanted to please her did they not do what they'd otherwise have done. I never asked for details—they'd be too painful for anyone to recount. But I've kept the story in mind.

So my "he" can do what he does in privacy without my prying or pulling strings, though I think about him all the time.

Chapter 13

Israel

As I write, the Trust has so far awarded more than $375 million in grants for Israel, and we'll have spent many millions more by the time you read this. We built the program from literally non-existent to massive. Though I don't keep track of such things, we are one of the world's largest private funders to Israel.

I'm often asked how frequently Leona Helmsley travelled to Israel and how many large gifts she gave there. The questioner is invariably surprised when I answer Never and None. I can sense the thought sinking in: You mean there was nothing there—no donations, no roots, no nothing—and then you became a trustee and suddenly there's this unbelievable infusion of money doing Israel a world of good? Aw-shucks, yes, that's what happened.

Why did I choose Israel as a program area for the Trust? Simple: Because I am a Jew; Israel is the homeland of the Jewish people, has been for nearly four thousand years, and is necessary for their survival. And because Israel is a democracy, embracing

Western values and flourishing in the midst of next-door and nearby countries' tsunamis of wars, chaos, and fanaticism, and the one reliable ally of America in that extraordinarily dangerous part of the world. Israel's contributions to the world in science, technology, medicine, the arts—you name it—are, like the country itself, miraculous. Investing in Israel is placing nearly can't-miss bets.

Being lead trustee of Helmsley's Crohn's and Israel programs equates to vastly different experiences. In Crohn's, trying to understand the medicine and science, and learning how painstakingly slowly they move; years without seeing concrete results; my general limitations and inexperience in that arena; the uncertainties of scientific research—all create a layer of frustration over the excitement of participating in a potentially life-changing or life-saving enterprise, fed by the tantalizing hope that the great scientific minds we fund will ultimately hit the elusive target and create the magic of a cure.

Israel, on the other hand, presents a vast sea of recognizable and more readily attainable opportunities.

Israel is not just a piece of land. It is a people. In Israel, every person—Jew, Christian, Muslim, other—counts. If you've never been there, go; see for yourself. Until then, I'll share some snapshots.

Ruthie and I travel to Israel twice a year, and I've figured out how to get quickly through El Al's vaunted security at the check-in. Invariably, an Israeli security guard asks: Hebrew or English? Ruthie answers in Hebrew and they exchange a few Hebrew sentences. The guard then turns to me and says: Hebrew? I say no. The guard says: How come? I answer "*Ahnee chamor,*" and the guard always smiles and lets us right through. It means: "I am a donkey."

Shortly after becoming a trustee, I contacted the office of Israel's then-President Shimon Peres, explained my role, and scheduled a meeting for my next trip there.

The President's residence and office are in the heart of Jerusalem. Security is, as you might imagine, very tight. His office is at the top of a long, winding staircase. The walls of the staircase were decorated with pictures showing the history of the man and the nation—Peres as a twenty-something aide to Israel's first Prime Minister, David Ben-Gurion; his evolution through virtually every major government position in the country, pictured with the great figures of Israel's history; and finally—at the top—the entrance to his private office. There stood the President, greeting us and asking whether we wanted tea or coffee.

He welcomed us with warmth and eloquence. He was eighty-eight years old and intellectually vibrant.

We began by my embarrassing Ruthie. I said, Mr. President, thirty-five years ago I uprooted a flower from Israel and stole her to America. I've been seeking forgiveness ever since, and the President of Israel seems about as high as I can go to ask. He said that on behalf of the State of Israel, I was forgiven.

I thanked him for the absolution, and got down to business. I told him I had asked to see him because of the unique opportunity I now had to direct significant money to Israel; that although everyone seems to have opinions about what the country should do and what its needs are, the view of the country's challenges and needs were far less clear from my office in mid-Manhattan than from his in the heart of Jerusalem and as a central figure in the nation's history; and I would welcome his suggestions as to how the substantial resources of the Helmsley Trust's Israel program could best serve the needs of Israel.

President Peres replied, What distinguishes us from the rest of the world is how we use our heads. Invest in our brains.

Some of Israel's best brains are in its universities, which seemed like a good place to start. I was concerned about doling out large amounts of money thousands of miles away—would it be wisely and honestly spent, or wind up where it didn't belong?—and these were large, highly reputable institutions where the odds of Helmsley money being put to its intended purposes was very high. Moreover, giving to preeminent universities for world-class projects wouldn't be rocket science or atomic physics, particularly since they have some of the world's preeminent rocket scientists and atomic physicists. So it seemed like a good area to get my feet wet.

I had a great idea, one that turned out to be dumb. With all the untold millions of dollars at the disposal of the Trust's Israel program, I became enamored by the thought of developing a world-changing initiative. I spoke with the presidents of several Israeli universities about the Trust funding a Los Alamos–type project: gather the leading researchers involved in developing alternative sources of energy, metaphorically lock them in a room, and fund their efforts until that grand moment of geopolitical impact—the end of the world's dependence on fossil fuels, of kowtowing to despotic countries lucky enough to sit on oceans of oil, while simultaneously helping create climate-friendly energy.

But that's not the way topflight science works, I learned. The Weizmann Institute is one of the world's preeminent basic research institutions. Its president, himself a physicist, explained to me that Weizmann doesn't tell its scientists what to study—they go where their curiosity leads them. And none of the other university presidents I spoke with stood up and cheered for my idea.

Weizmann scientists' curiosity eventually led them to a joint project with Israel's Technion, another of the world's premier scientific institutions. Technion's technology and engineering expertise, combined with Weizmann's basic science research, formed a unique opportunity for potentially groundbreaking, globally significant discoveries. We made a joint grant to the two institutions: $15 million to develop alternative sources of energy. We've also given the Technion $5 million to help develop lighter, more efficient, and longer lasting batteries and other methods of energy storage to help reduce the world's dependence on fossil fuels. Hopefully, their work will one day help achieve world-changing results.

By the way, those big numbers don't come out of the blue. They're spread over the three years of each project. And the institutions have to itemize the costs for each new piece of scientific equipment (they don't come cheap), the salaries of scientists, postdocs, and others who'll be working on each project, necessary outside services, construction and renovation costs, the requisite chemical, biological, and other supplies, travel expenses, and all the other stuff that goes into substantial scientific projects like these.

We eventually gave millions of dollars to every university in Israel, all for specific purposes, never simply for them to do with as a whim strikes—for stem cell research, research into the brain, robotics, medicine, technology, engineering, and scientific fields and equipment I'd never heard of. (Nanotechnology, in case you're curious, is the manipulation of matter at a molecular level; and if you've never heard of magnetoencephalography, a two-photon microscope, or a confocal microscope, they are all very expensive.)

I met with the presidents of all the universities and many of their academic superstars, Nobel Prize winners included. All of these people are, of course, far above my own intellectual abilities. But their humanness rather than their brilliance was what has stayed with me.

Bar Ilan University had recently opened the country's fifth medical school—the first in forty years—in Tzefat, one of Israel's oldest cities, located in the northern region called the Galilee. On a trip we had taken there a decade earlier, the town looked like it had fallen on hard times: poor, tired, lifeless. A medical school there could turn Tzefat around, help revive the North, and ameliorate Israel's shortage of physicians, especially in the periphery, and attract young Israelis to the north. The development of the medical school included a cancer research center, which needed funds. We examined the need, and contributed $5 million. Shortly after the grant was made, Ruthie and I visited the center.

We arrived on a late Friday afternoon, after most personnel had left for the Sabbath. We were greeted by the director of the center with embarrassing deference—a deep bow, and repeated thanks for the grant. He walked us through the center, and showed how the Trust's money was being used.

After the tour, the director invited us to his office. The conversation, as most conversations between Israelis, turned personal: How many generations in Israel does your family go back; what did your parents do; the hardships they faced growing up; are your parents still alive?

The director's father was not. He had died in the 1967 war. He fought in the Sinai, and his jeep had run out of gas. He and the troops with him began walking, and came to an abandoned car a short distance away. The key had been left in the ignition. The Israelis scrambled into the car, the director's father in the driver's seat. He turned the key in the ignition.

Ruthie and I were in Jerusalem to look at some projects the Trust had funded there, and several possible new grants. We coordinated our trip to coincide with an international conference being held in the name of President Peres; the Trust was a sponsor. Dignitaries from all over the world attended—former U.S. Secretary of State Henry Kissinger, former British Prime Minister Tony Blair, several heads of state, and others.

We were in a taxi and the phone rang.

The President would like to see you if you are available, the caller said, and gave me the address. I said we weren't dressed for the occasion, but was assured that was not a problem. So, half an hour later, we were escorted into an office in the conference center in Jerusalem, and greeted warmly by President Peres. As he reached down to kiss Ruthie, he asked her not to get lipstick on his collar. He greeted me like a friend.

We chatted about the conference, the country, a talk that had been given by one of several Israeli Nobel Prize winners a day earlier, and the state of the world. After half an hour, one of his aides reminded him of his next appointment, and we all stood up to exchange goodbyes.

Mr. President, I said, may I take up another thirty seconds of your time?

Of course, he said.

Me: I'm sure that with the important affairs of State you're involved in, you don't get out to the movies much?

President Peres: No, I don't.

Me: Do you know the movie *Zelig*?

President Peres: No.

Me: *Zelig* is a story of how a regular Joe somehow pops up in the midst of great historical moments—he appears at the Kennedy assassination, sits with the Pope at the Vatican, and is spliced in consorting with other historical figures. An hour ago I was in a taxi, got a call, and here I am with the President of Israel. I feel like Zelig.

He laughed, and said we'd meet again soon. He asked how

long Ruthie and I had been married, and offered some unsolicited personal advice: The key to a good marriage, he said, is to be a little deaf.

P resident Peres invited us to his office for a social call next time we were in Israel. Again, he gave a warm greeting to Ruthie, exchanging pleasantries with her in Hebrew. Then he turned to me: You still don't speak Hebrew?

Mr. President, I said, I've been working for years on one sentence which I intend to master during my lifetime. When I've got one breath left, I will look up at Ruthie and tell her, in flawless Hebrew, "I've understood everything over all these years."

We sat down with him over tea, and discussed Israel and the world. Toward the end of the meeting, he asked if I would do a favor for him.

I said, Mr. Peres, I'll be glad to answer that question, but may I first ask: Does anyone ever say "No" when you ask for something?

He answered, When I was Prime Minister, all I heard was "No." As President, all I hear is "Yes."

The favor was to read some materials about an agricultural initiative the President was interested in, and to meet with the people in charge. I promised I would.

W e were late for a meeting with Prime Minister Netanyahu and half-a-dozen American philanthropists, missing the introductions. When the meeting ended, Ruthie and I approached him and introduced ourselves. He immediately began talking in Hebrew with Ruthie. When she said she was from Petach Tikvah, one of the country's oldest cities, within seconds they realized that they shared several old friends and acquaintances and were familiar with the same schools. Though I didn't understand the words, they obviously were discovering a common background.

I said to the Prime Minister, Everyone in the country is within six degrees of separation.

No, he said—in Israel, it's only one degree.

The same thing happened the first time we met Reuven Rivlin, successor to President Peres as President of Israel. We were in a receiving line. When we reached President Rivlin, Ruthie told him that her mother had grown up in the same neighborhood in Old Jerusalem where Rivlin had grown up. They traded stories about the neighborhood, and the receiving line came to a halt, to the consternation of the host. But Rivlin was interested in recalling the sights and sounds of his old neighborhood. His family had lived in Old Jerusalem for more generations than he could count. Ruthie's family had lived there longer.

The one degree of separation reinforced itself vividly at a national birthday party for President Peres. The celebration took place in a packed auditorium. Security was beyond tight. After everyone, including the President, was seated, Prime Minister Netanyahu entered the hall, surrounded by four bodyguards, each within a few feet of him. After the Prime Minister sat, a series of speakers recounted the President's illustrious career and key roles throughout Israel's existence as a nation.

Then the Prime Minister went to the podium to speak. Recent press articles had reported tensions between him and the President.

The Prime Minister spoke highly of the President. The one degree of separation was his saying: When terrorists kidnapped Israelis and

Jews in 1976 and flew them to Entebbe, Shimon Peres—then the Minister of Defense—had to make a difficult decision whether and how to try to rescue them. My brother Yoni was killed in the rescue. Shimon Peres made the tough decision, and he was right.

T hings change quickly in Israel. On a subsequent trip, we were scheduled to meet again with Prime Minister Netanyahu. Earlier that day, a missile fired from Syria killed two Israeli soldiers and wounded seven on the Golan Heights. Retaliation or full-scale war were possibilities, and our meeting was cancelled. The Prime Minister's office warned us to stay away from the north.

Two days later, Israel had not retaliated and the situation seemed calm. We drove to the north, and stood on the heights overlooking Syria and Lebanon. The air was fresh, the flowers blooming. The continual booms of explosions across the Syrian border broke the silence.

A United Nations observer was standing alone on a ledge, calmly munching a sandwich and occasionally peering across the border through large binoculars. We asked him what the booming noises were.

Artillery shelling, he said. It's fine as long as they keep the killings over there.

We asked to look through his binoculars.

Use the ones over there, he answered, pointing a few feet away to a pair of binoculars mounted on a stand. Put five shekels into the slot and watch those lunatics kill each other.

T he next time I met the Prime Minister was on his visit to

Manhattan to address the UN General Assembly. Ruthie and I joined him at his midtown hotel, taking the elevator to floor X, being checked by security, then escorted through a stairwell to floor Y, past another security post, then through a warren of corridors, more security, and finally to a suite, where the Prime Minister, surrounded by aides, invited us to sit down and chat.

He said he'd heard we'd been doing good work for Israel, and asked for the details.

I had brought with me a copy of *The Aleph Solution*, inscribed, and handed it to him. Before I answer you, I said, I have waited for nearly forty years to give this to you. I told him I'd begun writing it on July 4, 1976. I knew that everyone in the room recognized the date of the Entebbe rescue.

Netanyahu took the book and read the cover flaps outlining my background and the plot. The room was quiet. I hoped I hadn't been insensitive with a man I barely knew, and that he'd understand the deep respect intended by the gift.

He finally looked up at me. When did you study at Harvard?

I told him.

I was there a few years later, he said. I will read it. I promise you.

He asked for specifics about the Trust's program in Israel. I gave him a quick north-to-south synopsis. He said we'd been so low-key that though he'd heard we'd been doing wonderful work, he hadn't appreciated the scope, and said he was very impressed and grateful on behalf of the country.

I asked for his suggestions about how we could do even better. He said he'd give it some thought, and that we'd meet again and he'd share his ideas. Then we talked about the country, and the way it was facing its extraordinary challenges. The Prime Minister was scheduled to address the UN the following morning and our meeting had been scheduled for ten minutes. After half an hour, an aide reminded him that his next appointment was waiting, and we left.

Several months later, the Prime Minister addressed a group of major Jewish philanthropies in Washington D.C. One of his aides approached and said the Prime Minister would like to see us afterwards.

We went to his hotel, with a similar labyrinth of super-security. This time, we met in a small anteroom, with only the Prime Minister.

Netanyahu was suffering from a bad cold, coughing and wheezing and apologizing for it. If it were me, I would have been in bed with a blanket over my head.

I've been thinking of all you're doing for the country, he said, and was specific enough to convince me he really knew. But his cough was getting worse, and I sensed we should make the meeting short. My legal training hadn't prepared me for the question I was now confronted with: Does one offer a half-used packet of mints, which I had in my pocket, to a head of state? Does he have an official taster? I figured the man is sick, offer him what's left of the packet of mints, and I did. He took it and read the label— "Sugar"—and politely declined.

I received an email: My name is Esther Wachsman. Maybe you've heard of my son Nachshon. I'm connected to Shalva, which runs a center in Jerusalem for over five hundred mentally and physically challenged children. I live in Israel but will be traveling to the U.S. in a few weeks. May I meet with you? And may I bring the director of the center?

Two weeks later, I met her: a slight, sixty-ish lady; five feet tall, if; with a gentle face and a soft voice, born in a displaced persons camp in Germany. She said she has six sons, one with Down Syndrome. For years, that son has attended Shalva.

The director of the center came with her. He and his wife have a son who was vaccinated at infancy with a contaminated vaccine that left him blind and deaf. Miraculously, the boy had learned to communicate through letters placed in his hand—a Helen Keller story.

Mrs. Wachsman and the director described the strains not only on children suffering such afflictions, but the impact on parents, spouses, and siblings of the twenty-four-hour needs that such children have. They described the needs' relentlessness: no time off, no safe haven, no temporary respite. So these two people established, in 1990, a facility to provide day care for their children and others similarly stricken; providing an education the children can absorb, with a modicum of social life, in a facility staffed with caring people. Maintaining such a facility in clean and fresh condition costs money. Mrs. Wachsman and the director were wondering whether the Helmsley Trust might help. I told them I'd let them know soon.

After the business part of the meeting ended, we sat and schmoozed. I told Mrs. Wachsman that I knew who she was and what happened to another of her sons, and she filled in the details.

She had been born in Brooklyn, and moved to Israel over forty years ago. In 1993, she'd had seven sons, not six. One of them, Nachshon, was a young soldier. He was given a one-week leave and came home to his mother. On a Sunday night, he left to travel north for special military training. He told his mother he'd be back the following night.

He hitched a ride to get to his base—a common way young Israelis get around. A car stopped to give him a lift. Inside were several young men dressed like orthodox Jews, wearing yarmulkes, with Jewish prayer books visible on the dashboard and Chassidic music playing on the tape deck. In Israel, cars registered to Arabs in the West Bank have distinctive license plates, for security reasons; but in Jerusalem, all residents receive the same type of plates. The car Nachshon entered had regular Israeli plates.

Nachshon did not return home Monday night. On Tuesday, an Israeli television reporter came to Mrs. Wachsman's home and showed her a video the studio had received: of Nachshon, bound hands and feet to a chair, with a Hamas terrorist, face hidden behind a kheffiya, pointing a rifle at his head. The video threatened that Nachshon would be shot on Friday at 8:00 p.m. unless Israel were to release the so-called spiritual head of Hamas, who was being held for terrorism in an Israeli prison, and two hundred other terrorist prisoners.

The policy of Israel is to not negotiate with terrorists. Israeli intelligence agents captured and interrogated the driver of the car, and learned that Nachshon was being held in an apartment ten minutes from the Wachsman home. As the Friday deadline approached, tens of thousands of Israelis assembled in the streets to implore the government to free Nachshon by releasing the terrorists, and prayed for him at the Western Wall; in Israel, every soldier is everyone's son or daughter.

Early that Friday evening, an elite group of Israeli commandos approached the apartment where Nachshon was being held. The intelligence they had amassed for the operation was considerable but imperfect, and seconds needed for the element of surprise were lost. Nachshon and the leader of the commando unit were killed— in Israel, the leader doesn't say "charge," but "follow me"—and ten other commandos wounded. The terrorists who had been holding Nachshon were killed in the operation. The multitudes of Israelis who had prayed for Nachshon now mourned.

Twelve years later, a young Israeli soldier named Gilad Shalit was captured by Hamas terrorists who infiltrated Israel through an underground tunnel from Gaza, and was held hostage for nearly five years. Neither the Red Cross nor any other organization was permitted access to him. He was finally released, emaciated, in exchange for Israel releasing 1,027 Palestinian prisoners, including hundreds of terrorists. It was a gut-wrenching concession felt by nearly all Israelis. Esther Wachsman implored Prime Minister Netanyahu to release the prisoners so that another Israeli mother would not have to feel the pain that she had carried for so many years.

Mrs. Wachsman's face and personality conveyed anguish and grief, perseverance and hope. She was devoted to Shalva. President Peres and Prime Minister Netanyahu were supporters of the facility. Both used the same expression: The measure of a civilization is how it treats the helpless. The Helmsley Trust granted Shalva $1 million for construction of a dining hall and events space in a children's center. You can see Shalva as you drive up the hills of Jerusalem. And, had you been in Israel at the time, you could have watched and heard the eight-person Shalva band—some blind, some cognitively impaired, some otherwise disabled—performing at the Eurovision music competition and bringing down the house.

Natan Sharansky was going to be in New York, and wanted to know if I'd meet with him.

Decades earlier, Sharansky had stared down the Soviet Union. In the early 1970s, when he was in his twenties and a mathematician living in Moscow, Jews were not permitted to emigrate. Sharansky became a spokesman and the most prominent public face of the "Refuseniks"—Jews whose applications to leave the country were refused by the Soviet government. He was arrested in 1977, and convicted by a kangaroo court on phony charges of treason and spying for the United States, and sentenced to thirteen years' imprisonment.

Though out of sight, Sharansky remained in the public eye throughout his years of imprisonment. Before he went to jail, his wife, Avital, had gotten out of the Soviet Union and moved to Israel. Sharansky had promised he'd meet her there soon.

When he was imprisoned, Avital campaigned indefatigably all over the world for his freedom. Photos of her—a slight, unassuming woman meeting with President Reagan and other heads of state—appeared for years in media around the world. So too did photos of Sharansky's elderly mother, standing in the freezing cold Siberian snow, alone, outside the stone prison where her son was kept, protesting his imprisonment. Rallies were held across the globe, for years, protesting the refusal of the Soviets to permit Jewish emigration in general and the unjust continual imprisonment of Sharansky. Even President Carter, whose anti-Israel views later became apparent, broke a long-standing policy of American presidents not commenting on Soviet spying charges (since denying an allegation against one could create an adverse inference from a later refusal to comment regarding another), unequivocally denying that Sharansky ever spied for the United States.

After serving nine years of his sentence, much of it in isolation, hard labor, and in the gulag, for "crimes" he did not commit, and after incessant American and international pressure, Sharansky was released in 1986. He was flown to meet Avital in Germany. When he saw her for the first time after all those years, he apologized: "Sorry I'm late."

Sharansky and Avital flew to a hero's welcome in Israel, greeted there by thousands, including the heads of the Israeli government. In the United States, he was awarded the Congressional Gold Medal and the Presidential Medal of Freedom. Following his release, large rallies protesting the Soviet refusal to allow Jews to leave were held around the world. The Soviets eventually allowed a million Jews to go to Israel, and another half-million to the United States and elsewhere.

Sharansky served in Israel's government for nine years, and

then became chairman of the Jewish Agency For Israel, an organization which rescues and protects Jews all over the world, and
helps Jews who voluntarily emigrate to Israel.

My office intercom announced: Mr. Sharansky is here. I walked
out to the waiting room, and there he was, just like in the pictures.
I extended my hand to him and said, Sorry I'm late.

"Nice line," he answered.

We walked to my office and he explained why he'd come to see
me.

Several weeks earlier, a terrorist had murdered a thirty-year-old
rabbi, two of his children, and another child at a Jewish school in
Toulouse, France. Natan explained that Israeli authorities have
ways of knowing the who, where, and when of many planned terrorist attacks on Jews throughout the world. But innocent people,
guilty only of being Jewish, were being killed because of financial
limitations on protecting them. The terrorists' reach was simply
too long and their financial resources too great—Israel and vulnerable Jewish communities did not have enough money to provide
protection such as security guards, equipment, protective windows, bulletproof vests, and other defensive materials. Natan
asked: Would the Helmsley Trust help?

I let his question hang unanswered for a time. I finally answered:
Life takes many odd turns. Decades ago, when I would think of
you in Siberia and see pictures of your mother waiting helplessly in
the snow outside the prison, and your wife sitting with world leaders asking their help in getting you released, I never dreamed that
a day might come when I would be sitting with you, long after you
became a free man, and you would ask me for help with something. We then discussed how funding by the Trust might help prevent deaths of innocent Jews at terrorists' hands.

Before he left, I asked whether he intended to reenter politics. He
said that he was one of the rare politicians who had gone to prison

before going into politics rather than after. He said that Bibi—Prime Minister Netanyahu's childhood nickname by which he was commonly called—had asked him to join the government, but that he had turned down the offer: I told Bibi that I spent nine years in the gulag and nine years in the Knesset, and both were enough for me.

Money-talk evolved into the personal. I asked about his years in the gulag, and he told me that it could have been much shorter. After the first six years of his imprisonment, under horrific conditions, he had gone on a protracted hunger strike when prison guards confiscated a makeshift menorah he had used to celebrate Hanukkah. Then, several leading American Jews negotiated terms of his release, without consulting him: He'd be freed if he would simply request release on grounds of poor health. But Natan refused. He would not permit the Soviets to transmute the injustice and anti-Semitism of his incarceration into a false act of Soviet humaneness. So he served three more years in Siberia, until being released on his own terms, unconditionally.

A t my first meeting with Natan, I remarked that his refusal to bend to the powers of the Soviet Union, and his ultimate release from the gulag, demonstrated the power of one person. The power of two, he said.

A year later, when Ruthie and I were in Israel, Natan invited us to join Avital and him for a Sabbath lunch in their apartment in Jerusalem. Our taxi driver, an Israeli Arab, got lost getting to the address, and when we finally arrived asked why we hadn't simply told him we were going to the Sharansky apartment—everyone knows where they live. No security. Natan had shopped in an open food market that morning.

At the apartment, I met Avital. After Natan's release from

prison, she had disappeared from public view, devoting herself to raising their children and living a quiet life in Jerusalem. The meal was overflowing, and as we got to know each other, they lifted the shutters of their lives a bit.

Avital's parents hadn't even told her she was Jewish until she was a teenager, fearing persecution if the family's Jewishness were known. And Natan told us of his beginning flirtation with Avital: When they'd met in Moscow and she wanted to enroll in one of the refusenik's Hebrew language programs, Natan told her there was a class for those who knew no Hebrew, and a more advanced class—his—for those who knew more than one thousand words. She said that was also her level. Turns out, she knew no Hebrew, and that's how Natan figured she might have a romantic interest in him.

I told Avital how Natan had corrected my statement that his ordeal had demonstrated the power of a single person, and joked that he had misinterpreted my statement—I had actually been referring to Avital, I said, not to him. But Avital corrected us both: Natan's release from the gulag had not demonstrated the power of either one or two—they had millions of Israelis with them.

The Sharanskys' warmth led me to occasionally forget the reality of what he'd endured. We met one evening for dinner in a restaurant. I asked the waiter to dim a low-hanging overhead light that was annoying me—must be like the guards used against Natan, I commented offhandedly to Avital.

No, she explained. That's not what they used. They put very bright lights right in his face and shined them directly into his eyes.

The Trust has given $4.5 million to the Jewish Agency for

protection of Jewish communities. Our first payment occurred shortly before a series of anti-Semitic attacks in Ukraine. Natan phoned me right after the attacks. I'm calling, he said, to thank the Trust for its money and to let you know that it came just in time: You have helped us save lives in Ukraine. I told him it was a great honor, and got goosebumps.

Several years later, the goosebumps recurred. On Yom Kippur in 2019, a terrorist attacked a synagogue in Halle, Germany. Fifty-one worshippers were inside. The door withstood multiple blasts from the terrorist's rifle. The people inside were able to see what was happening outside, through the synagogue's newly installed security camera system, so they barricaded themselves inside and called the police. The terrorist left, and randomly killed two innocent people in the street before being captured by police.

An hour later, I received a call from someone in the Israel Prime Minister's office saying "thank you" for saving those lives. A grant we'd made to the Jewish Agency for upgrading the synagogue's security system had helped prevent a bloodbath.

As the Trust's work in Israel grew, representatives of various media asked to interview me. One of those was a columnist for *Yediot Aharonot*, a leading Israeli newspaper. He was a journalist highly respected throughout the country; to-the-point, occasionally acerbic, and very smart. He had been a reporter and columnist in Israel for decades.

I met him for an interview on the majestic terrace of the King David Hotel in the heart of Jerusalem. He asked pointed questions about the Trust, Leona Helmsley, the Trust's mission in Israel, grants we had made and might consider, and me. We seemed to hit it off, and his resulting column was positive.

But our meeting had been uncomfortable for me, lest I make a comment revealing what was really on my mind. In anticipation of the interview, I had followed three basic rules for successful litigation: preparation, preparation, and preparation. Throughout the interview, my mind functioned on two tracks: our conversation, and what I had read about the journalist's background. Years earlier, he had been assigned by the newspaper to cover a terrorist bombing of a bus which had just occurred and resulted in horrible deaths and maimings. His editor suddenly called him back to the newspaper's office, to avoid his learning, at the site of the bombed-out bus, that his son was among the dead.

Because Israel is so small, lightning sometimes strikes twice. I met with the founders of Hatzalah, an extraordinary organization of first responders to medical emergencies, including, since this is Israel, terrorist attacks. In its earliest start-up days, the two founders were dispatched to a terrorist bombing in the heart of Jerusalem. Blood and body parts lay everywhere. They turned over one mortally wounded man. He was the uncle of one of them.

Retired colonel Ilan Egozi was the executive director of Beit Halochem, an organization dedicated to rehabilitation of seriously injured members of the Israel Defense Force and victims of terrorism. The organization was building a new rehabilitation center, and he asked to meet with me to explain their financial needs.

When we met, the first thing that struck me about Ilan was not that one eye and his right hand were missing; it was that his one functional eye and his smile were full of life, and that he carried himself as if he were the happiest, luckiest, and most secure man in the world.

Statistics showing large numbers of Israelis killed in wars and in terrorist attacks vastly understate the enormous physical and psychological toll suffered by Israelis—many tens of thousands seriously maimed, missing arms, legs, eyes, and other body parts. Those injuries remain for a lifetime, long after the headlines fade. Five rehabilitation centers in Israel—privately built and privately maintained, and provided without charge to all in need—have been built by Beit Halochem to help the seriously wounded.

Ilan described the work done by these centers, the substantial costs involved, and the money needed to complete the latest. I said I'd look into the possibility of Helmsley helping.

The most interesting part of funding projects in Israel is after the money talk ends and people feel comfortable enough to talk about themselves. What I hear puts the petty annoyances of everyday life into perspective. So it was with Ilan.

In 1967, faced with imminent attack, Israel defeated the combined Arab armies of its neighbors that were threatening to wipe it off the face of the earth. At the end of the war, Israel held several thousand Egyptian soldiers; Egypt held ten Israeli soldiers. In talks that might lead to an exchange of prisoners, Egypt released photos of all but one Israeli prisoner—Ilan, an Israeli Navy commando. The Egyptian authorities did not release any photo of Ilan because they had beaten him so severely during interrogation, they were not sure he would survive.

After Ilan's release, he continued to serve in dangerous clandestine operations that are part of Israel's 24/7 need for military vigilance. In 1973, he led a unit in an operation deep inside Lebanon, targeting terrorists in Fatah headquarters pinpointed by IDF intelligence. One of the soldiers under Ilan's command tossed a grenade toward a window at the terrorists. The grenade hit one of the window's grates and ricocheted back, unexploded, toward the troops. Ilan instinctively grabbed it and tried to toss it away to save his men. It exploded in his right hand, blowing off the hand, destroying his right eye, and severely injuring one of his legs. He ordered the soldier who came to help him to complete the mission and come back to help him only when it was done.

Despite his injuries, Ilan continued to serve as a Navy commando in later operations. He turned down a command position because he thought it could endanger his men. He received the IDF's two highest decorations for bravery.

The Trust granted $2 million to the Beit Halochem center being built in Beersheva, to serve the injured in the South. Saving wounded soldiers and victims of terrorists several hours of discomfort driving in a car to the north will mean that they in fact have access to a rehabilitation center. (We have since helped build other Beit Halochem centers with comparable funding amounts.)

When Ruthie and I visited the facility, Ilan greeted us and introduced us to a small, young lady in her mid-twenties who escorted us around the center. She wore a thin off-the-shoulder blouse—a style out of place in this environment. Men and women without functional legs played tennis and basketball in wheelchairs; paralyzed veterans were able to swim in the "Helmsley Charitable Trust Hydrotherapy Pool"; and families gathered together at tables on a lawn to capture a semblance of normalcy.

Ilan walked us to our taxi to say goodbye, and mentioned the girl.

What she wore was not a fashion statement, he explained. The girl had held a military command position in the IDF. During a drill, she was carrying a rifle nearly her size. She slipped, and the barrel of the rifle jammed forcefully into one of her shoulders, causing severe nerve damage. Any touch to her shoulder—even the softest cotton of a blouse—causes her excruciating pain, and so she is forced to dress that way.

A year later, Ilan sent me a magazine published by Beit Halochem. His face was on the cover and, inside, a brief history of his career. I flipped through the pages, looking at the pictures. On the pages following the article about Ilan were two pictures. One was of a handsome twenty-one-year-old soldier whose face was joyful and brimmed with confidence and vigor. On the facing page was a photo of an older man sitting in a wheelchair, slightly hunched, with a sparkle in his eyes and a warm smile.

Ruthie translated the article for me. The two pictures were of the same man. I finally learned what had happened to the heroic commando who had been shot in the spine forty years earlier during the Entebbe rescue. He was paralyzed from the neck down. Ilan told me the man regularly uses one of the Beit Halochem rehabilitation centers we helped fund.

Sallai Meridor had recently resigned as Israel's Ambassador to the United States. Now, he was International Chairman of the Jerusalem Foundation, a nonprofit organization dedicated to improving the lives of residents of Jerusalem—Jewish, Muslim, Christian, all. Shortly after the Trust's Israel program began its grant-making, Sallai and several colleagues came to see me about the Trust's possibly funding a project they had in mind.

Jerusalem, Sallai explained, though having one of the largest international press presences in the world, lacked any facility dedicated to nonpartisan, objective press reporting. The American

Colony Hotel in eastern Jerusalem served as the base of operations for Arab propagandists, functioning without any restraint, factual or otherwise. Foreign journalists would hang out there.

The Jerusalem Foundation, unaffiliated with any political party or ethnic group, proposed that a historic unused building sorely in need of renovation, in the center of Jerusalem, directly across the street from the stone walls of the Old City, be converted into a nonprofit press club, complete with modern media facilities. Journalists, foreign and Israeli, could congregate there, have access to high-level newsmakers, and use it as a professional base to see the country for themselves, factually and free of political influence. That, of course, would cost money, which Sallai hoped the Trust might provide.

He went on at considerable length to pitch the wisdom of our funding the club. What he didn't know was that what he was trying to sell, I, on behalf of the Trust, had been looking to buy: a "truth machine"—some way to let the world see, accurately, the truth about Israel—what it is and is not, how remarkable its people are, what are its considerable challenges, and how it surmounts those challenges and flourishes. Louis Brandeis, the first Jewish justice of the Supreme Court of the United States, wrote that sunlight is the best disinfectant. I wanted some way to help bring that principle to those who report about Israel.

When Sallai finished his pitch, he asked what I thought. I responded that the Trust is still new; we have to allocate very large amounts of money; we are just getting started and still trying to get traction; we don't move as quickly or nimbly as I'd ideally like; the project he was proposing involves a lot of money; there are other trustees involved; and so, I told him, getting back to him would take at least twenty minutes.

The Trust committed nearly $3 million to build the Jerusalem Press Club. A formal opening was held a year later, on a lovely

June evening in the courtyard of the club, overlooking the imposing floodlit walls built hundreds of years ago during the time of the
Ottoman Empire. The Mayor of Jerusalem unveiled a brass plaque
on the outside of the front door: Helmsley House, home of the
Jerusalem Press Club.

The mayor spoke first, to a gathering of over one hundred
Israelis, extolling the openness of Jerusalem and the country, as
personified by this new facility. Then Natan Sharansky spoke,
comparing Israel's freedom of the press to the Soviet system that
had robbed so many years of his life. And then I was asked to
speak, and began by observing that although the miracles of Israel
and Jerusalem were universally known, I had never imagined that
those miracles could include a guy from the Bronx sharing the
stage with the Mayor of Jerusalem and Natan Sharansky.

The Israeli consul general in New York City called to ask if I
would meet with Doron Almog. He said Almog was raising funds
for a nonprofit organization to establish a rehabilitation village for
mentally disabled people. He also said Almog was a renowned and
highly decorated retired IDF General.

I met with General Almog—soon, Doron—a few weeks later.
He had devoted his life to two commitments: protecting the State
of Israel, and helping Israelis unable to help themselves. How he
got there:

He and his brother, Eran, were young soldiers when Israel was
suddenly attacked by combined Arab armies during Yom Kippur—
the holiest day in the Jewish religion, when virtually nothing moves
in Israel—in 1973. Doron served in battle in the south; Eran served
as a tank commander in the north on the Golan Heights, where
Israeli soldiers were outnumbered nearly ten to one. Despite Israel's

ultimate military victory, there were thousands of Israeli casualties.

During the war, Doron's mother was notified by the government that Doron and Eran had been killed in battle. This was before the ubiquity of cell phones. When the war ended, Doron called his mother and told her he was alive. He learned that Eran had been killed; seriously wounded in battle, he had bled to death on the battlefield before finally being rescued days later, too late.

Under Israeli rules of conscription, Doron, as the son of a bereaved family, was eligible to end his combat service. He declined, and volunteered for heavy duty combat. He resolved never to abandon a soldier on the battlefield, regardless of risk.

Doron was part of the Entebbe rescue force. He flew in the first plane, landing secretly at the Entebbe airport with Yoni Netanyahu and other commandoes. Doron was the first Israeli soldier to set foot on the airport tarmac, and the last to leave. I'd read whatever was available describing the rescue, and was sufficiently affected to have co-written *The Aleph Solution* right after the rescue, but here was one of the heroes who had actually been there and done that.

Doron later served in numerous dangerous operations, saving many lives. He ultimately served as Major General in charge of the southern command for three years, dealing with thousands of terrorist incidents in the Gaza Strip and preventing every attempt by Palestinian terrorists in Gaza to infiltrate Israel.

A retired Israeli general who has served with such distinction has a glut of post-military opportunities. But when he resigned from the military, he devoted himself to raising funds for the creation of a rehabilitation village for people with severe disabilities. Doron's son, named after his late brother, Eran, had been born with brain damage. He would never be able to function normally. It took him three years to learn to lift a spoon to his mouth. He was unable to do anything for himself.

Doron described Eran as his professor—the person who taught this battle-scarred veteran about love, sensitivity, and caring, beyond what he had ever comprehended. Doron and his wife overcame initial feelings of shame, and resolved not to leave Eran, or others like him, on the battlefield of life.

From nothing, Doron spearheaded the creation of a village in the Negev for disabled people like Eran who were absolutely dependent on others. Eran died there at age twenty-three. Doron and his wife were determined that others like him would not be abandoned. They had developed plans to build a rehabilitation hospital there, and asked if the Helmsley Trust might help. The Trust contributed $2.5 million.

Doron knew of my interest in the Entebbe raid. Meeting by meeting, he told me more about it. Soldiers aren't permitted to reveal inside intelligence, and I wouldn't pry. But hearing the pieces put together by someone who fought in the middle of it, with other young soldiers, putting their lives at risk to overcome impossible odds and save dozens of innocent people, makes all the books and movies pale by comparison.

Hebrew University of Jerusalem is the second oldest university in Israel. It was founded a century ago by, among others, Albert Einstein, who delivered the first lecture at the university, on the theory of relativity. The university has fourteen schools on six campuses, and 23,000 students from Israel and dozens of other countries. Eight faculty members have received the Nobel Prize.

I met with Menahem Ben-Sasson, who had recently become President of the university, at the main entrance to the campus. He had served in the IDF, in an artillery unit. He had also served in the Knesset for nine years. Menahem is a soft-spoken man, a bit embarrassed with the deference given to him by most people we passed in the university.

We met with several scientists who worked on a variety of projects and whose research could be helped or accelerated by additional funding. The science seemed as difficult to Menahem as to me. He was a student of medieval times, having written dozens of books and articles on the topic. I know a bit about medieval times, he said, but could use some help on anything after the fourteenth century.

Among Hebrew University's treasures is that Einstein bequeathed his estate to the university. His handwritten notes and lectures are stored there. He wrote many of them in the same types of small softcover blue books in which I'd written out my final exams in college and law school. The curator handed several of the blue books to me. I turned the pages gingerly. These were Einstein's original penned entries—all Greek to me, and some of it in fact Greek. I'll explain the math one day when you've got some time.

Menahem walked us through Hadassah Hospital, which is affiliated with the university. The hospital brought back particularly poignant memories for Ruthie. She had served there in 1967 during the six-day war, tending to many of the injured. She would see young men wakening from comas or anesthesia realize that they no longer had legs, or arms, or eyes. Israelis know the taste and price of war.

Our tour of the campus ended at a sprawling lawn right outside the Frank Sinatra student cafeteria—the kind of place called "the yard" at dozens of campuses across the United States. The sun shined brilliantly on a few students still lounging there in the late afternoon. It was nearly impossible to imagine the scene at this oasis of tranquility on July 31, 2002, at lunchtime, when the cafeteria and grounds were packed with people, and Palestinian terrorists smuggled in and detonated a bomb that killed nine, maimed and wounded dozens, and left bloody limbs and ruined lives lying on the ground.

Not everyone associated with grantees is shy or retiring. We made a $4.5 million grant to Ariel University for a regional medical center. In honor of the grant, President Rivlin held a ceremony at the presidential residence in Jerusalem. Several dozen people attended.

After some introductory remarks about the importance of the health-care center to the region and thanks to me on behalf of the Trust for making it possible, the President named two people who, he said, deserved special thanks for getting the Trust to pay for the center. Both were former high Israeli government officials, internationally known. Neither had anything to do with the grant. One of them I'd never met, and the other I had met once, when he'd asked for Helmsley funding for a personal project of his and I'd immediately turned him down. They had both obviously taken credit for an important grant they had absolutely nothing to do with.

Ruthie, sitting next to me, was furious. Don't let them get away with it, she whispered to me. I was sitting next to the President.

When it was my turn to say "you're welcome" to all the thanks, I said: Let me tell you the genesis of this grant. I described how Ruthie and I had come up with the idea one night over dinner. The only people responsible for the grant, I added, are the people at the Helmsley Trust. And if that didn't make the point, I added: Nobody else had anything to do with it. I didn't know how to say "full of malarkey" in Hebrew. Then I thanked the President for having hosted us at such a wonderful tribute.

W e visited a large air base Israel had built in the Negev. The site had originally been only a runway, built shortly before the founding of Israel. It had been expanded over the years, and was now a component of a major project to transfer a large part of the IDF from the north of Israel to the south.

After our car passed through security and pulled up to a low-slung building on the post, a young man, probably in his early thirties, came out to greet us. He brought us into a reception area and introduced us to two even younger men. We made small talk about the drive down to the base. We had been told that we would be meeting the commanding officer, and waited for him to appear.

Turns out, the young man speaking with us was the commanding officer. He described the activities of the base, and explained some of the difficulties in a large-scale transfer of a major military facility from one area of the country to another.

Then he walked us outside, where, a few steps away, a camouflage tarpaulin covered a dozen small aircraft. A plane in the middle had flown to Iraq in 1981 and bombed Iraq's Osirak nuclear reactor. Standing next to that small plane, and realizing that two pilots had flown nearly a thousand miles over enemy territory with no protection but their skill and a few accompanying planes, was chilling.

The commander brought a small ladder next to the plane and offered me a photo op: to sit in the cockpit. It seemed sacrilegious to do so, and I declined.

After hearing our amazement at the bravery of pilots flying such tiny aircraft to protect their country from nuclear annihilation, one of the younger men—also a commander—led us to a small room inside an adjoining building.

Secretly, in the early- and mid-1980s, Israel rescued thousands of Ethiopian Jews from dire poverty, oppression, and desperation, and flew them to Israel. The younger commander showed us a grainy, green-tinged film taken of one rescue operation in real time: dozens of destitute Ethiopian Jews, carrying only their children and wearing threadbare torn clothing, being led in pitch blackness onto military planes in the heart of the Sudan, where they had been smuggled from Ethiopia by agents of the Mossad to a future of hope in Israel.

As the last of them boarded the plane, the film showed three figures visible in the distance jumping up and down excitedly, like children. I asked if those were Ethiopian refugees who hadn't been able to board. No, the commander answered, they were Mossad agents who had brought them out of Ethiopia to Sudan, jumping with glee at having gotten them to the safety of a flight to freedom in Israel.

Several years later, I saw the same rescue from a different angle. I met a retired Israeli Major General named Eitan Ben Eliyahu, who had been a fighter pilot for thirty-five years, had flown to Iraq as part of the operation that destroyed the nuclear reactor, and had served as commander of the Israel Air Force. He described having flown from Israel to Sudan, at low altitudes in order to avoid radar detection, to help rescue hundreds of Ethiopian Jews. In a remote area of Sudan, far from any airport or landing strip, he spotted some small stick-lights. They were held by Mossad agents, designating the area for him to land—not a landing strip, only a clearing on the ground. He landed, the Ethiopians were hurriedly ushered onto the plane, and Eitan flew them to Israel.

I told him of my having seen the real-time filming of the rescue: same miracle, but from a different vantage point. He and the others on the plane had been wearing the night vision goggles that cast the green pallor over the video.

I asked him to tell me about the bombing of the Iraqi nuclear reactor. It was simple, he said. The flight to Iraq took ninety minutes, over Jordan and Saudi Arabia through creases in their radar systems. The operation was a complete surprise to Iraq: The pilots dropped their bombs, destroyed the reactor, and flew back home, without drawing enemy fire. The mission had been simple, but only after it was over—his stomach was churning before we got going, he said. The hard part, he said, was the political will in decision-making by then-Prime Minister Menachem Begin in ordering the operation. Begin's job was much harder than mine, Eitan said.

Then he explained the different nature of a possible attack on the Iran nuclear facilities—lessons from an expert. What he didn't mention at the time but I pried out of him later were the plethora of other missions he'd undertaken. His bombing operations into Egypt during the war of attrition were much tougher than flying to Iraq, he said; the Egyptians were ready with anti-aircraft weaponry, and he had to parachute out of his plane when it was hit by Egyptian fire, curling his body into a ball with his knees pressed into his chest to minimize himself as a target from Egyptian fire as the parachute drifted down, and owing a debt of gratitude to the wind, which carried his parachute to the Israeli side of the fighting and avoided his becoming a POW or worse.

W hen I was eighteen, I was commuting to college; when Israelis turn eighteen, they're in the army. These days, I go out to the Hamptons during summer weekends, relax on the beach, and see occasional small planes pass by, advertising a concert or a beer or some other diversion; on the beach in Israel, you see planes constantly tracing the coastline, looking for terrorists trying to infiltrate. It's two different worlds.

I met the commander-in-chief of Israel's air force in the IDF's

large underground headquarters in the Tel Aviv area. Gaza terrorists had fired an unusually large number of rockets into Israel earlier that day, and I expected our appointment to be cancelled for
more important matters. It wasn't.

How come? I asked him.

We're used to these things, he said. We're prepared.

In my office are pictures of my family, and diplomas, certifi-
cates of bar admissions, and other memorabilia of a life in the law.
In the commander's office, he had one photo on his desk, of his
family. Three walls were bare. On the fourth wall, behind his desk,
was one photo: Jerusalem.

The Gaza Strip is a rectangular strip of land on Israel's western
corner. Its twenty-five-mile length abuts the Mediterranean. It is
seven miles wide at its widest, four miles at its narrowest. Following
Israel's War of Independence in 1948, the Gaza Strip was under
Egyptian military rule, but Egypt did not give its residents citizen-
ship. After the six-day war in 1967, Israel established paramilitary
enclaves in the strip. In 1978, when Israel, in exchange for a peace
treaty with Egypt, agreed to return every inch of the Sinai Peninsula,
Egypt had not asked for the Gaza Strip, leaving its problems and
dangers for the Israelis to sort out. Israelis began moving into the
strip, building homes and protected by Israeli soldiers.

In 2005, after decades of Israelis living in the Gaza Strip despite
thousands of terrorist attacks, the government of Israel, without
getting anything in return, ordered the withdrawal of all Israelis
living there, removing many by force and hoping Israel would now
be free from attacks from Gaza.

But thousands more terrorist attacks followed Israel's departure. Hamas, a movement dedicated to Islamic fundamentalism

and Israel's destruction, took over the strip, and years of unrelenting war followed—sometimes full-blown, always present.

We visited the small town of Sderot, less than a mile from the
Gaza Strip. From Sderot, you can see the wire fences and some of
the security apparatus used by the Israeli military to detect and
prevent terrorist attacks. But the attacks are incessant, and not
indiscriminate—they are aimed at civilians and children, the most
vulnerable groups in the area. Those attacks are constant—there is
no "peace time."

No rockets were fired during our visit to Sderot. The town was
peaceful. We visited a school in the center of town. Outwardly, it
was like any other school, with children in a classroom, teachers
teaching—except here, one of the rooms was a bomb shelter, and
many of the children's drawings were of bombs falling and body
parts flying.

There's a playground outside. In the center of the playground is
a sculpture of a long, tall, brightly colored caterpillar, unusual in
its size, hollowed out on the inside, that a handful of children were
running in and out of.

When rockets are fired at Sderot, Israeli high-tech sensors
sound an alarm warning that rockets will strike the ground in ten
seconds; every day, at every moment, every resident of Sderot must
be within ten seconds of a bomb shelter. There are many bomb
shelters in Sderot, and there is a monument for a young man who
didn't reach one in time and suffered a direct hit.

To the people who live there, Sderot is home. They won't be intim-
idated; they won't move; they won't desert the town. When rockets
hit, the Israeli army—their army—strikes back with force. The citizens are strong, proud, and unflinching. They know the enemy.

The big, ungainly, multi-colored caterpillar in the schoolyard is
a bomb shelter. The children are never more than ten seconds from
safety.

Other atttacks besides rockets were intended for Israel from the Gaza Strip. On a later trip to the area, we visited several new Israeli towns developed along the border, founded by new pioneers. These small communities were surrounded by protective fences. During one of the Gaza wars, Israel had discovered dozens of tunnels secretly dug by Hamas, providing hidden underground entry from Gaza into Israel. Many of the tunnels were connected to others in an elaborate underground network.

We entered one tunnel that the Israelis had preserved for the world to see—it's still there, go see for yourself. This tunnel was built more than thirty feet below ground, completely concealed. The walls inside were concrete, wired with electric lines and communication cables. We walked easily through the tunnel. It was wide and high enough for vehicles and equipment to pass through.

Several steps inside was a junction to another tunnel. We were in the remains of a highly developed underground roadway system for terrorists, emptying secretly into Israel. The thought of entering these tunnels in the midst of a war, not knowing who was hiding in wait or what hidden explosive device the next step might detonate, was terrifying.

The Gaza Strip is less than a mile away from the opening at the end of the tunnel on the Israeli side—about the distance of my walk to elementary school in the Bronx. The tunnels had been built invisibly—they began inside a house in Gaza, or a school or mosque there, dug straight down into the earth and then horizontally underground across Israel's border and opening into the soft underbelly of Israeli civilian communities. One of the tunnels had already extended under the dining room of a large kibbutz where hundreds of ordinary people eat every day.

When you see it, you understand the massacre that had been planned: Hundreds of armed terrorists simultaneously emerging with heavy weapons from tunnels, running, or on motorcycles driven through the tunnels, in a coordinated attack on civilians, murdering and kidnapping children, women, and men at will. The terrorists had also manufactured Israel Defense Force uniforms so that when Israeli soldiers would finally arrive they'd have trouble recognizing friend from foe. Standing in that tunnel, and emerging onto the quiet field steps from the small homes that dotted the area, drove home the stark reality: The entire community could have been decimated. And this tunnel was one of dozens. The massacre would have been Israel's 9/11.

A security guard with a machine gun slung over his shoulder described confronting a terrorist who had emerged from the tunnel. When the guard realized belatedly—a millisecond is "belatedly" when confronting a terrorist with a Kalashnikov—that the person standing there intended to kill him, he shot and killed the terrorist. Not until other residents rushed to the scene did the security guard realize he had been shot in the stomach and was bleeding badly.

These new communities were being built by people with deep ties to Israel. Many had ancestors in Israel reaching back many generations. They were literally, in the words of Ben Gurion, making the desert bloom: Fields of vegetation and greenery were surrounded by desolate land. We picked a carrot from the field and washed it off with bottled water; it tasted sweet as candy.

What could a charitable trust do to help these people? The law doesn't permit our buying guns or bullets for them to defend themselves; we are allowed to spend only for charitable purposes. So we helped them in other ways:

The communities lacked adequate medical care. They had a beat-up building that served as an occasional clinic, rarely visited by a doctor, and easy targets for rockets. To attract more families and develop, they needed a real medical center, which had to be

secured because it would surely be targeted by rockets. The Trust
gave $1.9 million to build one.

W e drove a few miles to a clinic in another small community
near the Gaza Strip. One room in the clinic was a bomb shelter,
built with Helmsley funds, so that patients being treated did not
have to flee the clinic when it was under rocket attack. The personnel expressed their gratitude. The shelter would allow residents to
seek medical help without fear of being killed there. We'd also
given them funds to buy two custom-fortified vans and protective
vests and helmets, to protect medical personnel traveling to patients
or transporting medical supplies.

The director of health care services in the area showed me a
map. In tiny Hebrew lettering, several dozen small Israeli villages
appeared as spots all around the border of the Gaza Strip. Twenty-
nine of those spots were circled in red. I asked the director what
the red circles represented.

Those twenty-nine towns, he said, all have clinics with bomb
shelters provided by the Helmsley Trust.

R ockets and tunnels were not the limits of the constant attacks
on these small border communities. The terrorists' tactics changed:
They began sending hundreds of incendiary devices, including flam-
mable balloons, into Israel, targeting hundreds of acres of farmland
and surrounding communities. We did our best to help there too. I
walked through acres of burned, blackened grass and crops that
had been destroyed just outside the Gaza border, until a security
guard who'd driven us there gave me a dose of reality: Get back

into the car, he warned, those are real snipers on the other side. When I returned to New York, we gave money to build dozens of bomb shelters to be interspersed in particularly vulnerable open areas in the fields, along with firefighting equipment, and money to fortify buildings in a college nearby—over $7 million in all.

Magen David Adom ("Red Shield of David") is Israel's national blood center, collecting, testing, processing, and distributing Israel's blood supply, including nearly all of the blood used in Israel's hospitals and by the IDF. It also provides ambulances, paramedical services, and disaster relief. The central blood bank had been built in the 1980s and was now outdated, unable to keep up with technological developments and too small for the current population. Moreover, it was not fortified to withstand rocket attacks from Gaza and, having been built between two geological fault lines, was vulnerable to possible earthquakes. They needed to build another blood center that was budgeted to cost $110 million, and needed a sizeable grant to boost them off the financial launching pad.

Ruthie and I drove to the existing center, met with the director and her staff, and asked how their fundraising had been going.

Not as successful as we'd like, was the answer. The reason: concern that full-scale fundraising would raise the center's public profile and make it an even more attractive target for rockets. The director said that targeting rockets at the center was self-defeating, since Palestinians from Gaza travel to the center every day for treatment.

I had heard of Gazans being treated at the center, and asked: Why doesn't Israel publicize the fact that it regularly provides medical care to the very people committed to its destruction?

Because, the director answered, if we did that, Hamas wouldn't let the people come to Israel for treatment anymore. We wouldn't be able to help them.

The Helmsley Trust gave $8 million to help build the new national blood center.

In Israel, 10 percent of the population lives in the Negev, the desert area in the south that comprises 60 percent of Israel's total land. There are only two full-service hospitals serving this entire area: Beersheva's Soroka Hospital in the northern part of the Negev, and a hospital at the southern tip of the country in the city of Eilat. Many people in the Negev live in poverty, with lower life expectancies and higher infant mortality than the rest of the country. Their health needs are primarily served by clinics and small hospitals.

Israel's largest healthcare organization is Clalit, which has a network of hospitals, clinics, and pharmacies throughout the country. Clalit sought funds from the Trust to build an electronic medical records system and an "e-pharmacy" program in the Negev's healthcare facilities. The EMR system would replace paper medical records and permit doctors to instantaneously access medical records from any other facility participating in the program, anywhere in the country. A patient treated at one hospital who might seek follow-up treatment elsewhere would be able to do so with the treating physicians having access digitally to all of the patient's medical history. The e-pharmacy program would prevent common mistakes in the prescription and administration of medications. Both of these electronic systems are technologically sophisticated and expensive to implement.

We drove through the Negev to get an on-the-ground sense of

their medical needs. We slept in a hotel in a sparsely populated town called Mitzpe Ramon, in the middle of the desert, built on the edge of an elevation overlooking a crater. In the morning, a cleaning lady came to our room, and Ruthie began speaking with her in Hebrew. The woman had emigrated to Israel from Romania five years ago. She loved Israel as a land of opportunity where she and her husband, through hard work, could lay the groundwork for a better life for their children.

But she had a problem. A daughter suffered from epilepsy. Whenever she had a seizure, she had to be driven to Beersheva, two hours away, because that's where all of her treatment records were. It was always a difficult journey: hours of driving, on difficult roads; waiting for her daughter to be examined, tests to be administered, records to be checked, and then driving back south to work. I wish there was a way for my daughter to be treated at the local clinic in Mitzpe Ramon, she said.

Later that day, Ruthie and I drove to Beersheva to meet with the heads of Clalit and the Soroka hospital. They toured us through the hospital and showed us the difficulties of treating patients without easy access to medical and pharmaceutical records.

The Trust granted Clalit $4.8 million to implement electronic medical records and e-pharmacy programs in its southern hospitals, which were later extended to hospitals throughout the country.

A reported Israeli missile strike in Syria killed a high-ranking Hezbollah commander, an Iranian general, and several other high-target terrorists. Hezbollah and Iranian leaders threatened ferocious retaliation. Israel raised its alert level in the north, and deployed Iron Dome anti-missile batteries there. Media reported tensions in the area to be sky-high. The U.S. government issued a security alert restricting its employees' travel in the north of Israel.

Ruthie and I were scheduled to fly to Israel the next day to visit a number of sites, including in the north, where the Trust had given several grants and was considering more. A colleague at the Trust asked if I intended to cancel our trip because of security concerns.

No, I said. What message would that send to Israelis? We'll send you money, but when it comes to real life you're on your own?

Israelis are used to living under such conditions, and reacted to the threats in typical fashion. A heavy snowstorm had recently fallen on Mount Hermon, near the Syrian border. The ski resort there was teeming with visitors. Iron Dome to the left, skiing to the right.

I was invited to a "think tank" conference in Washington featuring Israeli and American political leaders and other luminaries. During one of the breaks, I joined a conversation with a soft-spoken man who asked my opinion about several intractable aspects of the Israeli/Palestinian conflict. I deferred at first, saying that I live in the New York City area, as do my children, and was reticent about expressing opinions to someone whose family was on the firing line. But he pressed for my thoughts, and so I told him. He listened respectfully, asked me some follow-up questions, and seemed to take seriously what I had to say. We engaged in back-and-forth about who should do what to bring peace with security to Israel, and what that would look like.

When the break ended, he gave me his business card and told me to call next time I was in Israel. I looked at his card and recognized the name: Amos Yadlin. He was a former general in the Israel Air Force; had served as the IDF's Chief of Military Intelligence;

and had flown over 250 combat missions, including the destruction of the Iraqi nuclear reactor.

I've had other humbling experiences discussing war face-to-face with two chiefs of staff of the IDF—the commanders in chief of the Israeli military force.

Benny Gantz was the chief of staff during Operation Protective Edge, the 2014 war against Hamas in Gaza. He explained how Israel could have pulverized the Gaza Strip with overwhelming firepower that would have quickly destroyed the entire area and saved Israeli lives, but refrained from doing so out of concern for Palestinian civilians who were being used as human shields by the terrorists. Instead of applying full military power, Israel applied its military power like a dimmer switch, gradually increasing its force as Hamas escalated its bombardment of Israeli civilian populations; that is why the war lasted fifty-one days rather than just a few, and Israel lost sixty-seven soldiers and six civilians.

Gantz had spoken to his mother at the outset of the war. She had understood why Israel's defending itself militarily was absolutely necessary, but urged Gantz to make sure Gazans got fed during the war—fight them because you must, but feed them.

Gantz's predecessor as chief of staff was Gabi Ashkenazi, who later became foreign minister. When we met, he was chairman of a major charitable foundation dedicated to helping underprivileged youth in Israel. He, like Gantz, had an extensive and illustrious military background, and commanded troops in another Gaza war begun by Hamas rocket attacks.

Ashkenazi told me he was concerned about a weapon Hamas hadn't yet utilized. Israel can deal with military actions, he said, though at the cost of lives. But what if masses of Palestinian women and children were simply to walk to the Gaza-Israel border and attempt to breach it? A few years later, of course, that happened, with terrorists using women and children as human shields.

Ashkenazi was interested in the Helmsley Trust contributing to the foundation he chaired, for that foundation to use Helmsley funds for its own charitable work. I told him that his organization's work was outside our focus areas, and explained what we'd done, listing our grants—to whom, for what, and how much. Midway through the list, he interrupted.

Keep doing what you're doing, he said. Don't give money to us.

Ruthie looked up from her iPad.

Did you ever read Israel's Declaration of Independence? she asked.

I never had. So I did. Its principles could not have been more American—Israel "will ensure equality of social and political rights to all its inhabitants irrespective of religion, race or sex; it will guarantee freedom of religion, conscience, language, education and culture; it will safeguard the Holy Places of all religions: all within the Jewish State of Israel."

How many Americans like me had never read it? And wouldn't it be wonderfully educational if they did? Why not print it all over the United States?

So, on Israel's 66th Independence Day, the Israeli Declaration of Independence was reprinted in full in the *New York Times* and other influential American newspapers with a combined print and digital reach of over 14 million. We decided to have no accompanying text, simply a headline over the declaration reading: "Israel was established sixty-six years ago. Throughout those years, the United States and Israel have been partners in democracy, their people bound by common values and interests." We've run the text annually since, changing only the number.

We were in Israel on the day the ad first appeared. I received a phone call the next day from Israel's Ambassador to the United Nations. He had been to a diplomatic function the night before, and the ambassadors from several world powers had approached him and said they had read the Declaration from top to bottom; had previously been unaware of the founding principles of Israel; and were deeply impressed. I asked, Will it change the way they vote?

His answer: Not a chance.

I learned other lessons in realpolitik.

I MET A DEMOCRATIC Congressman who got chatty.

When the Iran nuclear deal was under consideration by Congress, he'd received a call from the White House, inviting him to visit President Obama.

So I got there, he told me, and an aide opened the door to the Oval Office. President Obama was standing there, alone, waiting for me. The aide shut the door behind us, and there I was, the President of the United States and me, alone for half an hour. We discussed the deal. He said he needed my vote. I said I can't. He asked what I thought was the worst part of the deal and how he could change my mind about it; I said letting the world's chief state sponsor of terrorism get tens of billions of dollars and a pathway to nuclear arms was not negotiable with me. He said he'd really like my vote. I said my conscience won't allow it. He asked me to let some time pass before announcing my opposition; I said I couldn't. The President wasn't rude or bullying, didn't threaten, and the meeting ended.

Shortly afterward, the Democratic speaker of the House stripped the Congressman of several powers he had as chairman of a House Committee.

THE MAYOR OF JERUSALEM arranged a private citywide tour for us by his advisor for foreign affairs and by an Arab-Muslim who worked in the mayor's office. Let's call the latter Abdul, so none of his brethren will hurt him.

Abdul drove us through several Arab neighborhoods in Jerusalem, and explained how Israel had dramatically improved the lives of Arabs there. Not more than a handful, he said, would prefer to live in an Arab country. Their lives are far better here, economically and politically. In Israel, they are free to speak and worship as they wish, and Israel improves even the most mundane issues in their daily lives.

Abdul drove us to a high school for Arab girls. The classrooms were ultramodern, with computers at every desk. Abdul said that no country in the Arab world provides such a high level of education for its children, and none makes any effort to educate females. While we were there, the headmistress of the school, wearing a burka, asked the mayor's advisor whether the school might get certain additional equipment, and the immediate answer was yes.

Abdul had driven us through some of the most volatile areas in the city, and had extolled the virtues of the Israeli government even there. Here, then, was an Arab grateful for the improved lives Israel had given to his people.

We talked some politics, and I asked him: Hasn't Israel done a great job governing Jerusalem?

It should be internationalized, he said, not governed by Israel.

The Rambam Hospital is a large healthcare center in Haifa serving 2 million residents in northern Israel, the IDF's Northern Command, the US Navy's sixth fleet, and thousands of Syrians wounded in their own civil war. It is a one-thousand-bed teaching hospital with medical institutes and a world-renowned medical center. It is also a prime target of Hezbollah missiles and rockets from Lebanon, even though many of the hospital's doctors and over a quarter of its patients are Arabs.

Because of its target-friendly status in the eyes of Hezbollah, and necessity being the mother of invention, the directors of Rambam decided to build a fortified underground emergency hospital that could continue to deliver medical care even in wartime. To that end, the hospital's underground parking garage—twenty-two feet below sea level—would be convertible into a two-thousand-bed underground emergency hospital within seventy-two hours, as operational as the aboveground hospital.

The hospital's director walked Ruthie and me through the garage. On the walls near every parking space were small doors for closets that would contain typical paraphernalia of a hospital: a prototype had oxygen supply, monitoring and other medical equipment, ventilators, dialysis equipment, operating equipment, blood pressure monitors—the entire panoply of medical equipment found near every hospital bed you've ever seen. It was built to serve patients from the Rambam and also those transported from other hospitals, and the possible inflow of wounded soldiers and civilians. The medical equipment for the underground hospital would cost $10 million. Rambam asked whether the Helmsley Trust might pay half. We did. A few years later, the garage was partially converted into the largest Covid-19 facility in Israel.

Other hospitals also needed fortification. Barzilai medical center in the southern city of Ashkelon, nine miles from the Gaza Strip, serves half-a-million residents. Thousands of rockets and mortars have been aimed from Gaza at the city's schools, hospital, and population center. The Trust gave $5 million to help complete a missile defense shield and protect operating rooms for the hospital. We later gave them $8.5 million for other pressing needs arising from their proximity to Gaza.

We helped change the literal and intellectual skyline of Haifa. Rambam, the University of Haifa, and the Technion wanted to establish a collaborative biomedical research center but needed a major donor's commitment to begin serious fund-raising. The overall cost would be $100 million, and they believed that the Helmsley name, by then widely known in Israel, would be a magnet for other donors. They were right. We gave $18 million (the number "18" represents "life" in Hebrew), and the Helmsley Health Discovery Tower is now twenty stories high, a towering building by Israeli standards.

This mayor says he's heard so much about us, we're doing great work, and wants millions for his town; this hospital director says we're doing great work, he's heard so much about us, and wants millions; this university president says he's heard so much about us, we're doing great work, he wants millions. The phone rings, the emails fly, the reach-outs-through-others continue—I've won the popularity contest. It's hard to keep perspective.

We're dispensing big money—$4 million, $5 million, what's the difference? Plenty. Millions here, millions there: To paraphrase the late Senator Dirksen, soon we're talking about real money. We've got to make sure all the money is necessary for its intended purposes and is spent that way, and that none of it falls into someone's pocket. It's tough to keep track of it all, but we've got systems in place to make sure the money is spent on what it's supposed to be spent on.

We did find one abuse and dealt with it forcefully. After giving several grants of millions of dollars apiece to a particular hospital, we learned that the hospital, unbeknownst to us, had given so-called "finder's fees" to people who weren't "finders" (we have none) and had no entitlement to any of our money. Our contracts require that every penny of our grants be used for grant purposes only, and many of our grants require that all of our funds be deposited into a special account for easy tracking. The hospital tried to circumvent us by paying over a million dollars to phony "finders" (Why? Who knows, but I can imagine.) who'd found nothing, out of other funds of the hospital. We terminated our existing grant to the hospital and made them pay back substantial amounts we'd already sent them—forfeiting nearly $5 million of our money. We weren't happy doing this—after all, our objective is to help, not hurt—but word travels, our actions received considerable publicity in Israel, and it was important for every institution receiving Helmsley money to know not to play around.

Did I mention? Leona Helmsley also had another small charitable foundation, with about $5 million in it. She named me one of its trustees, and we give the money out for charitable pursuits with smaller needs. So a $5 million foundation is small potatoes. Who'd've thunk it?

We've funded much more in Israel: a model farm to help Israel's farmers develop sustainable agriculture; other rehabilitation centers; additional facilities for the handicapped and disabled; providing hospitals with sophisticated medical equipment; research for agricultural innovations; colleges and other educational facilities throughout the country; bringing retired American generals and other influential groups to Israel so they can see the country for themselves and tell others what they see; advanced robotics development; emergency mobile medical services; at-home medical and dental services for the elderly; and much more. When Covid-19 struck, we knew the Israeli healthcare landscape thoroughly enough that without bureaucratic holdup we were able to quickly fund $12 million for hospitals throughout the country to build Covid-19 facilities and purchase desperately needed equipment. (We've done all this with a staff of four, all in New York City, headed by my former law firm associate who, at my request, switched professions to become director of the Israel program.)

But there are needs of a country that money can't buy, and people I wish we could help but can't.

Yom Hazikaron—the Day of Remembrance—is the national day dedicated to Israeli soldiers killed in wars, and Israeli victims of terror. It is not a Memorial Day holiday for barbecues. In Israel, everyone has a relative, a loved one, or a friend killed in battle or victimized by terrorists; nobody is immune. It is a day to visit cemeteries.

The day begins the night before, when sirens whistle eerily throughout the country for sixty seconds. Everything stops: Cars stop and drivers get out and stand at solemn attention; people stop whatever they are doing; complete silence, honoring the fallen. The following morning, sirens whistle once again, for two minutes. Everything, everyone, stops.

The mayor of Jerusalem invited us to join him at a Day of Remembrance observance that evening at Sultan's Pool, an open-air amphitheater whose origins extend to Roman times. Thousands of people packed the theater. The stage was empty—no curtain, just a few standing microphones, some large empty screens, and a few bouquets of flowers on the floor. I wondered: What performance on that starkly bare stage could capture the solemnity of the evening?

The lights went off. Then, a spotlight shone at an empty microphone in the corner. A young boy walked out and stood at the microphone. He had to speak up for it to catch his voice. On a large screen behind him, a face appeared, of a smiling young man, about twenty years old, as wholesome and innocent a face as you can imagine.

The boy behind the microphone began to talk. His voice broke as he began, but he spoke through it, and continued speaking through his tears. The young man in the picture was his brother. In battle, a grenade had been thrown in the midst of the troops he was with. It would have killed them all. He had thrown himself on it to save the others. It exploded and killed him.

The boy at the microphone finished speaking, and walked off the stage. There was no sound in the amphitheater.

The microphone was empty for a moment. Then, a young man limped out and spoke. A bomb had severed one of his legs. He had survived after a forty-eight-hour operation. The bomb had killed eight of his friends. He limped off. No sound in the amphitheater.

A middle-aged man approached the microphone. His face had been horribly burned by terrorists in an explosion but he was alive. He told of the explosion.

Several singers took the stage. They sang a cappella. Soft songs about Israel. When they finished, they walked off. No clapping, no sound.

A man approached the microphone. The face of a woman appeared on the screen. The man described having to tell his five children that their mother had been killed in a terrorist attack.

A young woman replaced him at the microphone. Another woman's face appeared on the screen. The speaker told of how her mother had been killed by terrorists, while pregnant with her. She knew her mother only by reading her mother's diary. People tell her that her face reminds them of her mother.

"Eemah" is Hebrew for "mother." A little boy sang a song about "Eemah." Her face appeared on the screen. Pictures were all that remained of her after a terrorist attack.

Sitting next to me was a large man whom I had talked with before the ceremony began. He had fought in several wars, and was scarred and looked like he was made of iron. The man's eyes closed and he swayed gently back and forth as the boy sang in Hebrew: "Come mother, tell me how dreams come true."

Another child approached the microphone, his father's face on the screen. The boy told of gasoline being poured on his father, and his father then being torched.

Several girls went to the microphone in the center of the stage and sang: This is my country; I have nowhere else to go. When they finished, silence. No applause.

A woman approached the microphone. A picture of a soldier nearly her age shown on the screen. It was her father. He had been killed in the Yom Kippur War, fighting in the Golan Heights when she was two years old. The Syrians had attacked mercilessly. His tank suffered a direct hit.

A group of singers took the stage, with guitars. They played several popular songs about Israel. When they finished, they walked off the stage. Silence.

The Druze in Israel have a different religion. Their culture and language are Arabic, but they serve in the IDF and some have high-level political and military positions. A Druze man approached the mic. He spoke about the five members of his family killed in Israel's wars. A musician played Druze music. No applause.

Eleven older men, my age, walked onto the stage. They sang together. Each had lost a son in war. Pictures of young men appeared on the screen. The fathers' chorus: We have suffered beyond words; we have lost beyond words; it is so hard; but we are staying here. They left the stage. No applause.

A blind young man was escorted to the mic. Shrapnel in his eyes. Numerous operations. He described it emotionlessly. He believes his eyesight will return.

Another young man's face on the screen. A father tells of a son who said he'd be back for Sabbath dinner.

Another father whose daughter, he said, knew every stone and flower in Jerusalem, killed by terrorists near Lake Kinneret eight years ago. The father built a temple and named it "The Song of Kinneret."

Another picture on the screen, of another young man. Another father approaches the mic. Tells about a knock on his door at 10:30 one night. "Suddenly, I'm on another planet." He and his wife promise each other they will continue to live. But it won't be on the planet they had been living on.

Another parent.

Another child.

Another song about the country.

Not a word of hatred or revenge, but an inescapable sadness.

And then all the singers return to the stage, and the audience sings with them "Hatikvah"—The Hope—to be a free people in our land, Israel.

The lights came on. No applause. The theater emptied.

Ruthie had begun whispering translations to me as each speaker began, but, with each, choked up and couldn't continue after a few sentences. I got a retelling the following day.

Yom Ha-Atzmaut is Israel's Independence Day. It immediately follows Remembrance Day, to remind people the price paid for independence. A special torch-bearing ceremony is held on Mount

Herzl in Jerusalem, beginning with a recital of the remembrance prayer in honor of fallen soldiers, and culminating in a torch-lighting ceremony featuring twelve Israeli citizens, drawn from throughout the country, representing the twelve tribes of Israel. The atmosphere is rapturous. Israelis learn to overcome indescribable sadness and continue with life.

I attended a forum where then-Vice President Biden spoke.

When I was a young Senator, he said, I met with Prime Minister Golda Meir. She described the existential dangers confronting Israel: surrounded by enemies armed with sophisticated weaponry, vastly outnumbering Israel's forces, and dedicated to eradicating the country.

Biden said to her: I fear for your country—you must be constantly terrified.

No, the Prime Minister answered. Because we have a secret weapon.

Biden was relieved. What's the secret weapon? he asked.

The Prime Minister responded: We have nowhere else to go.

After the Trust began donating millions in Israel, I became viewed by many Israelis and the press as the money spigot. Several major Jewish newspapers featured articles about me, one headline calling me "Santa Claus." Invitations became commonplace—to a groundbreaking, or an opening, or some other special event.

I did my best to keep things in perspective, but some of the plaudits were hard to resist. We had awarded $7 million to the University of Haifa, located in the north of Israel on the

Mediterranean coast, to establish a Mediterranean Sea Research Center, purchasing a remotely operated underwater sea vehicle to study the ocean and ocean floor, and hire necessary faculty and research labs. The university offered me an honorary doctorate. After speaking with the Trust's counsel, I accepted, but made certain that the award made clear that all the money we had given in Israel was Helmsley's, not mine. I'd passed up on a $25 doctorate at Harvard Law, but now had a freebie. (Confession: Time has softened me, and I ultimately relented and traded in my LL.B, becoming, without any further effort or increased knowledge or wisdom, a full-fledged doctor of laws.)

Ego has its limits, though. The President of Ben-Gurion University offered me the honor of accompanying her to lay a wreath at the tomb of David Ben-Gurion, Israel's first president, on the seventieth anniversary of the birth of the State of Israel. I told her it was difficult to imagine a higher honor, but that the honor was too great for an ordinary lawyer and accidental philanthropist such as me, and suggested she instead offer the honor to any Israeli parent who had lost a child to war or terrorism, or to any Israeli child who had lost a parent or sibling the same way. She asked me to reconsider, but I declined the honor.

Not everyone at the Trust is plugged into Israel and Jewish tradition. Nine days after my daughter-in-law gave birth to my sixth grandchild, I mentioned to someone at the Trust that I'd been blessed with a new grandchild and had been at the bris yesterday. The response: "How wonderful! Boy or girl?"

Chapter 14

Oh, the Rich Folks You Meet

In a supposed exchange between two literary giants, F. Scott Fitzgerald said to Ernest Hemingway: "The rich are different from you and me," to which Hemingway replied: "Yes, they have more money."

When you deal with billions, even though it's not your money, you occasionally hobnob with the rich and famous. In fact, most of the super-wealthy I've met over the last several years may not be different from you and me, but lead different lives.

Some are extremely generous.

Sheldon Adelson, if you haven't heard of him, was a multibillionaire casino operator. He and his wife, Miriam, gave more money than you can count to numerous Israeli institutions—many hundreds of millions of dollars. Among their gifts were several hundred million dollars—not an exaggeration—to Birthright

Israel, a charitable program that provides free trips to Israel for Jews between the ages of eighteen and twenty-six to connect them to the country. The Helmsley Trust contributed $5.5 million and I was invited to a meeting in New York for major donors.

I introduced myself to Sheldon, and told him I'd been trying to call him about our mutual interests in Israel but that I'd not been able to pierce the impregnable barrier of his loyal secretary. He gave me his cell phone number and invited me to call him directly whenever I'd like.

A week later, I was on the West Coast and called him. He invited Ruthie and me to join him and his wife for Sabbath dinner at his home in Las Vegas the following night, and I accepted.

We drove to Las Vegas. He gave us a grand tour of his home: an Olympic-size swimming pool (tiles imported from China); a full-court indoor basketball court; a racquetball court; and about every other amenity known to man.

You'd think owning an airplane would be more than enough, but Sheldon had numerous; not bad for someone who began as a kid selling newspapers on a street corner. We were joined at the dinner table by six of Miriam's friends, whom Sheldon had flown in from Israel.

The Adelsons were gracious and charming hosts. At the end of the evening I asked him: Why does a nice fellow like you get such horrible press?

Three reasons, he said. First, I own casinos, so people think there's mafia involved even though there's not. Next, I give to right wing causes, and the press doesn't like that. And third, I speak my mind, and I'll keep doing it. He told me how much money he'd contributed to Trump and other Republican candidates for public office. I'm not sure whether he intended for the number to remain private, so let's just say it was so large I nearly swallowed my fork.

The four of us met for lunch at a restaurant in New York soon after President Trump had moved the American Embassy in Israel to Jerusalem. The maître d' told us the specials of the day, and recommended sautéed shrimp. Miriam passed. I don't eat shrimp, she said. Since Trump became president, I believe in God and eat only kosher.

Several months later, we met again. Sheldon had recently broken several ribs, slipping on the wet surface of a boat in Macau. He wanted to sue the owner of the boat, until he learned that he owned it.

I received a call from Haim Saban.

Haim was born in Egypt in 1944 to a Jewish family, in dirt-poor poverty. They emigrated to Israel when he was young. He had pursued a music career, became a TV producer, eventually built an entertainment conglomerate, and was now a multi-billionaire. He says he earned an NPA degree—Never Poor Again.

Haim has a passion to which he devotes enormous amounts of time and money: Friends of the IDF, a nonprofit organization that provides support programs for young soldiers of the IDF and for families of fallen soldiers. It builds educational facilities, synagogues, and recreational areas; aids the thousands of widows and orphans who have lost loved ones in battle; helps the rehabilitation of wounded soldiers; and provides a variety of services to soldiers, veterans, and their families.

Notwithstanding his business successes and time pressures, Haim flies around the country like a traveling salesman soliciting funds for the FIDF. He does it for love of the country, and his sales pitch is very simple. Without the IDF there would be no Israel, and those who serve in the military should be supported when needed. His sales kit consists only of an iPad on which he shows prospective donors the everyday life of typical eighteen-year-old Israeli boys and girls suddenly thrust from teenagedom into defenders of the country, and the awful price that many pay.

Haim asked me to attend an annual FIDF dinner in Los Angeles. Several notables were in the audience, and Haim introduced them from the stage. But to me the most memorable moment was when a young man in his mid-twenties was escorted to the stage. When his hands were on both sides of the lectern, his escort walked away and left him there alone. He was touching the lectern because he was blind.

The young man's voice cracked as he spoke. His English was broken but easily understood. He explained what had happened to him.

When he was ten years old, he had gone with his family to a restaurant—a casual meal in Israel, like millions of families all over the world. A suicide bomber came into the restaurant. The explosion blinded the young man, and killed his parents, siblings, and a cousin. This blind young man, these years later, now served in an intelligence unit in the IDF, and wanted to thank the audience for supporting the FIDF.

He spoke matter-of-factly: That was who I was, that is what happened, and this is who I am. He added no flourishes; the facts spoke for themselves.

When he finished, the audience gave him a standing ovation, though standing seemed like the ultimate irony.

The following night, Ruthie and I had dinner at Haim's house with a few other guests, including the young speaker. He came with another young man, who physically guided him when necessary, and stayed close to him constantly. This young man, who sat wordlessly through dinner simply to be with his blind friend, was an IDF commander who led even younger soldiers in battle. At the end of the dinner, he told our small group how meaningful it was, to the troops under his command, to know that though the soldiers did the fighting, others around the world cared and supported them.

The Trust eventually granted $3.2 million to the FIDF, for college scholarships to soldiers who complete their military service in combat and combat-support units but can't afford college.

I attended the FIDF Los Angeles dinner the following year too, after our first grant to FIDF. It was quite Hollywood: Arnold Schwarzenegger was there, along with Sylvester Stallone, Barbra Streisand, and other glitterati; not exactly folks I hang around with. But Haim said it was important to the FIDF that I announce the Trust's gift and support of the organization, so I agreed to fly out.

The cavernous ballroom was filled with over a thousand people. Scattered among suits and dresses were several Israeli soldiers, in their simple tan uniforms, whom the FIDF had flown in for the occasion.

Nearly all of the soldiers were young—late teens, early twenties. Most stood shyly in pairs or small groups, saying hello and answering questions when approached. Two young soldiers standing together shook my hand when I approached, nodded awkwardly, and thanked me for nothing in particular. They were college age, by American standards, with the sweet faces of innocence. One introduced himself as Eitan; the other's last name was Goldin. Hard to imagine them in war.

A few months earlier, Operation Protective Edge in Gaza had ended. During a mid-war cease-fire, terrorists emerged from a terror tunnel and ambushed several resting Israeli soldiers. When the terrorists escaped back into the tunnel, the Israelis realized that

Hadar Goldin, one of the soldiers, had been abducted. A young lieutenant in the group sought permission to enter the tunnel to try to rescue Hadar, but his commander refused to allow it. Too dangerous. The lieutenant requested permission from the commander's commander, received it, and raced into the tunnel, alone. He emerged soon afterwards, carrying evidence that later helped the Israeli government pronounce Hadar Goldin dead.

Months later, when Haim asked that young lieutenant to attend the FIDF function in Los Angeles, he declined at first but later agreed. He made no speech about his heroism. He simply stood with another solider, shyly thanking people in suits and dresses for their support. Eitan was that lieutenant; the soldier standing next to him was the brother of the slain soldier Eitan had tried to rescue.

Not all my newfound billionaire friends are as giving or open as Sheldon and Haim, and often have their own unique quirks and foibles. Leona Helmsley for sure had her fair share of those. I'll give you some other f'r-instances. Let's call each of these folks "Bill."

IT'S DIFFICULT FOR OTHERS to understand, Bill explained, but there's a real difference between having two billion dollars and two-and-a-half billion. Bill's got twenty-one people serving him at home; the upkeep expenses for his airplane are enormous; the yacht always needs repair; and charities are always asking for money. With another half-billion dollars, he said, he wouldn't feel the pressure so much.

ANOTHER BILL INVITED RUTHIE and me for dinner at his sumptuous full-floor apartment. When we got off the elevator, we faced an open cabinet filled with several dozen pairs of moccasins, and a sign asking guest to please remove their shoes and put on whatever moccasins suit them; the floor inside scuffs easily.

WE HAD DINNER WITH a small group of superrich, including Bill, the co-founder of a large charitable organization. I'd never met him. He said he'd heard good things about the Helmsley Charitable Trust and wondered if the Trust might contribute to his organization. I told him that the Trust had already contributed over $5 million to his organization. He responded: "Really?"

ANOTHER DINNER, THIS TIME with a husband and wife who had inherited a fortune. During dessert, the waitress brought the check before anyone had asked for it. Without bothering to look at it, the wife disdainfully dropped it to the floor. The waitress picked it up and waited until the woman asked before re-presenting it. I left a larger tip than usual for our half of the bill—small token of apology.

WE WERE INVITED To the home of a super-wealthy businessman who had a large collection of armor, worn by knights in days of yore. He'd bought all the pieces from an auction house over many years. He told us that he'd wanted to test the current market value for such items, and asked the auction house if they'd resell one for him. They answered: Who'd buy it?

BILL WAS AN EXTREMELY generous philanthropist. He had considerable money left after his philanthropic largesse, and bought an enormous estate on which he created a private zoo with several dozen animal species: zebras, zedonks (offspring of a zebra and donkey, in case you don't know), alpacas, llamas, you name it. Among them was an oryx—an antelope with long straight horns—which passionately gored a zebra to death during mating season. I've had similar problems with my oryx.

BILL WAS HONORED BY a major hospital for a nine-figure donation, and was asked to say a few words. People ask me how I got so rich, he began. When I was a little boy, I picked an apple off a tree and sold it for a nickel. I used that nickel to buy two apples, and sold them for a dime. I used that dime to buy more apples, and sold them for even more. This went on for several years. Then, my father died and left me three-hundred-million dollars.

BILL INVITED RUTHIE AND me to dinner. He also invited his friend Bill 2. Bill hired a private chef to make the dinner. Bill 2 came with his own private chef to make *his* dinner. Too many cooks. . . .

WE ATTENDED A PARTY at Bill's home. At the door, a waitress stood with glasses of champagne to greet the guests; another waitress relieved the women of their handbags and stored them in a closet until departure time. Too many expensive trinkets decorating the home. . . .

I MET WITH ONE of the largest financial backers of J Street, an organization that regularly criticizes Israel. This billionaire's opinions about the country, its policies, and its people were radically different from mine, and he had opinions about everything. As I challenged everything he said, the thought began to dawn on me: The man really knows nothing about what he is talking about. So I asked him: When is the last time you were in Israel? I've never been, he said.

BILL AND HIS WIFE invited us to dinner. Then another, and two more. They were excited about their private philanthropy, and gradually worked up to The Ask. I told them that their work was very important but not what we do. I never heard from them again.

WE WERE IN A restaurant with Bill and his wife. She told us about a trip they'd once taken to some glamorous resort, and stopped herself midsentence to ask Bill one of the details she'd forgotten.

"That wasn't me," he said. "Must've been another husband, dear."

BILL WAS GOING To be feted by an institution to which he'd given grand amounts of money. We'd socialized several times before. He asked to meet with me.

They're going to announce gifts honoring me, he said, and I'd like them to announce a $5 million grant from the Helmsley Charitable Trust in my honor.

We don't give gifts in people's honor, I explained.

He came up face-to-face with me—cornered me—put his hands on my shoulders, and said: I'd love for the emcee to announce that Helmsley has contributed at least $2 million in my honor.

I repeated, politely, that we simply don't give gifts in people's honor.

He didn't lower his price any further.

Now maybe you're thinking: What a gold mine for a lawyer—billionaires galore, who doubtlessly have legal problems. What a great opportunity for financial back-scratching: I'll get the Trust to pay your organization a ton of money, and you'll throw business my way.

It doesn't work that way. The laws governing charitable organizations are very strict, and self-dealing is a No-No with serious consequences from the IRS and state tax authorities if you succumb to temptation.

Here's an example: Several major Israeli nonprofit organizations had invested with the Ponzi artist Bernie Madoff and got caught up in the ensuing litigations brought to sort out the mess. They spoke to me about representing them. It would've been right up my legal alley, but think about the optics: Helmsley grants millions of dollars to institutions that then pay legal fees to a Helmsley trustee. Doesn't smell so good, know what I mean? So I passed.

Decades ago, when I began earning a living, my father said to me: Rich or poor, it's good to have money, but there's no price for a good night's sleep. That's pretty good advice, and it's the best way to practice law or philanthropy, or, I'll wager, most anything else.

With all the money involved in giving grants and running the Trust, we have a strict set of ethical rules. Sometimes, when the amounts are small—a meal, a book, a trinket of nominal value when refusing would be awkward—accepting is permitted. But I've had to thank a few grantees for their thoughtfulness while explaining I couldn't accept. I've politely declined front-row seats to sports extravaganzas I'd've loved to attend, orchestra seats at entertainment events, home artifacts, and other goodies.

The ethical line-drawing can occasionally require creativity. Walter, one of my co-trustees, leads a program to help vulnerable children in sub-Saharan Africa. While visiting a remote rural area of Africa, he met with the local tribal chief, who gave him, as a present, a live goat. Refusing to accept it would be disrespectful. So Walter thanked the chief, accepted the goat, put it in the back of a pickup truck, drove to a children's clinic, and regifted it there.

Someone from the Friends of the IDF called to say a young reservist wanted to meet me.

We met in my office. He was in his mid-twenties but looked like late teens.

Can I give you a hug? he asked.

Why?

I'll tell you, but can I hug you first?

I said yes, and he did.

He explained: He'd been an officer in the IDF and commanded nearly one hundred soldiers. After his tour of duty ended, he tried to eke out a living as a waiter in a restaurant. One day a few years ago, while he was serving food, his phone rang. It was someone from the FIDF, telling him he'd been awarded a Helmsley scholarship. He was now in his last year in college, studying to become a lawyer. He was very grateful.

I brought you a present, the young man said.

I told him I can't accept presents.

You have to take this one, he answered. We went back and forth a few times until he reached into his beat-up knapsack and took out the present: his army dogtag. It was still covered with electrical tape, put on so the glint of the sun wouldn't reveal his position to the enemy.

I told him I was deeply moved but couldn't accept such a gift—he should give it to his girlfriend, or mother, but its's too valuable for me to accept. He insisted. From commanding troops in battle, to serving food in a restaurant, to studying law: he wanted to say thanks. I relented, and he draped the leather lanyard holding the dogtag around my neck.

I've kept that dogtag hanging on a cabinet behind my desk since then.

My "suspicious" conduct—uh oh—did once put me under "investigation" (or so they, or someone, said).

After we had sold nearly all of the estate's assets and transferred them to the Trust, we were required by law to file an accounting with the court. An "accounting" is a comprehensive report detailing exactly what happened to the assets of the estate: To whom did we sell the real estate and other property, for how much, and what did we do with all the money. Like executors of all estates, my co-executors and I were legally required to file the accounting, so the New York State Attorney General and the court could be sure we had properly exercised our fiduciary duties—that we'd paid the bequests, sold off the assets prudently, had transferred all that money to the Trust as required, and no money had gone where it shouldn't have.

As part of the accounting, we asked the court—as required by law—to determine our compensation for many years of work in liquidating assets worth over $5 billion. We asked the judge for what our lawyers thought would be considered appropriate, to be divided equally among us. The judge's permission was required before we could take a penny. We were legally required to send copies of all the voluminous papers to the Attorney General for review.

Once the Attorney General is involved in such a proceeding, he files in court a one-sentence document called a "Notice of Appearance"—a simple notice to the court that he has been given the papers and will appear in court. It is normal, routine, legally required, and signifies nothing of substance.

Because the Helmsley Charitable Trust had quickly become so prominent, and because "Leona Helmsley" was a name that always attracted attention, the New York Post, having learned that the Attorney General had filed a "Notice of Appearance" in connection with our submissions, called me and several other executors to ask about what the reporter characterized as the Attorney General's "intervention" in the Trust. We declined to comment, but authorized one of the Trust's lawyers to advise the reporter that the Attorney General's "Notice of Appearance" was routine and signified nothing. That did not stop the reporter, and the *Post* ran a story about a "probe" of the executors, claiming that the Attorney General was "sniffing around" the estate—even though the Attorney General had neither probed nor sniffed but merely filed a standard Notice of Appearance.

This is the internet age, though, and that tabloid invention spread virally and perversely. Shortly after the *Post*'s false story appeared, the Trust issued a routine press release announcing $9.6 million in grants to several important Israeli institutions. Rather than simply reporting the grants, a publication named *Jewish Business News*, with links to who-knows-how-many other websites, ran an article falsely linking the false *New York Post* story to these grants; falsely announcing, in a headline, that the New York State Attorney General was "Suspicious Of Helmsley's $9.6 million In Donations To Israel"; falsely claiming that the Attorney General was "investigating how they [the executors] disbursed more than $5 billion"; and, for good measure, falsely asserting that the Attorney General "is concerned about the conduct of the four trustees." Each of those allegations was completely made up: None had a feather's-weight of truth. Not a micro-millimeter. Zero. Zip. Nada.

I immediately contacted the publication and warned that the allegations were fictitious and libelous. The publication apologized and removed the article from its website. How many other websites ran the story before it was removed, and how many people therefore think that those major grants, or any of them—or the executors—were investigated by the Attorney General, I have no idea. Such are the dangers of a mixture of free speech and total irresponsibility. The price we pay for freedom. . . .

Chapter 15
Lawyering Redux

The mindsets of litigation and philanthropy are polar opposites. To properly prepare a legal case, you learn every facet of it, the facts and the law. If you've done your job right, by the time of trial you know more about the case than anybody else. At trial, you're single-mindedly focused on a single thing: winning. You live and breathe the case. During a trial, you're a captive in the courtroom, mentally and physically; outside the courtroom, you're still a captive of the courtroom mentally. You dream about the case. The case might not be important to the world at large, but it was vitally important to my client, and therefore to me. On the other side of the courtroom would be an adversary: someone fighting to stop us from winning. You look for his weak points, and drill down, exploiting them.

Philanthropy, at least on the scale of the Helmsley Charitable Trust, is totally different. The issues we address are large: helping fight diseases that affect millions of people, helping build hospitals, helping develop alternative sources of energy, helping people

in need, helping develop systems for providing medical services—
all of those have the potential to help vast numbers of people. Nor
is it necessary, or possible, to understand every facet of the "case"—
the problems we are trying to help solve. The doctors, the scientists, the experts are trained to understand it all, in full detail. I've
got to make the judgment whether the project is worthwhile and
has a reasonable enough likelihood of success to recommend it to
the other trustees, and then follow the grant through its conclusion. Everyone is rowing in the same direction; there is no adversary, no one determined to prevent me—us—from winning.

The differences between litigating and giving out multi-million
dollar grants are the difference between drilling deeply and plant-
ing broadly. Or, one day you're lifting heavy girders, and the next
day listening to a violin. In philanthropy as substantial as ours, the
opportunities for having a positive impact on people's lives—many
people—are virtually limitless and cover a broad range of human
endeavors.

The amounts we give out still make me gulp—over $3 billion
so far, and over $350 million every year. Though I'm the lead
trustee of our Crohn's and Israel programs, I've also got responsibility for all of our other programs—each of us does. None of the
trustees walks around with a checkbook in his pocket, approving
grants himself. We all vote on every grant recommendation for
every program. This means I've got to learn, quickly, about things
I'd never thought about before, in areas where I was ignorant.

We have limited ourselves to a few programs to achieve maxi-
mum impact. In addition to Crohn's and Israel:

A daughter of Mrs. Helmsley's grandson David Panzirer was
diagnosed with type 1 diabetes ("T1D") a few months before
David became a trustee (and his other daughter later received the
same diagnosis), and he has since devoted himself to improving
the lives of millions of patients suffering from that disease. T1D is

a 24/7 unrelenting disease which, like Crohn's, springs from causes that remain unknown; the body attacks its own insulin-producing cells in the pancreas, creating threats to life and serious long-term health problems. Our T1D program seeks to ease the burdens of living with the disease, improve the lives of those suffering from it, extend their lifespans, and fund research to better understand and treat the disease and, hopefully, help eradicate it.

Our other trustee, Mrs. Helmsley's grandson Walter Panzirer, has lived for many years in the upper Midwest and saw his new position as an opportunity to improve health care for that area's underserved population. He created and oversees the Trust's rural health care program, funding new networks of medical specialists working from a hub to serve hospitals, medical providers, and patients in previously underserved areas—push a button in some out-of-the-way rural midwestern community and instantly meet a medical specialist in Sioux Falls; and providing cardiac and cancer care, funding diagnostic equipment and behavioral health services, and attracting health care professionals all across the region. Walter's rural health care expertise led him to help establish and oversee our fifth major program—vulnerable children in sub-Saharan Africa—investing in increased access to essential health services, maternal and infant care, and improved nutrition and sanitation practices there.

We have the resources to fire at those targets with large cannon shots, and decided to do it. I hope we hit the targets. Feel free to second-guess—visit us at Helmsleytrust.org.

I used to consider myself a pretty good trial lawyer: got experience, learned how to examine and cross-examine witnesses, speak to judges and juries and establish what I thought was a fair rapport with them, and felt that I brought a certain level of credibility to my cases. Whether or not I won, juries and judges didn't think I was trying to fool them. You can't persuade people who think you're trying to pull the wool over their eyes.

Somewhere along the professional line, I became a litigator and not a trial lawyer. I'm not sure exactly when or how, but it happened. Many lawyers who litigate call themselves trial lawyers, but they are not. "Litigation" involves drafting reams of paper, fighting to wear down an opponent, conducting and defending depositions, using procedural devices to advantage, forcing the adversary to spend time and money and rue the day he or she got trapped in the maw of litigation and to ultimately cave in because of the weight of the evidence or the burdens and costs of the process. But actually trying a case—examining witnesses in a courtroom, addressing a jury, or a judge in front of a jury—being, in short, live in a courtroom with a jury watching every move—is a pastime most litigators simply don't do.

The end product of litigation that goes the full route is a trial (sometimes followed by an appeal); if you can do it—if you're a real trial lawyer, and present a credible threat of actually being able to try a case when the pretrial folderol is over—you've got a tremendous advantage over a lawyer who doesn't know his way around a courtroom in front of a jury. Only a handful of litigations actually go to trial. But when they do, the best opponent to have in a courtroom is someone who forgets that our native language is English spoken simply to people, not lawyerese spoken eruditely to scholars. If practice makes perfect (it surely didn't with me), lack of practice—"litigating" but not going to trial—amplifies imperfections.

As I began spending more time as an executor of the estate and trustee of the charitable trust, I spent less time in court, and even less time actually trying cases. The world of litigation was changing; law books were now passé, as cases and statutes and everything else were now digitized. Emails and the electronic world revolutionized litigation. The game of demanding discovery materials from the other side had now exploded, as electronically stored communications and documents had resulted in new subsets of pretrial issues.

I used to have a great technological advantage. I'd learned early to type when most folks couldn't, giving me a considerable leg up in generating documents. Typewriting was those days' technology. But the world changed, with computers now on every desk and everyone churning out his or her own papers; digital prowess is a tremendous skill which, to an abysmal extent, I lack. To me, a browser isn't a software application but someone with time on his hands, flipping through pages in a bookstore. I've wondered: What if phones were invented *after* emails; wouldn't we say: How great, I can actually talk with a person.

Even the courtrooms are now different. I took a respite from my executor and trustee duties to try a case in federal court in Manhattan. My clients, a successful independent record company named Ultra Records and its publishing arm Ultra Music, had been locked for years in a trademark battle with a successful music festival named Ultra Music Festival. Each side claimed that the other was infringing on the trademark in the "Ultra" and "Ultra Music" names and causing confusion in the music marketplace. Confusion surely existed: different designs and configurations of the name "Ultra" and the letter "U," differences between the names "Ultra Music" and "Ultra Music Festival," issues of who used what word first, were all ripe fruit for disputes.

The trial epitomized how courtroom lawyering had changed since my first cases decades earlier. Then, if you wanted to introduce a document into evidence, the court clerk would physically mark it with an exhibit sticker, the judge would look at it, and, if admitted into evidence, it would be passed among the jurors from hand to hand. As my cases became document-heavy, we'd bring loose-leaf evidence notebooks to court, one for each juror, for the adversaries, and for the judge, with dozens or hundreds of tabbed exhibits. Each juror would turn to the numbered tab when a document was introduced into evidence.

In the Ultra trial, documents were no longer on paper. Each side—and it wasn't just a lawyer: each side had three lawyers, sitting at long tables—had a computer expert at the end of its table. Each lawyer had a computer screen; the jurors and the judge had computer screens. To offer a document into evidence, you state the exhibit number, and the computer expert flashes the exhibit onto a screen visible only to the judge and the lawyers. If the judge admits the exhibit into evidence, it suddenly appears on the jurors' computer screens.

All of this seems like magic to me; it is surely far removed from the old days. Trying this kind of case is no longer a small exercise, and not for the poor.

The trial remains, though, as physically taxing as ever. For nearly two weeks of trial and several weeks of intensive preparation, I lived the Ultra case: appearing in court before 9:00, leaving after 5:00, returning to the office until midnight reviewing the day's events with the clients and preparing for the next day—interviewing witnesses, preparing cross-examinations, readying exhibits, researching legal issues that arose that day—and more.

I hadn't tried a case for a few years, and at the beginning of the trial I was like a rusty gate, not functioning very smoothly and somewhat creaky. As the trial progressed, the rust on the hinges began to scrape off, and I did okay. By the time of summations, I could see the jurors were following what I was saying, some nodding in agreement—though guessing jurors' inclinations is always only that: guessing.

At the end, right after summations, the parties settled, and the judge told the jury that each side had been frightened by the other side's summation. That was satisfying to hear, but the trial, which lasted nine full days, was tiring. Doing it at age seventy is different from doing it at twenty-five. You never forget how to ride a bike, but the hills seem steeper as the years go by.

Now I had a new point of comparison. As an executor, I'd been working intensively with lawyers in other specialties: trusts and estates, real estate, corporate law, taxation, and even large-firm litigation lawyers with armies of assistants ready to make the litigator's life easier. They all worked hard, but their professional lives were very different from the high-stress all-day tension of spending weeks on trial, fighting full tilt, every second, against adversaries, always careful to be deferential to the judge and not run afoul of some evidentiary rule or commit some perceived error. And the courtroom was a far stretch from philanthropy: Nobody tried to please me, no smiling flattery. The majesty of the courtroom spoke for itself: no baloney, no alternative facts, no phony smiles—real witnesses testifying in a crucible designed to find the truth. Just the facts, mister.

Occasionally, I'd be asked how I balanced practicing law, helping run a multi-billion dollar charitable trust, and being an executor of the estate. My stock answer was that I spent 100 percent of my time practicing law, 100 percent on the Trust, and 100 percent as an executor. But I knew that the time demands of the Trust and estate weren't permitting me to practice law at the same level as I'd tried to do throughout my career. Delivering honest services to clients requires full devotion. Emergencies arise requiring you to stop what you are doing and plunge into a legal crisis; you have to think about the cases all the time, whether or not you are in the office and often whether or not you're awake. Delivering honest legal services means being ready to spend weeks of undivided time actually trying a case and preparing for trial. One's head—or my head—contains only so many brain cells, and no day has more than twenty-four hours.

All of this philanthropy was taking a toll on my lawyering. Judges aren't interested in hearing "I can't be in court that day, I've got to give away $5 million," or meet with finance people, or oversee this or that. I was at the stage where I could do with my left hand what used to require my right, without the client noticing, but I knew that I wasn't delivering the kind of devoted all-in attention to cases as I'd done in the pre-billions days. I could fool others, but not myself. I needed support to keep delivering legal services at the level I was accustomed to. So after decades of running my own litigation practice, I decided that time had come for a change—change every forty or so years is a good idea in any event—and began to look around.

I didn't want to join a mega-firm; I'd sampled that environment decades ago after leaving the U.S. Attorney's Office, and hadn't liked the taste. A friend at one of those firms. which had recently hired its thousandth lawyer, commented that it wasn't the same warm and cozy place it had been with only 999. I wanted a mid-sized firm that could give both the support and flexibility I needed.

I called a top-caliber lawyer I knew, Dan Wallen, chairman of a fifty-plus lawyer firm named Otterbourg that was founded over a century ago by (you guessed it) a lawyer named Mr. Otterbourg and some colleagues. I told Dan that I wanted to continue lawyering but wanted to join a larger firm, and wondered whether Otterbourg might create a slot for me. Within a few days, we had worked out an agreement.

I quickly grew accustomed to my name not being on the front

door. Fortunately, my legal phone kept ringing. I got a call from Clive Gillinson, the Executive and Artistic Director of Carnegie Hall, probably the preeminent music institution in the world. The Chairman of the Board of Carnegie was Ronald Perelman, a multi-billionaire mega-donor to Carnegie and elsewhere, used to corporate wrangling and getting his own way. He had suspended Clive for alleged misdeeds; Clive denied the charges and hired us; and Carnegie hired an independent law firm to conduct an internal investigation of Perelman's accusations.

The press ran major articles based on evidently leaked information reporting Perelman's charges. Dan and I concluded that the allegations were bogus, but said nothing to the press, choosing instead to present our arguments and evidence to the investigator, who concluded that there was no evidence to support Perelman's charges. Carnegie's Board of Trustees publicly announced their full support of Clive, and Perelman resigned from the Board. Slaying the dragon still felt good.

I'd met Clive once before. Years earlier, he had contacted a mutual friend to arrange a lunch meeting, where he solicited a grant to bring the Israeli Philharmonic to Carnegie Hall. I explained that though both were world-class organizations, that type of funding wasn't our cup of tea. As we left the restaurant, I said to him: "I can't resist: To get back to my office, I turn left and walk east for a few blocks. How do you get to Carnegie Hall?"

I attended a dinner event and was seated next to the wife of a prominent New York City litigator. Decades ago, he'd co-founded what is now a large internationally known firm. In making small talk with the lady, I asked if her husband was still an active practitioner.

Are you kidding? his wife answered. Who would hire a seventy-five-year-old trial lawyer?

The answer struck me between the eyes. I was not that many years away from that age, and still thought of myself as, if not young, at least strong, healthy, and reasonably able to joust with the best—and certainly not old. Could it be that this lady's comment accurately reflected people's perception of when over-the-hillness might strike me?

For sure, the thrill of combat, the sport of litigation, had lost much of its luster and excitement over the course of decades. Trying a case was physically and mentally taxing, and very different from considering multi-million dollar requests for grants to help cure disease or help develop and secure Israel. But I've not yet become like a boxer whose constant fighting leads finally to his saying: "No more." I've reached the point where I say to myself: Not too much more—I still have what it takes, but I'll save it for special occasions.

I continue thinking of clients' problems when I go to bed, but not just through a narrow litigation lens, instead creating a broader range of possible solutions. And my answer is the same when people ask what legal field I specialize in; I tell them I think and I worry.

I still drag myself onto a basketball court from time to time, but the court seems longer, the rim higher, and nobody seems afraid I'll speed by him. When the children were kids, I'd race them and of course they'd always win; later, I swam laps against my son, Michael, and saw him, underwater, slowing down to avoid beating me by too much.

My father died at eighty-eight. Cancer. Very painful to watch. I should have seen him more than once every three weeks when I was a boy. I missed a father until I let him be one, many years late. Big mistake of mine. He had infinite patience, waiting outside the door of my life until I let him come in. I am lucky that he did.

When he turned sixty, I asked how it felt. "Great," he answered. "But I'd trade it for two thirties." If only he'd reserved ten or so minutes for now so I could bring him up to date.

My mother died at almost ninety-one. Seizures. Equally painful to watch. Once, toward the end, she phoned me. When I picked up, she said hold on a minute. Silence on the other end, until she got to the piano. She played a snippet from a Chopin etude she used to play more than sixty years ago on our piano in the Bronx. I never heard her play again.

I'm still married to the same beautiful twenty-six-year-old girl I met on that rooftop pool over forty years ago. (My great fortune: It wasn't raining; what if?) She hasn't aged a day. Our children are married, with families of their own. And our grandchildren—the greatest ever.[1] I'll show you pictures.

Time moves in only one direction. I recently attended my fiftieth law school reunion; how did that happen? The "In Memoriam" list grows longer every year, and once your name gets on, only a typographical error can get you off. Father Time and Mother Nature are a relentless, uncompromising couple, pushing me to the front lines, with no tolerance for fiddle-faddle. They can't be bullied, sweet-talked, bought off, or stalled. Life goes on. Oh sure, it can play some tricks. But all in all, in the good luck lottery that floats unpredictably in the cosmos, I hit the jackpot.

---

1. Ellie, Noah, Brooke, Alice, Chloe, and Ethan. Every lawyer's book is entitled to at least one footnote, and I've saved mine for them.